THE CRISIS OF
AMERICAN LABOR

BY

SIDNEY LENS

A Perpetua Book ∞

A. S. Barnes & Company, Inc.

New York

Perpetua Edition 1961

© 1959 by Sidney Lens
Library of Congress Catalogue Card Number: 59-7368
Printed in the United States of America

THE CRISIS OF AMERICAN LABOR

By Sidney Lens

Left, Right and Center

The Counterfeit Revolution

A World in Revolution

The Crisis of American Labor

Acknowledgments

IN PREPARING THE FINAL DRAFT OF THIS MANUSCRIPT I HAD
before me pages of notes and suggestions by four eminently
qualified men. Two of them were professors closely associated
with American unionism: Dr. Joel Seidman of the University of Chicago, who has written many labor books himself, and Dr. Bernard Karsh of the University of Illinois,
also a labor author of prominence. The other two were intellectuals with broader interests: Dr. Morton Gordon of
the University of California, a specialist in adult education
with a wide background in many fields, and Paul Scheffer,
the well-known Moscow correspondent of the 1920's and the
man who edited my first book, *Left, Right and Center*. To
all four I would like to offer my thanks.

In addition I would like to record in cold print my warm
and affectionate gratitude to my schoolteacher wife Shirley
for her patience, typing, criticism, encouragement . . . and
many other things.

CONTENTS

The Crisis of
American Labor

1
Little Labor, Big Labor

THE LATE DANIEL TOBIN, FORMER PRESIDENT OF THE TEAM-sters' Union, recalled in a moment of nostalgia a few years ago that he and the president before him used to sleep in the same bed in a $2.50-a-week hotel room to save the union money. Andrew Furuseth, head of the Sailors' Union at the turn of the century, lived an ascetic existence in a tiny room most of his life. On one occasion when he was arrested for picketing, he told the judge that he had no fear of going to jail because "there is no cell humbler than the room in which I live, no prison food any worse than what I'm accustomed to." John Fitzpatrick, president of the Chicago Federation of Labor, was usually to be seen at lunch spreading out the sandwiches prepared for him by his wife.

There were other union leaders, even a few decades ago, who had already lost their sense of devotion and their iden-tification with the humble workingman, but the tradition of self-sacrifice and selfless service is deeply rooted in the

American labor movement. The early unions had no full-time officials, hardly any treasuries, and few great victories to their credit. The first business agents, taken off the job to represent their fellow workers, were usually zealots, intensely idealistic. They looked on the labor movement not as a means of making a livelihood, but as the most noble cause worth serving. When the CIO was formed in 1935 a similar flavor of idealism permeated the house of labor. Thousands of fervid young men gave their time and effort, frequently without pay, on behalf of what they considered to be an evangelical "cause." They were fighting not for themselves, essentially, but for the millions of "injured and oppressed," the miners with silicosis in their lungs, the Ford workers laboring under ruthless "speed-up," the many victims of industrial tyranny.

At the grass roots of American labor the flavor of dedication to the "little" man and preoccupation with his problems still remains. In the late 1950's the labor movement was criticized for "bigness" and "corruption," but in the 75,000 local union offices around the country there are few features that are either "big" or "corrupt." Here tens of thousands of business agents, organizers, committeemen, shop stewards—paid and unpaid—toil ceaselessly to resolve problems that are seldom earth-shaking but are highly important to the rank-and-file members they affect. There are the annual, or bi-annual, negotiations for a wage increase, there are the hundreds of thousands of grievances and personal problems that filter through a normal union office: a worker is downgraded to a lesser job with a cut in pay; a job is reclassified and its rate cut; a man is laid off out of line of seniority or is deprived of an opportunity to bid for a better job *in* line of seniority; an incentive rate is timed wrong, reducing the earnings of pieceworkers; an employee is deprived of holiday pay or sick pay or vacation pay because of some twist of the contract or some foreman's whim; a member has a finger

cut off on the job and seeks advice on how to get his workmen's compensation; a worker in the hospital needs blood
and asks the union to line up a few voluntary donors. Little
problems like these, affecting millions of unheralded individuals, go the rounds of grievance procedure, arbitration,
union counseling programs. They never are inscribed in
printer's ink, except perhaps in the local union paper, but
they are the staff of American labor's life.

It is difficult to dispute labor's record of positive achievements: eighteen million union members usually receiving
annual wage increases, health and welfare benefits, job protection, and innumerable other rights they never enjoyed
before. This applies not only to workers in spot-clean unions
that are subject to rank-and-file pressure but to those who
are shackled in corrupt and undemocratic organizations as
well. The Teamsters' Union, for instance, may be as corrupt as Senator John L. McClellan or the AFL-CIO claims
it is, but who can deny the solid gains made by truck drivers
who, only twenty-five or thirty years ago, worked sixty or
eighty hours a week, slept in the cabs of their trucks, and
earned considerably less than a living wage?

In 1943, truck drivers and warehousemen were earning
$200 a year less than workers in factories, but by 1955 they
had improved their lot so much that they were earning $800
a year more than fellow workers in industry. In 1957, the
very year when the Teamsters' Union was stigmatized as a
result of the McClellan committee hearings, American truck
drivers and warehousemen—all honest and decent citizens—
were receiving average wage increases of fourteen cents per
hour. Everyone, except some extremists, recognizes that in
the matter of wages and working conditions American
unions have served millions of workers exceedingly well.
Few will deny, either, the contribution made by labor to
social reform and the national welfare. Unions have not
only pioneered for legislation to shorten the workday, but

have helped sponsor such measures as a free public-school system, abolition of child labor, antimonopoly laws, unemployment compensation, social security, workmen's compensation for accidents, foreign aid to underdeveloped countries, and civil rights legislation.

Yet, with all of labor's contributions to the social good there are some aspects of the movement that are unhealthy, some that are even shameful. Around a hard core of integrity there has been grafted a veneer of materialism, moral derelictions, and in some cases outright criminality. Around a hard core of "little labor" there has been grafted in recent years a veneer of "big labor." Around a healthy center that serves its members and society at least moderately well, there is a periphery that thwarts progress.

The question is: Why? What are the underlying factors that shape the labor movement? What is there about American labor that is different?

II

The most significant feature of labor unionism is that it operates within a framework of democratic capitalism. It is an instrument of *partial* revolt against capitalists and capitalism, which is indigenous to this one social system. Unions are sometimes allied with radical political movements that are committed to the overthrow of capitalism, but by themselves they are "reformist." They seek redress merely within the confines of the social system that generates them —capitalism. There are no legitimate unions either in the state-i-fied countries of the communist bloc, *etatist* Turkey, the various fascist and near-fascist nations, or in the underdeveloped countries where capitalism has no foothold. There were no unions in America before we had capitalism.

There can be no mystery, therefore, as to why some

unions have become big and some corrupt in recent decades. The pattern of union development adheres closely to that of the social milieu itself; its successes and failures mirror the ups and downs of that milieu. In good times unions prosper, in bad times they weaken—sometimes go out of existence. The rapid growth of the movement in the twentieth century is no more of a "success story" than the rapid growth of mass-production industry, Hollywood, or television. It is, in fact, part of the same success story.

By the time Daniel Tobin—who once slept in a $2.50-a-week room—retired from the presidency of the Teamsters' Union in 1952 he was earning $30,000 a year and the union was providing him with a $45,000 home rent-free, free trips around the United States and Europe for himself and his wife, a guarantee of a full-pay pension, and other emoluments. The man who succeeded him, Dave Beck, received $50,000 a year, plus unlimited expenses, plus free trips to Europe, plus a $50,000-a-year pension after he retired in 1957, plus the free use of a $162,000 mansion in Seattle. When Jimmy Hoffa took over the reins of the union in January, 1958, its treasury was a nice substantial $41 million, and its new building in Washington, D. C., was $5 million worth of lavish luxury.

Hoffa, Beck, and Tobin were all once poor workers, but like so many other Americans they had climbed the ladder from rags to riches. Their story was not too much unlike that of many industrial magnates who had started as factory workers at the turn of the century and ended as presidents of great corporations. Many unionists who think of their movement as more ethical than business have qualms about leaders who earn big salaries and live high; and undoubtedly they are right. But given the spiraling prosperity of American capitalism, there is a natural osmosis of that prosperity and that outlook into the blood stream of certain segments, at least, of the labor movement. If the unions were a *total* revolt against capitalism, a weapon to destroy the system, this probably would not happen. But unions as such are only a *partial* revolt, a means of *modifying* capitalism. They tend, therefore, to conform to the existing social system even while fighting it. And there are times when they conform to the point where their behavior becomes indistinguishable from that of the business community itself.

Partial revolt implies that there is also partial acceptance, partial accommodation to the forces of the status quo. The extent to which labor accommodates to the status quo or fights it determines its specific character at a given moment. Probably no feature of American labor history is so pronounced as the recurring periods of accommodation between our unions and business. For certain periods in our history unions and employers were locked in bitter class conflict, long strikes, and violence. But these have been followed by periods when the two contenders learned to "get along," periods of relative stability and even friendliness. This explains why so many unions have succumbed to business ethics and business mores, or why they have become institutionalized. When they are not "fighting," unions become soft, their treasuries grow, and temptation is put in the way of some of their money-minded leaders.

The process of accommodation between unions and management has not been, however, a uniform process. In the construction industries, for instance, there has been a considerable accommodation. In the agricultural industry, almost none. Various unions, for various reasons, have been more rebellious or less rebellious, have identified their interests with that of management or have been bitterly hostile to it. The result is a peculiar set of contrasts and paradoxes in the house of labor. The movement is rich and poor at the same time, strong and weak, corrupt and idealistic. Some of its leadership draws away from the rank and file, some is closely identified with it.

This duality is obvious in every facet of the labor movement. On the one hand are its positive achievements and intensely dedicated unionists; on the other a number of materialistic and money-hungry leaders. Labor has sheltered in its ranks not a few like William E. Maloney, former president of the Operating Engineers' Union, who squandered hundreds of thousands of dollars; or Dave Beck, former president of the Teamsters, who "borrowed" hundreds of thousands of dollars, interest-free, and who was callous enough to take a commission for collecting money for the widow of a friend. Labor's avowed goal of humanity and brotherhood has been cheapened by fortune seekers. Some decades back, "Big Tim" Murphy of the Chicago Building Trades' Unions defined his philosophy in these graphic words: "I'm still pretty much of a kid, but I made a million and spent a million, and I figure I'll make another million before they plant me." This is the mentality of a robber baron, rather than that of a harassed workingman.

Such gross materialism is an obvious feature of labor's present crisis. It clearly makes a mockery of the egalitarian ideals of the movement. But not so visible to the naked eye is a second negative aspect, perhaps even more damaging to labor's future: institutionalization.

In recent years, almost unnoticed, there has been a corrosion of labor's evangelism. Along with growth, wealth, and stability the major unions have become institutionalized. As used here, the term means more than the evolution of a rigid structure where every man has his "groove." It implies also that there has been a decline in the countervailing power of the rank and file and the secondary leaders, a weakening of the process of dissent, a loss in vitality, a failure to propound new and bold ideas. Not merely the corrupt officials and bureaucrats but the honest leaders of labor have drifted farther away from those they lead, and have lost part of that sense of identification.

III

After almost two decades of unparalleled prosperity in the United States—up to the 1958 recession—the center of gravity of the union movement has shifted farther away from revolt toward accommodation with the status quo. Its idealistic élan has been moderated so that its paradoxes and contradictions are more glaring than at any time in its history.

Leaders like David McDonald of the steelworkers, John L. Lewis of the miners, James R. Hoffa of the teamsters, George Harrison of the railway clerks, earn $50,000 a year or better —plus lush expense accounts. On the other hand the leaders of Joint Council 25 of the shoe workers—affiliated with the same AFL-CIO as McDonald and Harrison—are paid only as much as the average worker in their jurisdiction, $85 a week plus $25 in expense money. President George Fecteau of this international union is rewarded a bit better, $150 a week (no expense money), but the vice-president is paid only $100 and neither has a vote on the national executive board of his organization. That board is composed exclusively of men who work in the factories and who must take time off from the shop to attend national meetings.

At every turn labor is a study of contrasts.

A number of unions have treasuries running into tens of millions of dollars. Labor is therefore called "rich." But a few years ago, when sugar-cane workers needed a mere $700 to appeal an injunction case to the United States Supreme Court, they had to abandon their efforts because this piddling sum was unavailable to their small union.

Labor is called powerful, and there is no doubt that sections of it are. When David McDonald called the steelworkers out on strike in 1956 no one tried to cross the picket line. A whole industry was paralyzed. But when the same McDonald and the late Philip Murray, his predecessor, asked the steelworkers to vote against Senator Robert Taft of Ohio in 1950, the workers did just the opposite. A subsequent study by the political analyst Samuel Lubell indicated that most union members voted for Taft, many as a deliberate act of repudiating their union leaders. When John L. Lewis ordered the many miners' strikes of the last twenty years, his members followed him almost to a man. There were few or no strikebreakers. But when, in 1940, Lewis staked his career as head of the CIO on his support of Wendell Willkie against Franklin D. Roosevelt, the miners, by an overwhelming majority, voted for Roosevelt. The power of labor is a restricted one. The rank-and-file worker, who may give his union allegiance in economic matters, is as likely as not to by-pass its advice and leadership in political matters.

Consider another paradox. Labor's leadership in the United States is, ideologically, the most conservative in the world. Ours is the only labor movement that endorses the free-enterprise system. Elsewhere union politics usually meshes with some form of socialist or radical ideology for overturning capitalism. Yet, despite the moderate philosophy of American labor, in the economic sphere it is the most militant in the world. In an ordinary year it is involved in more strikes, for longer periods, than the rest of the legitimate trade-union movements put together.

What then *is* American labor? Is it George Harrison and his $64,719-a-year salary or the shoe worker official and his $85 a week? The rich steel union or the poor agricultural workers' union that could not afford a $700 injunction fight? John L. Lewis the strike leader or John L. Lewis the politician? The conservative words of the movement or its militant strike statistics?

Any sweeping estimate of American labor is unquestionably false, for labor is far from homogeneous. It is truly an agglomeration of many "labor movements," living together.

On closer examination there are at least four different kinds
of union leaders: racketeers, business unionists, social unionists, and radical unionists. And there are two main historical
threads which mark their lineage. Business unionism, which
has predominated as the main current of American labor for
decades, grew primarily out of the simple unionism propounded by Samuel Gompers and the AFL after its formation in 1886. Social (as distinct from social*ist*) unionism is
an offshoot of the radicalism of the nineteenth century and
the minority currents of radicalism in this century, particularly in the 1930's. Each of these union forms is really a
world apart, with different ethics, different ideologies, and
different orientations. At the center there are blends and in-
termixtures, but at the poles there is a universe between
Dave Beck and Walter Reuther. They do not speak the same
language or think the same thoughts. When Reuther was
forced to lay off 100 of the 750 staff members of his Auto
Workers' Union in May, 1958, both he and the other twenty-
four top leaders took a pay cut of 10 per cent themselves as
a gesture of solidarity. Such a thing would never have occurred to a Dave Beck. When Beck sold a secondhand Cadillac that belonged to his union, he pocketed the small sum of
money. To Beck, labor is a "business"; to Reuther and his
friends, business ethics are anathema. Yet both men are part
of the labor movement.

IV

The worlds of labor operate within and relate to the
worlds of capitalism. They do not slavishly accept the ethics
or mores of capitalism; but neither do they entirely reject
them. Unions emerge only as a by-product of industrialism
and political democracy. Their forms change as capitalism
itself changes. The first unions in the United States were
formed in 1794; those in czarist Russia, only a hun-

dred years later. In England, unions were contemporary with the industrial revolution and the political reforms of the early nineteenth century; but in Greece, unions emerged only fifty years ago; in Norway, in 1872; and in many Asiatic and African countries they are only now coming into being. In many of the nations of the so-called free world legitimate unions do not yet exist—Siam, Egypt, Turkey, to name a few. In those countries there is only a veneer of capitalism and little political democracy.

The saga of labor is a reflection of national history and national problems. Unions in Bolivia, for instance, are revolutionary. In the 1952 revolution which brought Paz Estenssoro to power, workers swept down from the tin mines in commandeered trucks to toss dynamite at the army. The unions they formed under the leadership of Juan Lechin drilled as "workers' militia" and were highly political and class conscious. These unionists were willing to fight with their lives for a better world. They were clearly more militant or radical than their contemporaries either in Britain or America. Yet they earned many times less than a British worker—let alone an American worker. Militancy, combativeness, unity, solidarity are necessary qualities for a labor movement, but in themselves they are not enough to win concessions. There must also be an expansive economy that has enough resources—enough "give"—to yield wage-and-hour gains. An American company that grants a fifteen-cents-an-hour raise may not enjoy doing so, but it is not irreparably hurt; it can stay in business—often without any loss of profits, since it usually improves its productive efficiency to make up the cost. American workers can therefore win their demands through collective bargaining or economic (as opposed to revolutionary) strikes. But a fifteen-cents-an-hour wage increase in Bolivia is impossible. The economy has no such "give." Almost no private employer and no government can concede so "staggering" a demand without facing bankruptcy. To win such a concession Bolivian workers would have to go over to revolution; they could not achieve it through normal bargaining or simple strikes.

The type of union leader, too, is a coefficient of the social milieu. A man like George Meany ideally fits the role of president of the AFL-CIO at this historical juncture. A strong devotee of the free-enterprise system, practical, honest, strongly—almost blindly—anticommunist, he once boasted before a meeting of employers that he had never personally been in a strike or walked a picket line. In a country where radicalism has virtually disappeared, Meany is an excellent catalyst for the more moderate forms of unionism which comprise his federation. But with his free-enterprise philosophy he could never be selected as union leader in Bolivia, or Britain, France, Italy, Germany, or Japan. The man who heads the British Trades Union Congress can only be a member of the Labour party and an avowed socialist. The president of the German Union Federation (DGB) could hardly be elected to that post if he were not a member of the Social Democratic party (SPD). Even Walter Reuther, who is considered an extremist in some circles in the United States, would have no chance to be selected as leader of most European trade-union movements because of his present nonsocialist philosophy.

The social milieu sets the limits for many features of the labor movement—its structure, collective bargaining methods, leadership, even its forms of opportunism. That explains why there are no Dave Becks or William Maloneys in the European labor movement. The leaders of labor overseas are not paragons of virtue, selfless and consistently idealistic; but their opportunism, where it does exist—and it naturally does—is of a different nature from the American species. It consists of a certain political moderation that accommodates itself to prevailing employer politics, rather than the use of the union as a vehicle for personal profit.

Leaders of European labor earn vastly less than their counterparts in the United States. A survey of British union leaders two or three years ago revealed that the average salary of the heads of the thirty biggest unions was only $3,360 a year. Few received more than $100 a week. There were no unlimited expense accounts, and officials who were given the use of an automobile by their organization were rare. Lower down in the hierarchy, the average organizer—equivalent to our business agents—earned only $30 to $35 a week. Bribes, pay-offs by employers, "sweetheart" contracts, and other vices that exist in some American unions are unknown in Europe. The social milieu, social values, and economic conditions are different from ours; therefore union morality differs too.

The less favored economic circumstances of the old world have left their imprint on the character of its labor movement. What stands out there is the lasting marriage of unionism and socialism. In the United States these two forces were divorced after the nation entered a period of rapid growth. But in Europe, with economic progress usually slower, unionism and socialist or radical politics have been inseparable. In most countries, in fact—in Scandinavia, Germany, Italy, France, Holland, Belgium—it was the socialists who first organized the trade unions. English unions followed a somewhat different course, associating themselves with the radical wing of the Liberal party (much as our American unions today are allied with the liberal wing of the Democratic party), until 1900-1906 when they formed their own separate Labour party. In 1918, under the political guidance of the Fabian Society and the Independent Labour party, the Labour party declared itself socialist in philosophy—though not Marxist—and it has remained so ever since. In Germany today the DGB is theoretically neutral, but in actual practice it is an abiding partner of the Social Democrats. In France, Holland, Belgium, and Italy where Catholic (and in one case, Protestant) unionism has a foothold, there are three or more federations of labor, each a satellite of a different political party. But at least two of these federations in each country is associated with either the Socialist or Communist parties, and within the Catholic federations there is, in most cases, a left wing which is also socialist in ideology.

The European economy for the most part did not achieve the viability of the American. It was broken into too many small units, each protecting its industry by high tariff walls, and each lacking the mass market that was such an incentive for industrial development in the United States. It was hampered in some countries, such as France, Italy, or Austria, by feudal social carry-overs which inhibited its growth, and incessant strife and warfare, culminating in two world wars which shattered not only the nations' terrain but their economies. The result was a wave of revolutions, near-revolutions, and sharp class struggles; three revolutions in Germany, the 1926 general strike in Britain, the sitdown strikes in France, and the defeated struggles of labor in Italy and Germany which paved the way for fascism.

Politics in Europe remained decisive for labor, and state power was its avowed goal. The workers, harassed by wars and involved in revolutions, were class-conscious and socialist-conscious to a degree unknown in the more placid terrain of twentieth-century America. European workers saw no solution for their problems except in fundamental social change. And their leaders could only come from a radical political movement which, regardless of merits or demerits, imposed mores, ethics, values, and ideas sharply at loggerheads with those of the business community. As members of the Labour party in Britain, the S.F.I.O. of France, or the Social Democratic party of Sweden, they could hardly preach socialism if they lived in $162,000 mansions or earned $50,000 a year plus unlimited expenses.

American workers, on the other hand, have never been pressed to the point of revolution, have never called a nation-wide general strike; and though they have been harassed and exploited, they have not been class-conscious in the same sense as their European brothers. A more bounteous economy and a general level of prosperity—though interrupted by periodic depressions—have cut the ground from under radicalism on these shores. The mores, ethics, values, and ideas of labor's leadership have frequently tended therefore toward those of the business community.

The specific forms of American labor are rooted not in the views or talents of its leaders so much as in the development of American capitalism. No one can deny the role—for good or evil—of capable men like Samuel Gompers, Peter McGuire, William Green, John L. Lewis, Philip Murray, Walter Reuther, George Meany, James R. Hoffa and many others, in forging the types of labor movements that have emerged in the United States. But the evidence indicates that these leaders were more the products of their milieu than its producers. The "fathers" of American labor are not so much individual men as social developments.

Yet at key historical moments "great" men can alter the course of events. A new philosophy can awaken the populace to take measures for basic change. In that sense the leaders of American labor are charged with offering their constituents new hopes and new goals for improving society. The great leader rises above his milieu; the mediocre one merely sinks into it.

The crisis of American labor consists precisely in the fact that while America itself is in a crisis, the leaders of labor have failed to rise above the narrowness and rote of their epoch. They have failed to chart a new direction.

To evaluate this crisis and to trace labor's two main currents—business unionism and social unionism—it is essential to dig deep in American history. For here one notes similar impasses and other attempts at solution, as well as the roots for the current forms of labor unionism.

2
The Radical Heritage

THREE MAJOR EVENTS FASHIONED THE UNITED STATES FROM thirteen divided and separate colonies into a modern industrial nation. At each of these historical turning points the country was at an impasse, doomed to stagnation if it failed to remove the historical roadblock, or ready to unleash great momentum, if it did. It seems to be inherent in the progress of nations that they must either meet these challenges head-on or lapse into suspended animation. Our twenty Latin-American neighbors are an excellent, though tragic, illustration of what happens when inner social contradictions are not resolved. Had the great dreamer of Latin-American unity, Simon Bolivar, been successful in welding the nations freed from Spanish and Portugese tyranny into one, or a few, viable nations, they too might have experienced substantial growth. As it was, they remained saddled with much of the feudal past—backward, poor, hungry, illiterate. And most of their labor movements, in harmony with stagnant or slow-moving economies, have remained either state-dominated and impotent as under Rafael Trujillo, Fulgencio Batista, Getulio Vargas, Juan Peron, Perez Jiminez; or become revolutionary as in Bolivia.

The United States has been more fortunate. As a result of the American Revolution, the Civil War, and the New Deal under Franklin Roosevelt, it has swept aside social impediments to make progress possible. Without these, it would never have pushed beyond the Mississippi, nor united into one coast-to-coast nation, nor established what has been called the American standard of living. Nor would it have laid the groundwork for the kind of labor movement we now have.

At the time of the American Revolution the thirteen colonies had reached a dead end; they could only mark time unless they removed the social and economic shackles of British rule. Under British policy the colonies were expected to produce cotton, tobacco, and other materials, ship them to England in British bottoms, and purchase finished goods from the mother country in return. They were not to manufacture on their own, except in limited amounts and under special permit. During the seventeenth century there were only eight iron centers in the whole land, none of them employing more than five workers. Parliament disallowed laws to aid American industry on the grounds that it would "interfere with the manufacture of this kingdom [and] has always been thought improper." Restrictions on settling the public domain confined the colonies and their expanding population to the East Coast; the British wanted their subject peoples concentrated into a relatively small area where they could be more easily controlled.

Economic life too—following European feudal and semi-feudal patterns—was often highly restrictive. Tenants had to sign compacts with their landlords not to trade anywhere but at the landlords' stores, to grind flour at their mills, to buy bread at their bakeries, lumber at their sawmills, and spirits at their stills. Many landlords were so powerfully placed they had their own insignia and flags. Their domains were fortified, armed with cannon, protected by paid mercenaries; and the tenant was like a chattel.

Wage workers were then few in number. Frequently they worked only in the off season, between crops. Those who did work all year around were usually bound to their jobs for a period of time—a year, for instance—prohibited from quitting, and limited to wages no higher than those prescribed by law. The Massachusetts Bay Colony proclaimed in 1633 that "carpenters, sawyers, masons, bricklayers, tilers, joiners, wheelwrights, movers and other workmen were not to receive more than two shillings a day, each paying his own board." On a number of occasions during the year a wage earner in some colonies might be required to work on public projects, and in others he had to help with the harvest. Economic life was rigid, inflexible, and centralized. Rapid industrial growth in such a social climate was impossible. And so were labor unions.

A group of fishermen off the coast of Maine were reported in a "mutiny" in 1636 when their wages were held back. In 1667, cartmen in New York refused to move dirt from the streets for the pay of threepence a load. In 1741, in the same city, bakers, in order to protect their price level, refused to bake bread. But these were episodic and spontaneous efforts by small entrepreneurs rather than wage workers, and uncoordinated through any union. For the first 187 years—or more than half of American history—there were no true labor unions. Our forefathers were not pacifistic men who suffered the whip without fighting. Life in the colonies was hard, and the frontiersman, the Negro slave, and the white indentured servant struck back frequently. There were revolts of the backwoodsmen such as that of Nathaniel Bacon of Virginia in 1676, John Culpepper of Baltimore in 1689,

Leisler in New York the same year, and others. There were scores of uprisings by indentured servants and harassed Negroes. These were "all-or-nothing" struggles, in which the price of defeat was sometimes death. But the instrument of partial revolt, the labor union, was impossible when there was so little manufacture, few wage earners, and no true political democracy.

II

The American Revolution resolved this impasse. After the victory of Washington's tattered army it was possible for the United States to evolve—hesitantly, it is true, but inexorably—along capitalist lines. The strictures on industry and trade were removed. Enterprise became free and businessmen "equal before the law," no longer restricted by guilds which prescribed prices and quality. The laborer was freed from bondage. He no longer was bound to his job for a specific period; he could quit when he wanted to and work where he pleased without being termed a vagrant. The Revolution changed the face of America. Labor-saving machines, carefully hoarded by Britain and France, were smuggled in from overseas, and a modest manufacturing industry arose side by side with the more bountiful commerce. The nation remained predominantly agricultural, but it was on its way toward industrialism.

In the wake of these developments, the first unions were minor and flimsy affairs. Workers agreed amongst themselves in secret meetings, usually under oath, to work only for established wage rates, and to assist their fellow workers when necessary. When there was a "turn-out"—a strike—the men merely stayed home, without bothering to establish picket lines, until their demands were met. Sometimes they put a notice in a newspaper, putting forth their position as against that of the employers, seeking to win public support. Periodically, in line with the then prevailing common law in Britain, such groupings were prosecuted as illegal "conspiracies," and disappeared from the scene—only to reappear again some time later. The first union, that of the Federal Society of Journeymen Cordwainers (shoemakers), established in Philadelphia in 1794, lasted but twelve years. Except for those of the printers and shoemakers there were no continuous organizations until the 1820's. The word, *union,* itself, was not used until 1825, when we first hear of a "mailers' union" and a "weavers' union."

These original, rudimentary organizations had to be craft unions in structure because manufacture was primitive. Division of labor was rare; the man at the workbench made the whole product from beginning to end. The unions then were also unstable and ephemeral; first, because there still existed strong ties between the worker and the employer, who himself was only one hairsbreadth removed from journeyman status, and secondly, because the amount of money needed to open a new business was insignificant. It was so small, in fact, that after losing a strike journeymen frequently united to compete with their former bosses. In 1806, following their conviction for "conspiracy" to organize, the shoemakers of Philadelphia opened their own warehouse. Journeymen often united for a single venture—say, to publish a book—and then returned to the workbench for their employers.

The first unions were primitive, uncertain of their future, unclear as to their direction. But once they had caught their breath and begun to coalesce into city central bodies, they became highly political and radical. The Workingmen's party in New York in 1829 polled 6,000 votes of a total of 21,000, probably a higher percentage than labor has ever polled since, as an independent political force.

One newspaper commenting on labor's agitation in 1830

said: "We discern symptoms of a revolution, which will be second to none save that of '76." At least fifty labor newspapers were founded in this period. According to historian Mary Beard, "political organizations along the old, familiar lines of county and ward committees and conventions were established; and radical agitators demanding revolutionary changes came to the front."

Equality was the byword of these movements. They demanded equal ownership of property, equal citizenship, equal opportunities for education through a free public-school system, abolition of imprisonment for debt, abolition of the militia system, and similar reforms. The New York Workingmen's party stated that "all human society, our own included as well as every other, is constructed radically wrong." It opposed both private ownership of land and inheritance of wealth. Other radical reformers such as Robert Dale Owen and Frances Wright proposed the formation of cooperative communities as a means of by-passing the evils of private property.

This was long before the day of Marx and Engels or the British Labour party, yet there is no mistaking the socialist flavor of American labor in its formative period. The words of the Working Men's Republican Political Association of Penn Township, Pennsylvania, sound like a foretaste of the *Communist Manifesto:* "There appear to exist two distinct classes, the rich and the poor; the oppressed and the oppressor; those that live by their own labor and they that live by the labor of others; the aristocratic and the democratic; the despotic and republican, who are in direct opposition to one another in their objects and pursuits. . . ."

When the second French Revolution took place in 1830, a line of unionists three miles long marched in a parade in New York City as an enthusiastic endorsement of the aims of that revolution.

The flair for independent labor parties lasted only a few

years, but even after their disappearance labor continued
to agitate for cooperation, free land, and other panaceas.
Some unions set up self-employing workshops, the profits of
which were to be equally divided among the men themselves. The Journeymen Molders' Union established a
foundry near Cincinnati, and the Tailors' and Shirt Sewers
formed similar producers' cooperatives. Though none of
these prospered for long, American labor in the first half of
the nineteenth century came back to cooperation time and
again as a means out of its dilemma. Utopian reforms, cooperation, and various other nostrums were more in the forefront of- labor's thinking than simple wage-and-hour issues.
Before the Civil War the demand for free land became insistent. Labor sought for such panaceas because it had no
faith, as yet, in either the stability or justice of the capitalist
system.

Union conventions listened attentively to the great radicals of the day: Horace Greeley, George Ripley, Albert Bris-
bane, Wendell Phillips, William Lloyd Garrison, Charles
A. Dana, William H. Channing, Robert Owen, and many
others.

From 1790 to 1845 one million immigrants came to America, and in the following decade another three million. The
frustrated revolutionaries of nineteenth-century Europe fled
to the United States, and here continued their radical
preachings, built unions and cooperatives, and agitated for
free land and agrarian reform. The line of demarcation between unionism and socialist politics or panaceas was quite
thin.

An unstable capitalism produced a radical labor movement, more radical than that of any other in the world at
that time.

In structure too, the tenuous unionism followed closely the
limits laid down for it by early capitalism. In 1800, it still
took two weeks—sixteen hours a day of hard riding by stage

coach—to reach Indiana from New York. It took six weeks to reach St. Louis. Under such circumstances neither capital nor labor could be highly integrated. Local unions tended to group into city-central bodies, and did not try to form national craft organizations. For the better part of a century these city bodies—composed of unions of different crafts in a single city—were to be the power center of the movement.

When the National Trades' Union was organized in 1834 it consisted of seven city bodies—not a single national craft union. The city bodies did the organizing of new workers, coordinated strike action, engaged in politics. Their leaders, like those of the local unions themselves, were usually men who worked at the bench in the daytime and conducted their union activity in spare moments, nights and weekends, without pay, and with little glory. Such a unionism could only be idealistic, and unsullied by the ills of bigness that were to plague not only labor but the rest of our society later on.

The emasculation of these city-central bodies toward the end of the nineteenth century, and their reduction to minor legislative roles today, lowered the curtain on a proud period in labor's history. Union protagonists can be permitted a moment of nostalgia for this "little" labor movement which no longer exists, nor can ever exist again, but which, while it lasted, was free of the specific problems that bedevil the labor movement today when by force of circumstance it has been separated a few notches farther from the rank and file.

III

The second major turning point in American history was the Civil War.

In the American saga this was, both for industry and labor, the bridge between "littleness" and "bigness." Osten-

sibly the most dramatic issue in the war between the states
was the freedom of the Negro slave. But at bottom, what was
at stake was America's future as an industrial nation, capable
not only of competing with, but outstripping Europe. In the
thirty-five years following this bloody intramural conflict,
production was increased by almost five, railroads by almost seven, times. From 1859 to 1899, the number of industrial plants tripled, the number of wage earners quadrupled,
the value of commodities increased by seven times, and the
amount of invested capital skyrocketed to nine times its
former level. In the same period in England the value of products inched up by only 50 per cent, in France 45 per cent,
and in Germany, then making the most rapid progress of all
Europe, by a mere 65 per cent. Favored by its geographic
position, safely wedged in between two oceans and militarily
impregnable, blessed with unbelievable material wealth
discovered in the West and the human wealth of millions of
new immigrants, the United States grew far more rapidly than the atomized, hemmed-in, warring nations of Europe.

But none of this American advance could have been
achieved if King Cotton in the South had not first been subdued. King Cotton was the halter around America's neck,
preventing a mercantile nation from becoming an industrial
one. The kind of America it sought was radically different
from the kind of America sought by an industry-conscious
North; and had it maintained its political grip on Congress
and the administration as in the previous decades, it would
have been fatal both for industry—and labor.

King Cotton, after the invention of the cotton gin, needed
new land to the North and West to replace the rapidly exhausted and poorly utilized land in the South. By wile and
guile, therefore, it opposed the opening of the public domain to the free farmer and pioneer for fear they might pre-

empt lands the South too wanted. It opposed state expenditure for roads, canals and other improvements which might benefit the capitalists to the North, but would only impose additional taxes on Southern Bourbons. It saw little sense in high tariffs to protect infant industries because its own *modus operandi* was based on selling cotton to England in exchange for cheaper goods from a more mature British industry. What the North wanted in high tariffs, new roads, subsidies to railroads, the South could not grant except at its own expense. The conflict therefore was "irrepressible" and the victory of the North indispensable if America were to be converted to giant industry, corporate management, and coast-to-coast abundance.

The Civil War, catastrophic as it was to both North and South, was from a historical point of view a vitalizing event. It did not bring the Negro slave full freedom nor did it obliterate all vestiges of Bourbonism in the South; but it did open more free land to the West for anxious pioneers, it did push the "iron horse" and highways inexorably westward, and it did give nascent American industry the tariff protection, the mass markets, and the subsidies it needed to bloom and flourish. As one of its side effects it also plowed the field for the simple, "business" unionism, that was a special American brand—unknown elsewhere.

Few people, either in industry or labor, understood the long-term implications of the Civil War at the time. Employers, for at least two decades, continued their frontal attacks on the labor movement, smashed scores of strikes, and forced many unions out of business, particularly during the depression of 1873-1878. Jay Gould, the railroad tycoon, typified the more harsh and perhaps prevailing management attitude when he said: "I can hire one-half of the working class to kill the other half." Class lines were drawn taut; hundreds died in the struggles between the Molly Maguires—

a secret organization of coal miners—and the coal operators, in the railroad strikes of 1877, the Haymarket Riot in Chicago in 1886, and other disorders.

For their part, union leaders had little faith in the new capitalism or little hope of advancing the cause of the workingman within its framework. Most of them de-emphasized the simple bread-and-butter approach in favor of panaceas, "uplift," and socialism. The socialist content of unionism remained more important for many key union leaders than the wage-and-hour demands.

William H. Sylvis, one of the great unionists of this era and the architect of the first federation organized after the Civil War, the National Labor Union, believed that formation of producers' cooperatives would eventually undermine the capitalist way of life. "We must adopt a system," he said, "which will divide the profits of labor among those who produce them." Disillusioned with simple union objectives after his Molders' Union—the most important union of this period—was defeated in a strike, he organized the Troy Cooperative Iron Founders' Association. This approach had considerable appeal and was followed by many other unions— Bakers, Coal Miners, Printers, Machinists, Shipwrights, Shoemakers. It seemed like a simple answer: why let the employers pocket the profit sweated out of the workers' hides, when the workers could and should have it all to themselves? The amount of capital needed for business ventures was still not prohibitive; the program of producers' cooperatives was thus more attractive than that of striking for higher wages.

The International Labor Union, formed in 1878 by socialists and anarcho-syndicalists, attacked the problem in a different way, but all to the same end: the abolition of capitalism. The leaders of this group, Parsons, Schilling, Wedemeyer, Sorge, called for such an increase in wages "until wages represent the earnings and not the necessities of labor;

thus melting profit upon labor out of existence, and making cooperation, self-employed labor, the natural and logical step from wage slavery to free labor."

Cooperation and uplift were also the theme of the successful Knights of Labor, which grew by 1886 to 700,000 members. The Knights spoke of "harmonizing the interests of capital and labor," and had little faith in strikes or in the struggle for wage increases and shorter hours. Terrence Powderly, the vain, platitudinous "Grand Master Workman" of the Knights, refused to endorse the eight-hour-day movement in 1886 (one of the reasons for the decline of his organization) on the grounds that such gains were illusory. The end goal, he said, must be to abolish the wage system itself through cooperation, not to try to improve the system.

Few people, either on labor's or management's side, seemed to foresee the day when some *modus vivendi* could be established, or when labor could be appeased within the context of capitalism.

America, then as today—though not in the same proportions—was a study in contrasts, big and little, rich and poor. "There are too many millionaires and too many paupers," cried the *Hartford Courant* in 1883. President Cleveland, in his message to Congress in December, 1888, spoke of "the existence of trusts, combinations and monopolies, while the citizen is struggling far in the rear or is trampled to death beneath an iron heel." Samuel Gompers complained in 1883 that wages were lower than in 1870. The United States Census of 1880 estimated per capita income at $300, whereas a decade earlier it was $400. Despite growing prosperity there was also great poverty; side by side with the concentration of capital into large aggregates, there was unemployment and wage slashing.

Under the circumstances it is quite understandable that many unionists could see little hope in the prevailing social system. For the most part they were fighting defensive

battles to prevent wage cuts or to win wages back, once they
were cut. Strikes were incredibly harsh affairs, and unions
disappeared in depressed years as if into a squall. In the depression year of 1877, for instance, there were three million
unemployed. Of the newly formed national craft unions only
twenty-two of thirty survived. Cigar makers lost four-fifths
of their membership; New York's union roster fell by eight-
ninths, from 44,000 to only 5,000. Textile strikers in Fall
River, hitting back at wage cuts, lost two bitter strikes after
almost a half year on the picket line. The 1877 railway
strike, across the nation, reads almost like a revolution:
twenty-six workers killed by troops in Pittsburgh, thirteen
killed in Reading, $5 million in car shops and other property
set afire in one city, the workers in St. Louis so aroused that
for two weeks they took over the city itself. Yet all the
strikes of this period were beaten. In the midst of a mush-
rooming capitalism came depressions; and in the midst of
depressions the labor movement suffered a severe setback.

But the setbacks of one decade were followed by insistent
new efforts—and new setbacks—in the next. After the depressions of the 1870's the wheels of industry began to grind
forward once more in the 1880's. The number of factories
grew from 253,852 to 355,405, their capital from 2.8 to
$6.5 billions. In a more prosperous period many strikes were
won. Strikes against Jay Gould's railroad system were victor-
ious, and in their wake labor added hundreds of thousands
of members. But another strike, against the McCormick Harvester factory in Chicago, ended in the Haymarket Riot and
the eventual hanging of four anarchist leaders. Now the
offensive against labor mounted again. Thousands of unionists were blacklisted, many driven off company property at
gun point. Committees that went in to discuss grievances
with employers were as often as not told to leave the premises. Spies were introduced by the hundreds, and Pinkerton

agents were used in large numbers both for espionage and to break strikes.

The mere assertion that this was a decade of great industrial growth does not accurately picture the turmoil and unevenness of this development, the heartache and tribulations of the millions of immigrants and native workers who sought security in the factories and railroads being built by the "robber barons." To such men industrial tyranny was real, and the theories of socialism and radicalism not unattractive. Did anyone really believe that the Vanderbilts and the Goulds could be "put in their place," made to yield wage increases of five cents and ten cents an hour without near-warfare? The facts seemed to belie it. Did anyone really think that the recurring depressions almost each decade could be stopped so long as the titans of industry were politically so powerful? A large segment of America, in addition to the labor movement, had no such confidence. This was the era when Populism was sinking roots amongst the farmers, when the West manifested deep hostility to the corporations of the East. Something more radical than "higher wages and shorter hours"—important in themselves—seemed on the social and political agenda. Producers' cooperatives lost their appeal as the years slipped by, but more mature forms of socialism gained stature with the laboring man, particularly in depression times.

In 1893 the United States experienced another depression, and in 1894, there came—again as a defensive measure against wage cuts—one of the most bitter strikes in American history, labeled in the press the "Debs Rebellion." Eugene V. Debs, a tall, kindly, humane railroad worker, later to become the leader and presidential standard bearer of the Socialist party, in 1893-1894 organized 150,000 men into the American Railway Union. Before the group could stabilize, however, it was confronted with its first—and last— major test.

The trouble started at Pullman in Illinois, where the maker of sleeping cars, George Pullman, ruled an empire strongly reminiscent of feudal days. His workers lived in Pullman tenements, paid him exorbitant rents, bought at his high-priced stores, sent their children to his school, attended his church, took relaxation in his theater or park, and lived a life completely circumscribed by the likes and dislikes of the "boss." Needless to say, Pullman was against liquor, sin, and unionism. In the midst of the 1893 panic about one-third of the labor force was laid off and the rest took wage cuts ranging from 25 to 33 per cent. A committee of the men met with Pullman to seek rent cuts and restoration of the wage cuts, but to no avail. Debs tried to moderate the actions of the workers, but when three of their leaders were discharged they struck.

A month and a half later railroad unionists throughout the country refused to handle Pullman cars, cutting off the sleepers and sidetracking them. The employers, through their General Managers' Association, responded with discharges and the ensuing strike paralyzed a large amount of railroad traffic throughout the nation. Before it was over the Association had deputized 3,600 men, who, in the words of a federal commission that investigated the matter, were "armed and paid by the employers and acted in the double capacity of railroad employees and United States officers." Two thousand railroad cars were wrecked, $50 to $100 million in property destroyed, a general strike was called in Chicago, scores of injunctions were issued, and 10,000 federal troops were mobilized by President Cleveland to break the strike.

A decade later, in 1903-1904, another American depression interrupted the steady spiral upward. In its wake, another radical force came into being, the picturesque Industrial Workers of the World, or, as they were popularly known, the Wobblies.

IV

Inexorably, however, the lure of radicalism was being dimmed. Capitalism's development was uneven and the division of its bounty far from just, but from decade to decade it stabilized at an ever higher plateau. In the wake of phenomenal progress it was able to yield important benefits to the workingman. Beginning with 1886, it spawned a new type of unionism—simple, bread-and-butter unionism—a unionism that eventually separated itself from socialism. Such a development could occur in the United States because, compared to Europe, there was far more resiliency in the American economy, far more possibilities of appeasing the laborer, particularly the skilled laborer. Poverty remained—and remains—a blight on the national conscience. Franklin Roosevelt could talk in the 1930's of the one-third of the nation that was ill-fed, ill-housed and ill-clothed, and even after World War II, at the height of the economic swing, four of every ten families were living on standards below what the United States Department of Labor considered minimal—$75 to $80 a week. Yet, it is undeniable, despite depression and setback, the system stabilized to the point where it could grant considerable concessions to sizable groups. It opened safety valves and deflected the laborer's horizons from panaceas to simple demands for "more"—more wages, more leisure, more security. A conjunction of interests between segments of the employing class and segments of the laboring class encouraged and solidified the new unionism. As usual, this conjuncture resulted not from the connivings of any unionists or the philosophical meanderings of any groups of employers. On the contrary, it emerged naturally from the "give" in American capitalism. The piling up of wealth released the tensions between the capitalist in construction and other industries, and the skilled workers, making possible a policy of accommodation rather than attenuated and ceaseless class warfare. But this policy of accommodation evolved in the course of a number of decades; as a natural concomitant of rapid economic growth, it was part of no preconceived plan or conspiracy.

The men who formed the AFL in 1886 were not altogether simple unionists. Peter J. McGuire, who became its secretary and who headed the largest affiliate, the carpenters, was a lifelong and fiery socialist. Before he was twenty he had been in and through most of the radical groups on New York's East Side. He had helped found the Socialist Labor party and he remained socialism's friend within the AFL ranks until the beginning of the new century. Samuel Gompers, first president and architect of the AFL, belonged to no political party but he also originally considered himself a socialist and an advocate of the class struggle. "The man," he said, "who would accuse me or charge me with being an anti-Socialist says what he don't know anything about, he does not know Sam Gompers. I say here broadly and openly that there is not a noble hope that a Socialist may have that I do not hold as my ideal. There is not an inspiring and ennobling end that they are striving for that my heart does not beat in response to." In 1887, he defined his philosophy in concert "with most advanced thinkers" as the "abolition of the wage system." In contrast to the theories of the Knights of Labor about the harmony of interests between labor and capital, Gompers insisted that "the interests of the employing class and the workers are not harmonious . . . the struggles of labor cannot be obviated in the future." The Federation itself proclaimed in its preamble that "a struggle is going on in all nations of the civilized world between the oppressors and the oppressed of all countries, a struggle between the capitalist and the laborer."

These were obviously not the words of simple unionists. What motivated McGuire, Gompers, and their colleagues to form the AFL was not a desire for more tepid unionism, but for a more militant type. The Knights of Labor, at the time, had become openly hostile to craft-union walkouts and, in line with the theory of class harmony, had helped undersell and break many strikes, including one by Gompers' cigarmakers. Organization of the AFL was an act of self-defense by the unionists within the Knights, who were prevented from taking decisive action for higher wages and shorter hours, and who therefore coalesced with craft unions outside the Knights to form the AFL. On their banner in 1886 and for the following decade was the then radical demand for an eight-hour day. McGuire's carpenters sparked a great demonstration in 1890 for this objective and won a substantial victory not only for themselves but for other unionists as well. This effort was in conjunction with May Day demonstrations by socialists throughout the world and it brought forth jubilant estimates by Marx's collaborator, Frederick Engels, about the unity of the "proletariat of Europe and America." Though their immediate goals were economic—higher wages, shorter hours—many of the first AFL leaders considered these as the first step toward the broader goal of abolishing the wage system, capitalism, itself. Socialists like Daniel De Leon exercised considerable influence on the AFL in its first days, and the socialist group remained a potent minority force within the organization for a few decades.

The men who led the AFL in its first period were selfless zealots. Eugene V. Debs, who became one of its most virile critics in later years, said of them: "The labor agitator of the early days held no office, had no title, drew no salary, saw no footlights, heard no applause, never saw his name in print and fills an unknown grave."

Mother Jones, one of the colorful contemporaries of this formative stage, wrote in her autobiography:

These early leaders sought no publicity. They were single-minded, not interested in their own glory nor their own financial advancement. They did not serve labor for pay. . . . Never in the early days of the labor struggle would you find leaders wining and dining with the aristocracy, nor did their wives strut about like diamond bedecked peacocks; nor were they attended by humiliated, cringing colored servants. The wives of these leaders took in washing to make ends meet. Their children picked and sold berries. . . . In those days, labor's representatives did not sit on velvet chairs in conference with labor's oppressors. They did not dine in fashionable hotels with the representatives of the capitalists such as the Civic Federation. They did not ride in Pullmans nor make trips to Europe.

Until the time Sam Gompers became president of the AFL he had never held a salaried job with a labor union. His wage as the head of the new federation, frequently unpaid, was less than $20 a week. The AFL treasurer received only a token salary of $100 a year. Labor's struggle for existence was still so hard, and the sacrifices imposed on rank and file and leader both so great, that only a dream of a beautiful tomorrow could sustain the union leader in his task. Whatever else their faults or blind spots, neither Gompers nor any of his associates could have conceived of the vulgar philosophy of Dave Beck: "I run the union just like a business. We deal in one commodity—labor." Nor could any of them dream of a day when men like William E. Maloney of the operating engineers would earn $55,000 a year, plus an average of $56,000 a year in addition for expense money.

It was only in the following decades that American prosperity became the magnet to draw union leaders, in increasing number, away from their idealism and self-sacrifice to "business unionism." Capital investment in industry, which had increased ninefold from 1860 to 1900, doubled again in the next decade, and by 1919, it was six times what it had been in 1900. The value of manufactured products, which doubled from 1900 to 1910, tripled again in the next ten-year period. This was a setting ideally suited for that special and unique unionism which jettisoned the noble ideals of labor's pioneers in favor of the rugged individualism of the business community.

The Civil War and the general prosperity which it initiated was the true father of business unionism; just as it was for the "robber barons," the monopolies, and that peculiar American philosophy; "every man for himself, devil take the hindmost."

V

This second major turning point in our history eventually was followed by a third. After the 1929 depression, America reached a new impasse. The wheels of industry ground to a halt, the majority of the working class was reduced to unemployment or partial employment, and a whole new set of government principles and measures was necessary before the impasse could be breached. The New Deal was a face-lifting of America, another stage of the American revolution; it was also the precursor of a new type of unionism—social unionism—that would eventually give business unionism its greatest challenge. We shall return to the New Deal era later in our chronicle. But two generations were to elapse between the birth of business unionism and this challenge. In that period it sank roots so deep that it made a shambles of many labor ideals.

3
The Business Agents Take Over

IN 1883, ACCORDING TO LABOR LEGEND, A NEW YORK CARPEN-
ter, James Lynch, became the first union "walking delegate."
Union affairs, hitherto, had been handled by a job steward
in his spare time, before and after work. Now Lynch was
taken off the job and paid by his fellow workers to walk
from place to place policing against piecework, enforcing
apprentice rules, collecting dues, organizing new workers,
and handling other sundry tasks. The hiring of Lynch was a
response to a practical challenge. Fly-by-night subcontractors
in New York were hiring nonunion men to install doors,
stairs, or windows in half-finished buildings on a piecework
basis undercutting the hourly union rates, and the union had
little machinery for enforcing its rule against this practice.
Before its job stewards knew what was going on, the windows or doors were installed and the nonunion men had van-
ished. The walking delegate could uncover these projects
far more efficiently.

By 1890, according to Robert Christie's book, *Empire in Wood*, there were full-time walking delegates handling the Carpenters' Union affairs in 100 cities. Other organizations too found it feasible to hire one of their members away from his regular job to work exclusively for the union. For a variety of reasons a growing labor movement needed full-time functionaries in addition to the nonpaid volunteers such as the job stewards. After the Chicago Haymarket Riot in 1886, employers initiated a campaign of blacklist and discharge. Active unionists who discussed a grievance with their foremen were often fired on the spot, and their names given to other employers so that they found it difficult to get work. It was felt therefore that someone else, an outsider, was needed to speak to the boss. There was in addition the bothersome jurisdictional conflict. As construction techniques became more complex, craftsmen argued with each other as to which unionist was to do the new types of work.

The Carpenters' Union insisted that "once wood, it is always the right of the carpenter to install it. . . ." But what about wood processed by machine, or wood substitutes, fiberboard, plastics? What about wood that required metal trim? For fifteen years carpenters and sheet-metal workers fought over the right to set metal trim in fireproof buildings. As the years went by, the Carpenters' Union was involved in jurisdictional squabbles with the machine woodworkers, elevator constructors, tile layers, wire and metal lathers, painters, asbestos workers, car workers, hod carriers, plasterers, machinists. The union that wanted to keep its men at work had to jealously guard its "jurisdiction." The circumstances seemed to demand that labor become more "efficient"; and the full-time walking delegate—or business agent as he was later to be known—seemed to be a major step in that direction.

In itself there was nothing sinister about this. In other countries too, professional organizers replaced nonpaid officials as the labor movements grew in size and power. So long as the business agent was responsive to the checks and balances of union democracy there was no danger. In many unions, that remained the case. In many others, however, the business agent—because of the favorable economic conditions in America—drifted away from his members and became not the union's humble servant but its master.

Once a union leader becomes a full-time functionary there is an inevitable gulf between himself and the membership. The leader has a year-round rather than seasonal job, he does not have to worry about being unemployed, is not subject to the whims of foremen and employers, and is freed from the drudgery of normal work. There is something interesting, even romantic, about his activity. Ordinarily, however, the gulf is bridged by a sense of dedication on the part of the leader, an almost religious identification with the rank and file just as if he were still working. When John Fitzpatrick, president of the Chicago Federation of Labor, died some years ago, his wife, a dedicated unionist in her own right, refused to accept a pension. "My husband," she said proudly, "was adequately paid for his work."

The belief that a union leader should receive no special privileges because of his position nor live on a scale beyond that of his members, is part of a humanist or socialist or "labor" philosophy that welds the leader to his followers. Thousands of union officials, through the years, have accepted this discipline because they devoutly believed that the cause of social progress pivoted around the labor movement. Their attitude can perhaps be summed up by the clumsy term "idealistic." The union leader who is idealistic insists, as a matter of principle, that the rank and file must have the power to decide on all issues and that nothing must be done without its consent. The first business agents, men like James Lynch, undoubtedly shared these ideals, and were close both in ideology and personal relations to the men on the job they served.

The gap that grew between the rank and file and their leaders in the American labor movement must be attributed not to the fact that unions accomplished little for their members, but because they accomplished, at least in the economic sphere and for a limited number of skilled workers, so much. As the members' wants were *relatively* satisfied they became apathetic to the inner working of their organization. The union leader who did not or could not accept an idealistic discipline, accrued to himself many of the prerogatives formerly exercised by the rank and file. Little by little his union became institutionalized. The member could still dissent, still speak his piece at meetings, but such was the apathy of his fellow members and such were the changes in union structure that he could not effectively *oppose* his leader's policies.

Eventually the union leader draws so far from his members that he adopts the ethics of business; he still serves his workers, still wins wage increases and reductions in hours, but the union becomes for him a vehicle for personal enrichment as well. He no longer is concerned with labor as a *movement* or with broad social problems. His union post becomes a job or a position, rather than a "cause." The rank-and-file member now loses not only his right to oppose but his right to dissent as well, and the union is no longer ruled by its members but by the machine. The area of decision narrows. The broad decisions are no longer made by the local union members, but by their leaders. Eventually they are no longer made by the local union officials either, but by the national leaders. The base of the labor pyramid loses its important prerogatives, confining itself more and more to secondary problems, while an entrenched bureaucracy at the top is predominant.

If America had not made such rapid economic progress, beginning with the 1880's, there might not have evolved a business-minded type of unionism. The very successes of the skilled craftsmen in gaining economic benefits resulted in a decline of interest in the internal affairs of their organization and gave many business agents and the top leaders an opportunity to dominate the unions. The economic climate in America was propitious for business unionism. Though often challenged by more socially minded organizations and by radicals inside and outside, business unionism grew almost uninterruptedly. The unskilled worker usually had to look for help beyond the AFL to revolutionary unions such as the Industrial Workers of the World, or the independent textile unions that sprang up from time to time. Needle-trades organizations such as the International Ladies' Garment Workers' Union or Sidney Hillman's independent Amalgamated Clothing Workers' Union (later to become a keystone of the CIO) were avowedly socialist. But the main current in the movement veered ever more to the philosophy and insularism of business unionism.

Even after the formation of the CIO, business unionism continued to flourish, actually reaching a peak in both membership and power. Today it encompasses almost all of the building trades unions' three million, many of the printing trades unions, almost all of the service industry unions, the large teamsters' organization, the mineworkers, many of the railroad unions (a notable exception being the small but vibrant Sleeping Car Porters of A. Philip Randolph), and many of the entertainment unions. Within these ranks, admittedly, there are hundreds of dynamic, democratic local unions which are a tribute to the movement, but they do not predominate, nor is their voice decisive in the top echelons of their organizations.

II

Inherent in the business agent's post was such a reservoir of power that he could, if freed from checks and balances, achieve a status far beyond his rank-and-file members. Using the argument that surprise was a necessary factor in strikes, he asked for and usually received the right to call strikes without consulting the men involved. Gradually too he gained another hold over the members: he became, in a sense, a labor contractor supplying skilled craftsmen to the employer. The craftsman who depended on the business agent for work was chary of offending him lest he be given poor jobs or seasonal rather than year-round work. Conversely, many a union man was willing to associate himself with the business agent's machine to get better work. The business agent's job enlarged to the point where he was recruiting workers, negotiating contracts, settling grievances, levying fines, and handling other administrative details with less and less control by the membership.

In the early history of the AFL there is clearly visible the conflict between full-time leaders who wished to capitalize on this inherent power of their posts, and those who, still bound by the idealistic discipline, insisted on the dominance of the rank and file. The subjugation of the rank and file was not accomplished in a day; in many old unions— the typographical workers are an outstanding example—it was never achieved. But in a significant segment of American labor the professional organizer, looking on the union more and more as personal rather than collective property, did take over. The vibrant and dedicated character of the movement was thus diluted in favor of "practical" business unionism.

The process of change is perhaps best illustrated by developments in the Carpenters' Union from 1890 to 1900. At the head of the union in that period was a socialist, Peter McGuire, who had built the organization from the ground up and who commanded the firm allegiance of the rank and file. They worshiped his integrity and spell-binding oratory. Opposed to McGuire were the new men of power, the business agents, who sought to control the executive board. Up to this time the leading body of the union was composed exclusively of men who worked at the trade, with the professional organizers excluded. But the professionals, already entrenched in their districts, insisted on the right to be elected to the national executive board. At the 1890 convention McGuire resisted this demand and won his point; for the time being power was still vested in the nonpaid union leader, elected by a convention.

This was a time of bitter conflicts with the employers. The National Builders' Association, formed in 1887 to offset the union's successes in the campaign for the eight-hour day, was on the offensive. By lockout and other devices it broke strikes and weakened the union in many places. At one point the union lost fully half its members. In the minds of the business agents the answer to all this was to centralize power in their hands.

At the 1892 convention the professionals altered their strategy somewhat, suggesting that the national executive-board members be elected by the delegates of each district rather than the convention as a whole. The business agents, as already noted, were stronger at this level since they organized new locals and led them in strikes. Had this proposal carried, the working members of the executive board would have been replaced by the professionals; but McGuire, still commanding a great personal following, was able once again to defeat the resolution—though by a small majority. Two years later McGuire suffered a setback; the business agent supporters captured the convention, and voted to shift many prerogatives to the union president: the right to suspend all officers on charges, the right to order or call off strikes, issue charters, adjudicate between individuals and locals, and approve all local union rules. The president was also to have the right to appoint all full-time organizers and generally to "run the union." In 1896, these issues were put to national referendum and once again McGuire prevailed. The membership voted down the proposals in favor of continued veto by the rank and file.

It took the professionals another fifteen years before they finally achieved their objectives: At the turn of the century McGuire became a hopeless drunk and in 1902 was forced to resign because of charges of embezzlement. His popularity was still so high, however, that his resignation was accepted by a margin of only sixty-one votes of 335 cast. But the change had been made.

The man who replaced McGuire, William Huber, was of a different viewpoint entirely: a sharp critic of socialism and a devotee of practicalism and machine rule. In the person of McGuire the union had combined socialist philosophy and democratic safeguards with a practical quest for shorter hours and better wages. Huber condemned the radical philosophers as "visionary, their schemes and isms . . . only the mouthings of a lot of irresponsible, imaginative fantastical doctrines." At the 1902 convention he won the right to appoint organizers, with or without the approval of local bodies. The seven-man executive board remained a body of members at the trade, but the handwriting was already on the wall.

At the local level the business agents were entrenching themselves further, some like Sam Parks becoming extortionists and racketeers. At the national level Huber appointed swarms of professional organizers at $4 a day (good wages at that time) all beholden to him and all working to whittle away the power of the executive board. The conven-

tion committees now were appointed by the president, paid
$10 a day, and rigged in his favor. After ten years of factional
strife with leaders of the executive board the battle was decided. A strong residue of democratic spirit remained in the
union, but the democrats were becoming tired. In 1912, Huber's proposal to make executive board members full-time
and salaried was carried, and the board was further reduced
to impotence by being placed under the supervision of the
general president. The president and secretary were now
added to the executive board with voice and vote; and henceforth the apparatus of the union was firmly in the hands of
the officialdom. The rank and file had lost its countervailing
power.

Though Huber himself quit in 1915, the machine found
itself in the firm hands of William L. Hutcheson, an em-
peror so powerful that when he retired in 1952 he was able
to pass on his domain to his son, the current president, Maurice A. Hutcheson. By then the rank and file was thoroughly
subdued and the original radicalism of the organization converted to business unionism. On the back cover of its 1949
constitution the Carpenters' Union still carried the historic
relic of a socialist past, the ancient demand for "public ownership of all public utilities and transportation to be conducted in the interests of the people." The union, however,
was now fully bureaucratized, dominated by one man and
the professional organizers who were either under his thumb
or powerless to oppose him.

Anticipating our story, we might note that there is some
parallel between the developments of the first few decades
of the AFL and that of the CIO in our times. The same
process of lifting the professional organizer above the rank-
and-file worker, the same decline of factionalism and dissent
are evident in the newer unions today. The CIO too started
with a large tinge of radicalism and is now in a stage of
moderation. In its early days its membership was active and

vigilant; today it is much further removed from the workings of the union. The institutionalization of the CIO—again, using the term broadly to imply a loss of countervailing power, etc.—has taken different forms from that of the AFL, because American capitalism has changed in the interim and because the CIO unions are for the most part in centralized rather than decentralized industries. But the corrosion of idealism and dedication is evident in the ex-CIO unions today, just as it was in the carpenters' and other unions a few decades after the organization of the AFL.

The saga of the Carpenters' Union is typical of what can happen when the "give" in capitalism makes possible a policy of accommodation with employers. What began as a moderately radical organization was altered in a few decades into a moderately conservative one, drawing ever closer to the ethic of business and away from the inherent cooperative ethic of unionism. The prosperity of the first quarter of the twentieth century gave the business agents their great opportunity and they took full advantage of it.

The record shows that almost invariably—just as with the carpenters—the old AFL unions went through a turbulent period of factional strife in the first part of the century. Consider the case of the Boot & Shoe Makers. In the eight elections for president of that union between 1904 and 1917 there were bitter contests seven times. John F. Tobin, a well-known socialist, held the post from 1895 until he died in 1919. By contrast, John J. Mara, who followed Tobin, was unopposed in the four elections—over a twenty-five year period—that followed. It is interesting to note that with the decline of opposition, union conventions were spread out over longer intervals. While there were eight elections in an eleven-year period from 1904 to 1915, there were only four in the twenty-five-year period from 1919 to 1944.

From 1910 to 1944 no candidate opposed a president in the Bridge, Structural and Ornamental Iron Workers'

Union. "As is to be expected," says Professor Philip Taft, in his book, *The Structure and Government of Labor Unions,* "the opposition is concentrated largely in the earlier years of the union." President P. J. Morrin served for thirty years from 1918 to 1948.

Once factional opponents are defeated, the tendency has been for business-union leaders to stay on in power indefinitely. John L. Lewis has been president of the mineworkers since 1918. During the 1920's he had vigorous opposition from socialists, communists, and independents like John Brophy and Alex Howat; but once Lewis expelled these forces and set up trusteeships over most of the districts in his union, his power became unassailable. A union leader who dared oppose him in 1944, Ray Edmundson, president of District 12, never even reached the floor of the convention. Though he had support from a hundred locals in Illinois and a smaller group in West Virginia, he was expelled before he got started.

George L. Berry was president of the printing pressmen from 1907 until he died decades later. Joseph V. Moreschi, president of the hod carriers, was *appointed* to his post in 1926; there had been no election in his union since 1911 and there was to be none for another fifteen years after Moreschi was appointed. In 1941, when a convention was finally held —after thirty years—the incumbents were all elected. Moreschi was still president in 1958. Dan Tobin remained president of the teamsters from 1907 until he retired in 1952. Joseph P. Ryan, of the International Longshoremen's Association had himself elected as president of the union for life.

III

The power over the membership by some of labor's leadership is by now fully sanctified in their constitutions.

The United Mine Workers, which succumbed to business unionism only after bitter struggles by socialists and communists in the 1920's and 1930's, provides in its constitution that the president "may suspend or remove any International Officer or appointed employee for insubordination or just and sufficient cause . . . may appoint such organizers, field and office workers as may in his judgment be necessary." The president interprets the meaning of the constitution and can appoint trustees to control errant locals and districts. At one time fully twenty-one of the thirty-one districts in the United Mine Workers had lost their autonomy and existed merely as "provisional" districts run by an appointee of the president, John L. Lewis. Since the national executive board was composed of the presidents of all the districts, Lewis was actually making a mockery of the clause in his union's constitution which provides that he is answerable to the board. The board became his *alter ego,* an assembly of his hirelings who owed their jobs and their livelihoods to their leader and who would as soon depart from his directions as a vassal from the directions of his feudal lord.

Article 7 of the constitution of the Marine Cooks' and Stewards' Union stated that "the president shall hold office until two-thirds of the entire membership decide by a referendum vote that his services are no longer required." This is about as close to the divine right of kings as you can get. Such a union may have a host of "democratic safeguards" in its constitution, but few men will avail themselves of these safeguards. The president is most often the officer who decides whether a local union can or can not strike, whether to give or not to give it strike benefits, whether to approve or disapprove its contract, whether to assign or not to assign it organizational help. What local union will risk offense to a president on whom it is so dependent and who is virtually entrenched for life? The chances for success here are so small that only the most hardy will fight back.

The rights of some business-union leaders today stagger
the imagination. No Indian potentate was given more
powers, for instance, than those of the president of the American Federation of Musicians. James C. Petrillo, who retired
in 1958, claimed that these provisions were written decades
before he assumed the post in 1940 and that he used his
powers to set aside the constitution only twice—once to re-
lease veterans from paying dues and another time to permit the Boston Symphony Orchestra to recruit musicians
from other locals. The very existence of such powers, however, reflects autocratic thinking on the part of those who
bestowed or took them. Article I, Section I of a long 218-page
constitution provides:

It shall be his [the president's] duty and prerogative to exer-
cise supervision over the affairs of the Federation; to make decisions in cases where in his opinion an emergency exists; to give
effect to such decisions he is authorized and empowered to pro-
mulgate and issue executive orders which shall be conclusive and
binding over all members and/or locals.

If these powers are not sufficient, the president "may
amend and set aside" the constitution "or any portion
thereof except such which treat with the finances of the organization." These powers are "hereby made absolute." The
president has the right to call strikes, appoint all committees,
make any rules, sign any contracts, and remove any local or
member he desires. And if such acts don't fit into the narrow
interpretation of the constitution, he may change the constitution itself, without conventions or referendums.

With such prerogatives in hand, there are really few occasions when drastic discipline must be taken; the rank-and-
file member knows that he is powerless and that resistance is
next to useless. A number of writers have concluded that
there is, on the whole, "adequate protection for the rights of
members." They list innumerable appeals to the presidents
of international unions and many favorable decisions for the

individual member. But this is begging the question. The real issues are not whether some members do appeal but: (1) how many members *don't* appeal because they feel the cards are stacked against them; and (2) how significant are the appeal cases, how much do they really threaten the real power of the leaders?

In the most harassed business union one can find scores of examples of local unions that operate democratically, indeed with considerable idealism; but the area of decision of the local union has been circumscribed, and too many top union presidents permit this free play by subordinate bodies and individuals only so long as they do not challenge their established over-all authority. For instance, a worker who insulted other unionists for "stealing his work" was fined $75; on appeal to the international union the fine was cut to $37.50. This is hardly a challenge to the power of the leadership. A carpenter who worked on Saturday without permission of the business agent was fined $100. The international president reduced the fine to $25. Control is hardly involved in such an appeal either. The important thing for business unionism is to keep power centralized; those who have such power can afford to be generous in secondary disputes and to permit all kinds of leeway, so long as power itself is not challenged.

The essence of business unionism is that it converts the union from a cooperative venture on the part of its members, in which workers collectively decide their own fate, into a service industry, in which the business agent and union leader sells a service *to* the membership. This is not too much different from the many other service industries in America. The average policyholder in the Metropolitan Life Insurance Company receives substantial benefits and security from his policy but he has little to say in the affairs of the great company. The same is true of the average member of the average business union. He receives great benefits and he is permitted minor areas at the local-union level where his decision is still respected; but in broader decisions he is almost as voiceless as the insurance policyholder.

It is this progressive emasculation of the democratic process which typifies most business unions. To call it honest or dishonest is irrelevant; first, because most business unionists are personally honest, and, second, because there is neither more nor less integrity in this form of business than in any other. Business unionism converts the union from an evangelical effort on the part of the underprivileged to raise their status, into a business venture. It is in that respect no more crooked than business itself and no more lamentable than the prevailing mores of the business community generally.

IV

The business agent who illegally took for himself powers that belonged to the members made the first breach in the democratic structure of the labor movement. A second was made by the subjugation of those bodies in the union hierarchy closest to the man on the job—the local union and the city central body. Local unions were, of course, the first rudimentary means of union organization. Beginning with 1827, city central bodies became the power center of labor; they were, as pointed out, the pivot of strike action, strike relief, new organization efforts, and political action until the end of the nineteenth century. The first national federations of labor were composed primarily of city bodies. The ties of the local union to the national craft union, even where one existed, were weaker and less significant than those to the city and state central bodies. Many, if not most, of the local unions were unaffiliated to any national union, their only ties with labor being through city and state bodies.

But once the AFL was organized in 1868, Samuel Gompers set a deliberate course to whittle the power of the city bodies. He concentrated first on forming national craft unions out of isolated locals, and second on securing predominance of the national union. When the AFL was founded there were thirteen national unions in its fold: carpenters, molders, cigarmakers, bricklayers, boilermakers, miners, and so on. In 1891, Gompers assembled various local unions into two more national craft organizations: the electricians and coopers. From 1896 to 1901 he grouped together an additional thirty-five national unions: laborers, lathers, upholsterers, stationary firemen, teamsters, and others.

To de-emphasize the role of the local and the city central body, Gompers pushed through a series of resolutions at successive AFL conventions. At the 1886 meeting it was agreed to exclude all local unions where a national union was already in existence. In 1887, the voting powers were juggled so that national unions received one vote for every hundred members, but city and state federations of labor were limited to only one vote for their total membership, no matter how large. Thus, by way of example, at the 1911 convention there were 349 delegates. Of these, 118, or one-third, represented city and state federations, unaffiliated local unions, and fraternal organizations. But the national unions had a preponderance of voting strength of 17,104 to a mere 136.

After 1897, city central bodies were prohibited from accepting membership of a local union unless it was part of a national union or directly affiliated to the AFL; hitherto they could enroll any organization they saw fit in or out of the AFL. In 1901, city bodies were prohibited from originating boycotts—an important union activity at that time.

The city federations fought back but the fight was hopeless. In 1900, resolutions were introduced at an AFL convention for reversing the power relationship, to reduce the national union vote to only one per delegate while the city federations were to vote their entire membership. The resolutions were defeated. In 1902, socialist Victor Berger of the Milwaukee city federation issued a call for a national convention of all city federations (many of whom were not affiliated with AFL), but Gompers was able through the pressure of the national unions on their locals to frustrate this venture. As a result one city central body after another was incorporated into the AFL and its wings clipped. More and more, the city bodies were limited in their activity until today they are a negligible force confined to minor legislative and lobbying actions.

The Chicago Federation of Labor, under the presidency of John Fitzpatrick, one of the great humanitarians of the American labor movement, held out longest in its efforts to maintain independence. Fitzpatrick, who had purged the Chicago central body of corrupt elements, refused to slavishly follow AFL policy. He sponsored industrial-union campaigns in the packinghouse and steel industries during World War I. Later he was active in various local, state, and national labor-party movements, even though the AFL itself opposed such politics. But with the loss of the 1919 steel strike and the decline of the labor-party movement after the defeat of Progressive party's Senator LaFollette in 1924, the star of the Chicago Federation of Labor also descended. It took its place with the rest of the city bodies: a follower of "official policy," with no independent power of its own.

In the circumstances of American industrialization and with the integration of capital, national unions were obviously inevitable. It no longer took two weeks to reach Indiana from New York; the railroad was cutting time and distance drastically. The corporation, first severely limited, was breaking out of its bounds. Originally these companies were restricted as to the amount of property they could own, were confined to one type of business in a specific area, and were chartered only for a definite period—usually twenty or thirty years. Our forefathers were deeply worried that corporations would develop into monopolies and that individual men would lose their freedom of action—a fear that events proved all too justified. For eventually the corporation grew so large that it far outweighed all other forms of property ownership combined; it spanned not only the nation but the whole world, and it became a trust in perpetuity rather than for a limited period. Gompers was certainly farsighted when he insisted on grouping weak, local unions into more centralized bodies, to match economic power with integrated capital.

National unions were inevitable and necessary too because of the centralization of collective bargaining. From 1898 onward, multi-unit bargaining pyramided. In that year operators from the central coal-mining fields met in joint conference with the United Mine Workers. By 1903, district bargaining with the UMW spread to the southwestern field. The International Longshoremen entered into district agreements with the Lake Erie Dock Managers, the Lake Carriers Association, the Lumber Carriers Association, the Great Lakes Towing group. Lithographers, coopers, hatters, wallpaper workers, machinists, newspaper workers, and many others entered into collective-bargaining agreements for whole cities or districts, rather than individual companies. As capitalism tended to integrate, labor had to follow.

There is in a sense an objective logic to the centralization of the AFL under Gompers. Unions had to integrate to keep pace with capital. But greater powers could and should have been left in the hands of the local unions and the city central bodies. The delegates to the national AFL convention (and today the AFL-CIO convention) were not elected by the members in the local unions, but usually appointed by the national union leaders. The men who spoke for labor, who wrote its resolutions on legislation and foreign policy, did not discuss these issues with their members in advance and did not put their positions to the test of a rank-and-file vote. They were free to do almost as they pleased. A wiser policy would have deliberately provided for greater countervailing power by the local-union members and the city bodies at the grass roots. Had the delegates to AFL conventions been directly elected by the local-union members and the city bodies the national unions might have remained more democratic. Had the city bodies been given autonomy in organizing new shops, helping strikes, guiding local unions, and in political affairs in their areas, there might have been greater involvement of the rank and file in union affairs. As it was, the national unions became all-powerful and to a considerable extent inflexible.

This is best illustrated perhaps by the resistance of the national craft unions—which dominated the AFL—to industrial unionism. In 1897, a National Building Trades Council was formed outside the AFL to seek "closer amalgamation of building trades workmen." But in the face of this cry for industrial unionism the AFL continued to charter national craft unions in scores of subdivisions of each craft, so that in six years up to 1904 it had issued seventy-five new charters. The result was a wave of jurisdictional disputes that had the AFL in ceaseless turmoil. To resolve some of these problems the Carpenters' Union in 1903 set up a Structural Building Trades Alliance composed of nine large craft unions. But the Alliance neither merged with the National Building Trades Council nor took steps on its own to amalgamate into some industrial structure. Gompers was able to arrive at an understanding with the Alliance by which a building-trades department was formed within the AFL and the jurisdiction of the larger craft unions was enlarged to include many of the new technological tasks. Craft unionism remained the religion of the AFL until the 1930's.

In a few of the more progressive unions, such as the International Ladies' Garment Workers' Union, a form of industrial unionism prevailed, closely akin to that of the National Building Trades Council. Formed in 1900 by Jewish and Italian immigrants who carried their socialist ideology over with them, the garment workers consolidated different crafts, such as cutters and operators, into city-wide councils which coordinated collective bargaining for the skilled and unskilled alike. The needle-trades unions, however, were of a different current from the main stream of labor in the following decades—militant, radical, and welfare oriented. The core of the movement within the AFL remained rigid, inflexible, and dominated by the national unions with their craft philosophy.

V

Gradually the towering structures of the national unions stood like iron curtains between the individual workers and their union leadership. The time between conventions, previously one year, was increased to two years, three years, even to four or five. The Marine Cooks' and Stewards' Union did not hold a convention for the first forty-four years of its existence.

Constitutional amendments put the fate of local unions and individual members in the hands of an all-powerful international president or secretary-treasurer. This concentration of power was illustrated in a survey of international union constitutions made a few years ago by the American Civil Liberties Union. In about half the unions, the study showed, the authority to suspend local unions was in the hands of the international president. In others it rested with the executive board, which in most cases was merely a rubber stamp for the president. Of fifty-four constitutions examined, forty-four provided for control of local-union policies by international officers. Most provided that locals might not strike without permission of their international, nor enter into bargaining agreements without international approval. According to Professor Philip Taft, in the Winter of 1946 issue of the *Harvard Business Review,* "most unions explicitly prohibit the existence of factions, cliques or political parties organized to discuss union business outside of official meetings as proof of the establishment of a dual or opposition union which can be penalized by expulsion." The situation since 1946 has not grown better, but worse.

In Lodge 113 of the machinists, the union headed by Al Hayes, chairman of the AFL-CIO Ethical Practices Committee, a group of dissidents in 1958 published a newspaper detailing their grievances. The lodge was under trusteeship for more than a year and the dissidents were trying to win back their autonomy. The newspaper apologized for the fact there was no union label on the publication. It explained that "the paper was printed at a union printer by union printers, but we asked them to leave the label off for fear that the administrators of Lodge 113 will be able to trace the paper and take action against the Lodge members who put this out. The administrators have threatened to discipline members for much less, as for example asking questions at a Lodge meeting. We cannot afford to let them identify us." The machinists are one of the better unions in America today, and perhaps the matter is out of Hayes's hands, being handled by a subordinate or a regional vice-president. But this apology is indicative of a pervasive fear in so many unions that mere expression of differences or disapproval of the policies of the leadership is subject to reprisal.

Who can challenge the top union leadership where it is so entrenched? Business unionism has eliminated the give and take between leader and rank and file. Not in all unions, of course. Many still remain religiously democratic. The Typographical Workers' Union has a two-party system which contests elections with vigor and integrity every two years. The Progressive party and the Independent party each maintain separate caucuses, publish papers and leaflets of their own, and strive for leadership posts. This is a model of union democracy that is unequaled anywhere else in the American movement. But the Typographical Workers are a breed apart; the trend has been in the other direction. In fact the mere criticism of union leaders has become a "crime" in some business unions.

A New Jersey teamster, some years ago, was expelled after nineteen years of membership in the organization for "derogatory remarks about the local's president and vice-president." A member of the Paint and Varnish Workers' Union was expelled for "seeking to remove" the president of the union. A marine engineer who declared himself a candidate for secretary and business agent was expelled because he gave out a pamphlet attacking the union leadership he was opposing. The leaders ruled that he had "publicized" union business "without permission of the officers," in violation of the constitution. The outgoing president of another union was declared an "agitator" by the new leadership, expelled, and fired from her job.

Once the rank and file were subdued, the leaders of business unionism developed endless techniques for consolidating their monolith. Two such techniques were the granting of "paper" charters, and trusteeships.

Local charters now are sometimes issued to friends or business associates of an international-union president, even though no union actually exists and it has no membership. Armed with such a charter, the owner can then legitimately organize in his jurisdiction or he can use it as a means of signing collusive "sweetheart" contracts, which provide for subpar conditions or no improvements at all. Under either circumstance, however, the charter becomes a means of solidifying machine rule, both at the local and the international level. For instance, when Dave Beck issued seven paper charters to John Dioguardi, a New York hoodlum, these seven local unions were thereby alloted forty-nine votes in the New York teamsters' council, enough to hold the balance between two rival candidates for presidency of that council. A paper union can seldom be retrieved for the membership, even after it succeeds in organizing a few shops. Before a single member is enrolled there is already in existence a set of by-laws drawn by an attorney that provide dictatorial power to the owner of the charter. The rank-and-file member has few rights from the outset; the union leader does not have to go through factional fights to win them away from him. This is hardly in harmony with the concept of unionism as a co-operative venture. Even under the best circumstances, it is a service business, with the membership relegated to interested but impotent bystanders.

Trusteeship has also been used as an invidious technique for machine rule. Trusteeship is sometimes necessary where a local union flaunts union policy, as, for instance, when a local union of the Auto Workers permitted its committeemen to act as bookies and take bets in the shop. In some unions the rights of the top leaders to impose trusteeship are clearly defined and limited: Charges must be filed, a trial held, and a time limit placed on supervision by the international. In machine-dominated organizations, however, the trusteeship becomes an instrument of dictatorial rule. At one time Dave Beck had under trusteeship to him enough locals of the Western Conference of Teamsters to dominate it. William Maloney, ex-president of the Operating Engineers kept Local 150 in Chicago under trusteeship to him for nearly thirty years. During that whole period the members could make no decisions on contracts, strikes, grievances—anything. Maloney's decision was unchallengeable. Of the 283,000 members of this organization, twelve locals, with a total of 51,000 workers, were under trusteeship in 1958, and another 101,000 were in "branch" locals which had no voting rights; more than half the membership had no say in how their organization was to be run. When Hoffa became president of the Teamsters' Union in January, 1958, there were 107 local unions out of 891 in trusteeship. At one time this number was even higher. In the Carpenters' Union as late as 1937, 130,000 members were classed as "non-beneficial, non-voting."

The ingenuity of business unionists in jettisoning democratic practice is often remarkable if not for its ethics, at least for its deviousness. Thus in the same Operating Engineers' Local 138, only 550 members were permitted to vote. Of these, according to a reform leader, Peter Batalias, at least 169 were employers friendly to the administration. Four hundred and forty "apprentices" were kept in a separate local, 138-A, 300 shop and maintenance men in Local 138-B, and between 500 and 1,000 "permit" men paid $2.50 a week for the right to hold a card in the local, but had neither voice nor vote at meetings. Thus, in a group of perhaps 2,000 workers the union could be machine-dominated if the president mustered 107 votes in addition to the 169 employers who were in his back pocket.

In his own inimitable style, Dave Beck once defined union democracy this way: "We have the most democratic union in the world. But sometimes you can have too damn much democracy and it interferes with your welfare . . . and my biggest trouble comes from the elected secretaries of some locals, because since they're elected they're not always the best men for the job. Plenty of times, I say to the boys, 'Do you want to elect your officers for this regional council or local union, or do you want me to appoint them?' More often than not, they'll say: 'You appoint them, Dave,' because they know I'll choose the best men."

On another occasion Beck enlarged on this topic. "Unions," he said, "are big business. Why should truck drivers and bottle washers be allowed to make big decisions affecting union policy? Would any corporation allow it?"

4

The Labor Business

ONE OF THE UNION LEADERS ACCUSED AT THE SECOND CONVENtion of the AFL-CIO in December, 1957, of "unethical practices" was the suave, articulate president of the Bakery and Confectionery Workers' Union, James G. Cross. Standing on the dais, delivering his defense in measured tones, he epitomized the tragedy of so many unionists who had reaped a harvest of success. Jimmy Cross had originated in the coal-mining region of Illinois, where militancy, radicalism, and socialism were miners' bywords. He himself had been a socialist, poor, self-sacrificing, and intelligent. During the mid-thirties when CIO unions were involved in scores of sitdown strikes—taking over key auto, rubber, and other plants—seeking union recognition, Jimmy Cross was leading similar sitdowns in Detroit bakeries for an AFL union. As a reward for his efforts he rose to local-union leadership, and then step by step he moved up the union ladder until in his early forties he had reached the top of the pyramid, president of an upstanding, untainted union of 135,000 members.

In many respects Cross's career paralleled those of Walter Reuther, James B. Carey, and scores of other American labor leaders. From worker to top union leader in a few short jumps. Unlike the untutored and insensitive officials of so many old-line unions, Jimmy Cross knew, understood, and in his early days revered every basic principle of the labor movement. He had been weaned on militant unionism; and he believed that there was a conflict of interests between labor and capital. Though his union was small and he seldom basked in the newspaper or television limelight, like Reuther or Carey, Cross was no easily beguiled innocent finding his way in the movement, but an exceptionally capable and brilliant man who could hold his own with any union official in the country—Reuther included—on most intellectual subjects. His speech at the AFL-CIO convention was well put together and well delivered. It undoubtedly made an impression even on the delegates who voted against him, an impression so strong that only George Meany's forceful counterpolemic could dispel it.

But after two decades, Cross was stigmatized publicly before the McClellan Committee and then before the AFL-CIO. The unethical practices that he was charged with included such items as accepting a $6,550 Cadillac from a local union which was under trusteeship, and concealing this gift as an "organizing expense"; spending $40,000 for "expenses" in one year; and taking loans of $56,700 and $40,000, respectively, from a wealthy businessman to purchase two homes, one in Washington and the other in West Palm Beach, Florida. There were many innuendos involved in these charges which were personal and which fortunately were toned down, but nothing could erase the blot of the two loans. The man from whom Cross borrowed the money was Martin Philipsborn, a former owner of Zion Industries, Inc., with whom the union leader had negotiated contracts for a number of years. Though the AFL-CIO Ethical Practices Committee conceded that Philipsborn had sold his interest in this firm in 1948, seven years before the loans were made, it pointed out that he was still associated with the firm as "general manager" and was being paid $72,000 a year plus expenses.

"While neither President Cross nor Mr. Philipsborn personally participate any longer in regular negotiations covering this company," the report read, "they did hold a top level meeting on the labor contract as recently as November 9, 1956"—just about the time, it should be mentioned, Cross made his second $40,000, loan.

In his defense, Cross said that he didn't know Philipsborn was still with the Zion company and that, furthermore, the contracts with Zion were in no way substandard. There was, he implied, no *quid pro quo* of $96,700 in loans, in return for a "soft," "sweetheart" contract. It was all aboveboard, a mere personal matter between two men who had known each other for twenty-five years, who had been visiting each other for five or six years, and had evidently established a close rapport.

Whatever the merit to Cross's defense, his story sheds interesting light on how business unionism itself has emerged. It is, in a sense, a condensed history of the phenomenon.

Here was a man who began his career as a fighter, a dreamer, and an idealist. His union was one of the most spotless in the nation. There never had been a taint of racketeering in its top echelons, and Cross himself had an admirable record—not generally publicized—of fighting off attempts by the crime syndicate to penetrate his organization. No one, by the remotest stretch of the imagination, could pin the label of "hoodlum" or "associate of hoodlums" on James G. Cross. But within two decades he had changed character. The poor, harassed youngster of the thirties was now a man who drove expensive Cadillacs, lived luxuriously in plush homes, mixed with the mighty, and spent $40,000 a year for expenses in addition to his substantial salary. When he needed money for a home he didn't go to a bank or to friends in the labor movement, but to a businessman with whom he should presumably have been at odds.

To Jimmy Cross, business and businessmen were no longer the "enemy," nor their mores totally alien, but were now acceptable and their mores even imitated. The notion of "fighting the boss" was moderated to one of "getting along." Perhaps in relations with employers other than Philipsborn, Cross took a more firm position. Perhaps, too, he may mend his ways now that his union has been expelled from the AFL-CIO and is forced to go independent. There is certainly a virtuous strain in Jimmy Cross that can be—and may be—reactivated. But the lure of the market place, of high living, and the easing of management pressures combined to subvert this union leader's sense of dedication.

Cross was not the first militant to succumb to such lures. The American climate of ever-pyramiding prosperity has drawn many others away from idealism toward the business ethic. Voting against Cross at the AFL-CIO convention were not a few leaders with far worse records—for instance, William Maloney of the Operating Engineers who was later to resign his own post under pressure of a Senate expose, and a threat by the AFL-CIO to suspend his union unless he were removed. A half century of business unionism—parallel to business prosperity and social theories of "rugged individualism"—has blurred the labor ethic.

II

The effect of long periods of prosperity in American history has been to make our unions and their leaders relax. When wage increases can be won consistently from year to year, the labor leader is under less pressure. His membership is satisfied enough usually to let him run the affairs of the union with little interference. The union itself becomes stable, builds a substantial treasury, and begins to operate like a well-oiled machine.

In the decentralized industries, where unions were first organized, the result of this process has been the evolution of a specific American form of unionism called business unionism. In its excesses business unionism is something unsavory; it consists of the taking of bribes, collusion with management to sign "sweetheart" contracts, and the like. At its extreme tip it blends with the outright racketeer who belongs to or is a "fellow traveler" of the national crime syndicate. But essentially business unionism is based on the philosophical and moral approaches of our times; its outstanding characteristics are moderateness and pragmatism.

The overwhelming majority of business unionists have never received a pay-off, nor carried a gun or a pair of brass knuckles. They are simple, direct, practical. In talking to workers they put the issues squarely and clearly: "Sign this card and I'll get you a $6- or $8-a-week raise." That is primarily what the business unionist sells—more money; he doesn't try to peddle uplift, ideals, or socialism. He seldom tries to implant propaganda about the need for solidarity, unity, or other standard union principles. Instead, his talk is of more earthy matters: "Our scale is $2.60 an hour. Join the union and I'll go to your boss tomorrow and hit him up for this scale." He doesn't negotiate with a committee and a stack of leaflets for his members. He meets with the employer by himself and either gains or loses his point after a short talk.

Nor is the average business unionist necessarily "soft" in wage agreements. Usually the wage level in the most business-minded union is among the highest. Most of the building-trades unions, for instance, are machine run and business-minded. But what other jobs command such high wages —wages gained through the strong unions in this field? Bricklayers, electricians, carpenters, plumbers, all earn between $3 and $4 an hour—$6,000 to $8,000 a year on a fifty-two-week basis. This is considerably higher than the wages of the average schoolteacher in America, $1 to $1.50 an hour higher than what the average factory worker earns, twice as much as the average retail employee receives. It is substantially more than what the auto or steel workers earn, and no one can say that these two unions have not done an outstanding job in raising wages in their industries. Business unionism does win benefits for its members. For those who feel that unions should be nothing else but a service industry, business unionism in America is ideal.

Nor are the business unionists—even those convicted of crimes—always unpopular with their members. The attitude of workers seems to be: "We got ours, why should we object if he got his?" After Sam Parks, a New York building-trades leader, was indicted in 1903 for extortion, he was elected business agent with the highest vote of any of the candidates. Despite his depredations the men had some solid victories to show during his administration. When he became business agent in 1896, wages were only $2 a day and the union was next to impotent. Under his leadership the union gained full job control and wages of iron workers jumped to $4.50 a day by 1903.

In their *History of Labor in the United States,* Volume 4, Selig Perlman and Philip Taft summarize this point with keen insight:

Charges of widespread graft in the building industry have frequently been made. . . . Evidence that the business agent has often extorted money payments through threats of strikes has been produced. Nevertheless, the business agent has been neither the sole nor the chief beneficiary of the system which made graft possible. Favored employers also benefited. Contractors and ma-

terial men have used the grafting business agent to gain monopolies, to harass competitors, or to escape penalty when unable to
complete the work on the date specified. . . . Grafter though he
was, the grafting was incidental to his activities in behalf of the
membership. The sympathetic strike, his chief instrument for
levying tribute on the employer, was at the same time an effective
leverage to improve wage and other standards of employment.
. . . Furthermore, the graft came out of the pockets of the
builder, and ultimately the consumer, and as long as wages and
job conditions were improving, the building tradesmen, far from
feeling oppressed by the leader, viewed him as an efficient fighter
for their interests.

A misconception exists too that business unionists seldom
hold meetings, seldom give financial accountings, and always
have some tough guys around to threaten anyone who dis-
agrees. Sometimes such things are true. But very often the
most rock-ribbed old-line unions have much better attendance than those of the new mass-industry unions. Certainly
the meetings of the painters or carpenters or electrical
workers or bakers are better attended than those of the ex-
CIO steelworkers. On occasion a bureaucratic machine stifles
discussion, but the mechanism of bureaucracy is usually
much more subtle. It resides in the bureaucratic *powers* of
the leadership and in the feeling on the part of the rank and
file of "What's the use?" or "It doesn't really matter."
    In the sphere of politics the old-line unionist knows all
the important officials of government and has connections,
either personally, or through other leaders of labor and his
lawyers, with the ruling political machine. He is "in politics," not out of any basic love for the politicians or any desire for social reform, but purely for what he can get out of
it. He wants no trouble from police or the district attorney
when there is a strike; he wants immediate recognition and
good wage contracts for the union members who work for
the city or state; he wants protection against unfavorable

local and state legislation; he wants a whole host of little favors. In return he solicits votes and funds for politicians in power.

He has no compunctions about dropping the Democrats and becoming a Republican, or vice versa, as the occasion demands. If necessary he will even support a Socialist, just as he supported Democrats and Republicans in years gone by. His outlook is formed by the answer to two questions: Can the candidate get in? What can he do for me? In the matter of politics the modern business unionist has identically the same morality as the modern lawyer or industrialist; he is merely defending his empire and, in his own way, his membership. By and large, he has far fewer illusions about politicians than most people.

The business unionist is practical, but not necessarily insincere. If he is an opportunist, he is not lacking in principles. But his principles are based on the belief that the leadership of labor must have more power in order to do things *for* the rank and file. He considers such arrogation of power to himself as a blessing, rather than a hindrance, to his membership. Most often he is personally honest and as devoted to labor as the average churchgoer is to the church. He has a certain peculiar type of liberalism which, while it has no social depth, as a matter of course fights restrictive legislation. His career, his business, is labor; and in his own way he intends to protect the rank and file.

III

The tragedy of business unionism is not that it fails to do a good economic job for its individual members, but in its tepid philosophy, its lack of solidarity, its loss of evangelism, and its excesses.

The practical business unionist is interested primarily in his own union. Just like a businessman, he is building his own business and is little concerned with other "labor businesses" or with social reform. He is no longer the fervid advocate of "labor solidarity" that was so characteristic of the early labor pioneers. Crossing a picket line is no longer a cardinal sin but a simple, practical, strategic problem. Sometimes you do, sometimes you don't, depending on circumstance.

Business unionism has reversed the theory of solidarity. There have been literally thousands of instances where one union has refused to support another in its gravest crisis. A skilled tool-and-die makers' local of the Machinists' Union has lost three strikes in recent years because the production men in these shops, also members of the Machinists' Union but in a different local, have crossed their picket lines.

Perhaps the classic example of *non*-solidarity was provided in the 1947 strike of Local 16 of the Typographical Workers' Union against Chicago's newspapers. After nearly a hundred years of unionism this group had established a wage scale of approximately $100 for a thirty-six-and-a-quarter-hour week, and had many other outstanding working conditions. When the Taft-Hartley law was passed, however, the union, for one reason or another, felt that its very existence was in jeopardy. It could not come to terms with the newspapers on such issues as "struck work," seniority, new equipment, and wages. In November of that year, after extended negotiations, the union struck. Twenty-one other unions, all members of the same AFL with which the Typographical Workers were affiliated, came to work each morning, surveyed the picket line, exchanged a few pleasantries with the pickets and went in to work. The local Hearst paper (now owned by the *Chicago Tribune*) advertised that "twenty-one loyal AFL unions bring you today's *Herald American*." The mailers, members of the same international as Local 16, crossed the line of their own brothers. As conscience balm they contributed large sums to the strike; so did many other workers who crossed the picket lines.

One of the craft unions that crossed the line, the photo-engravers, could have forced the employers to heed Local 16's demands with little extra effort. The varitype process used by the newspapers as a substitute for linotype required much more work on the part of the photoengravers. They were earning fabulous wages working overtime. If they had only refused the overtime, let alone refused to work the new process, they could have tilted the scales in Local 16's favor. But they didn't, and the typographical men had to picket for almost two years before they came to agreeable terms.

There are naturally areas where in pure self-defense the business unionists must pool efforts—in opposing, for instance, right-to-work laws or antipicketing legislation. But by and large, their philosophy is the rugged individualist philosophy of the old robber barons: every man for himself, devil take the hindmost. Thus in America the gap between skilled (organized) workers and unskilled (less well-organized) workers is wider than in any other country in the world. The business-union leaders have served their own members well but have permitted other segments of labor to fend for themselves.

Traditionally, business unionism has been less than luke-warm about organizing the unorganized or spending money to help weaker affiliates. "Let them take care of themselves" —so runs the theme. The thesis of "wages solidarity" espoused by unionists in Europe, is frowned on here. Many European unions give priority to the lowest-paid workers, in an effort to lift them above the subsistence level. Norwegian unions, since the war, have raised the wages of low-paid fishermen and agricultural workers more than those of the rest of the working class. But in America it is "every union for itself": the better-paid and more highly organized workers have received large wage increases; the lower-paid and poorly organized groups have either stood still or fallen behind the rise in the cost of living. The lowest 20 per cent of American

workers in 1951 received only the same share of the wage
pie they received in 1945 and 1939. But the more highly
paid laborers and craftsmen improved their position not
only relatively but absolutely.

IV

If any reason is sought for the special character of our
American business unionism, it is primarily in its underlying
philosophy, or perhaps lack of philosophy. In the course of
the years, business unionism has become reconciled to the
free-enterprise system so that its thinking on many subjects
parallels that of the employers. That is most evident in its
concept of ethics.

Al J. Hayes, chairman of the AFL-CIO Ethical Practices
Committee, told a Notre Dame audience in March, 1958:
"What might be admired as no more than 'sharp practice' or
'clever dealing' when it is engaged in by an employer, becomes corruption and unethical practices when indulged in
by a trade unionist." This is undoubtedly a correct statement
of the labor ethic, but far from complete. It is not only sharp
practices or clever dealing that subverts labor ethics, but the
normal code of ethics of the business community—the exaggerated quest for money, profit-consciousness, the autocratic
mentality. While condemning the misuse of union funds,
Hayes does not see anything wrong in labor leaders earning
so much more money than their followers that they lose a
feeling of sympathy for their members. And while condemning investments by union leaders in stocks and bonds that
create a "conflict of interest," Hayes fails to criticize the official who has business investments and real estate that conflict with the fundamental labor *outlook*.

Business unionism has an ambivalent, and ambiguous, attitude on the matter of ethics. In its over-all philosophy, un-

like most European unions, it has steadfastly endorsed the free-enterprise system. Years ago John L. Lewis wrote: "Trade unionism is a phenomenon of capitalism quite similar to the corporation. One is essentially a pooling of labor for purposes of common action in production and sales. The other is a pooling of capital for exactly the same purpose. The economic aims of both are identical—gain."

George Meany, writing in *Fortune* in 1955, said: "We are dedicated to freedom . . . through a system of private enterprise. We believe in the American profit system."

If unions are dedicated to the profit system, what then is wrong with union leaders also making a "profit"? If there is no basic cleavage between management and labor, why shouldn't union officials and employers find some *modus vivendi*, some basis for mutual aid rather than incessant conflict? Labor's top leadership, though honestly perturbed by corruption, finds itself wrestling with this illogic.

A. H. Raskin, labor analyst for *The New York Times*, underscored the dilemma when he wrote in *Commentary*:

> The real significance of the racketeer is not that he is a crook, but that he is a pathological expression of the kind of labor-management cooperation toward which industrial relations are headed. The most universally applauded precept of labor statesmanship is the notion that the welfare of the worker is inextricably bound up with the welfare of the industry in which he works. Hand in hand with this goes the concept that one cannot prosper unless the other prospers. If the identity of interest is so complete, what is wrong with the head of a union running a business? Why shouldn't the president of the Bakery Union operate a bakery, or the president of the Teamsters Union own a fleet of trucks?

Business unionism, to use the words of C. Wright Mills, has a "basic affinity" with other forms of business enterprise. It is an accommodation to businessmen by union leaders, and vice versa, in which neither is interested in labor as a class or in society as a whole but in mutual peace or mutual gain.

There are many strange instances of this affinity, both in practice and outlook. Jimmy Cross was thrown out of AFL-CIO for having borrowed money from a businessman. But unionists sometimes make questionable loans to employers. The teamsters once loaned $1.2 million to a Minneapolis department store that was being struck by a retail clerks' union. A Chicago unionist named Angelo Inciso loaned $40,-000 of his union funds to an employer when the latter ran low on cash.

The same Inciso, when asked by Senator Paul Douglas about a trip he made to Europe at the union's expense, explained: "I fight for them to get them the best of everything, and I'm sure that when I travel they should give me the best of everything." When asked by the senator the purpose of his trip, he replied that it was a "good will tour"; and when pressed further as to whom he was spreading good will for, he answered laconically, "Myself."

Even more specific on labor ethics was Anthony Doria, former secretary-treasurer of the United Auto Workers, AFL (now called the Allied Industrial Workers and not to be confused with Reuther's UAW-CIO). This was the colloquy between Doria and Senator Douglas:

Doria: "I think labor representatives today are entitled to the position they hold."
Senator Douglas: "To diamond rings?"
Doria: "If the man sitting across the table from me wears a diamond ring, I think I am entitled to the same thing. I represent my people on the same level."

Doria didn't see anything odd in the concept that his living standard ought to be closer to that of the employer he supposedly fights than to that of the worker he supposedly represents.

The affection some unionists bear for businessmen is more

often than not reciprocated. Dave Beck, for instance, despite his derelictions as head of the Teamsters' Union, was far from a pariah with either politicians or employers. At one time he was regent of the State University in Washington. *Business Week* (in January, 1948) calmly noted that his methods "have endeared Beck to an ever-widening circle of local businessmen on the Pacific Coast. To them he is the businessman's labor leader." And *Time* (in the same year) seconded this estimate: "The great majority of employers (in the Northwest) think he is wonderful and applaud like happy seals when he speaks to the Chamber of Commerce." Conceivably, it is possible to endorse the free-enterprise system and still look at labor unionism as a public trust. Some unionists do this. But the endorsement of the profit system is not a cause of business unionism but its effect. Having narrowed its sights from the interests of labor as a class to that of a single union or group of unions, business unionism has also narrowed its philosophy. Instead of a conflict of interests, it sees an identity or near-identity of interests. Instead of a policy of struggle it operates on a policy of accommodation. Praise of the profit motive, trimmed to its essentials, is but a convenient apology for business unionism's own *modus operandi*. It is in a sense the rationale of its own ethic; and when George Meany, a thoroughly honest man, endorses it, he is caught in the contradiction of trying to ride two horses at the same time: either the profit motive is a good ethic for *both* business and union officials, or it is a good ethic only for business, while labor must have a different ethic.

V

The policy of accommodation between business unionism and business took form at the end of the nineteenth and beginning of the twentieth centuries. It was not a subjective,

coldly calculated process but in part an automatic development. In a booming period of capitalism there was an atmosphere that lent itself to accommodation. Employers making
substantial profits were under less pressure to fight the unions; it was cheaper to grant concessions than to lose business
during a strike. After the long and bitter battles of the last
half of the nineteenth century there slowly evolved a general
feeling in certain industries that such tactics were costly and
unnecessary. Why engage in expensive wars when there was
enough in the pot for everyone? Why resist wage increases
when there was a sellers' market and the cost could be passed
on to the consumer? Why try to save a few dollars in wages
when far more could be gained if the union official and employer collaborated? The idea was not to destroy the union's
power, but to harness it.

What happened, therefore, was that employers agreed to
demands that brought stability to unions and union leaders,
in return for stability or some trade advantage for themselves. It was a simple *quid pro quo* that seemed natural under the circumstances of prosperity. The employer helped
the union leader, the union leader helped the employer.

In 1897, the Carpenters' Union in Chicago secured a
closed-shop contract from the employers' association. Under
the provisions of this agreement the contractors pledged not
to hire any one who was not a member of the union. In return the business agents agreed they would refuse to supply
skilled craftsmen to those employers who were outside the
association. This was an excellent arrangement for both
parties: the business agents were assured security of their organization; the employers were able, with the help of the
union, to drive low-cost competitors out of the industry. Soon
the closed shop was extended to bricklayers, painters,
plumbers, steamfitters, and many others. The business agent,
while performing a service for his members, also performed
one for the employers. To enforce the pact, he sometimes

had to use violence against workers who wouldn't "go along." When Sam Parks organized his Housesmiths' Union Local 2, ninety beatings occurred in a period of two months. Recalcitrants who refused to heed Parks's dictum were literally slugged into the union. Usually, however, violence was unnecessary since the worker received solid benefits from union membership.

In most instances what the employer gained from the closed shop and friendlier relations with the business agent was peace. The costly strikes ended. The union organized the whole industry, and labor costs were taken out of the sphere of competition: all employers in the same area paid the same scale. What the unionist gained was also peace and stability. He no longer had to fight as hard as he did in the days of the blacklist, the Pinkerton thugs, and the employer offensives. Nor did he have to contend with as much opposition within his union. Control of jobs made it possible to mold an effective ruling machine.

Under such circumstances many business union leaders just relaxed. A few were content with just having peace; they gained little monetarily for themselves. Even their salaries were not too far out of line with that of their members. At the other pole, some became wealthy by collaborating with employers in shady joint ventures. Most, however, did nothing dishonest, took no bribes, made no collusive agreements. Though little concerned with the rest of labor or social justice generally, they continued to gain concessions for the members of their own unions. Their salaries pyramided to levels beyond that of their members, they joined the best clubs, lived well, worked only a few hours a day, took frequent vacations in Miami or Hot Springs or some other such spots, and became respected and inoffensive members of the community. They bought real estate, stocks, even small corporations.

The peace gained through stable relations with management made it possible to grow relatively affluent without accepting bribes. Union officials soon were responsible for huge sums of money, and found many ways to earn sizable amounts for themselves. The most obvious method was raising their own salaries and expense accounts. With a moderately satisfied and relatively apathetic membership this was hardly a problem. Sam Parks, who was a crook, received a salary of $48 a week—good pay in 1901. But he also received out of the union treasury $40,000 in expense money in 1901, $60,000 in 1902, and $50,000 in 1903. Salaries of business agents and above all of top union officials have steadily increased. The gap between the rank-and-file worker and union leader has grown until in many unions the leader is earning eight or ten times as much as the highest-paid worker, not including his expenses. In the highest echelon there are a few $50,000 salaries—not including unlimited expense accounts. But even in the lower ranks, there are many officials earning $15,000 to $25,000 for just managing local unions.

The business unionist has other opportunities as well. If his union builds a headquarters, there are always ways of making a commission by placing the building contract in the right place. If his union is covered by health and welfare insurance with a commercial insurance company there is always a way of earning a gratuity. A unionist in a Midwestern city was sent to jail because he did not report income tax on about $1,000 worth of painting done on his own house by a thankful contractor who had received many thousands of dollars in union work from him.

Dave Beck, who administered the $41-million Teamsters' Union treasury before he decided in 1957 not to run for president again, once made a loan out of union funds of $1.5 million to the Fruehauf Trailer Company and then turned around and took a $200,000 personal loan from the company.

Perhaps characteristic of both the opportunities available and the techniques used for enrichment is the story of the bizarre business ventures of the Brotherhood of Locomotive Engineers in the 1920's. The Brotherhood had so much loose money around that it founded twelve banks, with resources of over $53 million; eleven investment houses, with $34 million; it purchased the Equitable Building in New York for $38 million, the Standard Bank Building in Cleveland for $6 million; and spent $16 million for development and promotion in Venice, Florida. To top it off, its officials purchased, in the name of the union, the Coal River Collieries for $3 million and operated it with *nonunion* labor.

By 1932, the whole series of investments had collapsed and the Brotherhood found itself $9 million in debt, while its workers had lost $30 million. The union officials, however, had made tidy sums from all the financial maneuvers. Warren S. Stone, union head, and his successor William B. Prentner, each received $50,000 from the nonunion collieries alone. When the Equitable Building was sold, the new owners were so grateful for the bargain that they made a present of $2,000 to $2,500 to each of the fourteen Brotherhood officials. The callousness of these officials is perhaps best illustrated by Prentner's reply to a delegate who objected to such dealings: "I took mine," he said, "and it's nobody's damned business."

That seems to be the point: Is it "nobody's damned business"? Can the labor movement survive on the ethics of business?

In extenuation, some writers point out that the ethical lapses of business are far more formidable than those in labor. That is undoubtedly true. From 1951 to 1957, the federal government had to write off $150 million in withholding taxes, deducted from workers' wages by employers but never turned over to the Internal Revenue service. Dishonesty in banks and business takes a half billion dollars a year. *Life* magazine estimated that "as much as $5 billion probably changed hands in kickbacks, payoffs and bribes" amongst business and professional men. Many hundreds of millions more "evaporated in retail chiseling" and "a half billion went down the drain in home repair frauds alone." *Fortune* noted that embezzlers steal $500 million to $3 billion a year. In one study of 1,001 such men it was found that 270 were trusted company supervisors or executives.

For better or for worse, however, the dishonesty in business—tax cheating, embezzling, bribes for business orders, and similar practices—are taken as a matter of course in our society. Perhaps a business system can not exist any other way, although business morality in Britain seems to be higher. But when the labor movement apes the mores of business it can no longer attract either public opinion or the millions of unorganized workers outside its ranks.

Edwin A. Lahey, chief of the Washington bureau of the *Chicago Daily News* and ordinarily friendly to labor, put his finger on the problem when he reported on the AFL-CIO executive council meeting in Miami, February, 1958. This was a period of recession. The Bureau of Labor Statistics had just reported that 1,120,000 workers had lost their jobs in the month before.

"By unfortunate coincidence," wrote Lahey, "a good many working-class families will be planning a long stretch of fat back and lentil soup, during the same week that the labor leader is relaxing over an $8 steak on Collins Avenue (in Miami Beach). . . . The leaders of that movement have had it so good for so long that they forget what it is to get fallen arches waiting in a soup line, or to hold a local union meeting under a viaduct, with one guy posted as a lookout for the cops. . . . If they [examine themselves] seriously, they will find the problem of 'materialism' high on their list of defects. And if they look at it closely, they may reaffirm the ancient belief that the labor movement as a career is a vocation of service, not a 'business' in which one keeps up with the Joneses in matters of high living."

VI

Most business unionists, as indicated, are guilty of nothing more than aping the mores and accepting the philosophy and ethics of business. Some, however, have gone further. They have entered into arrangements with employers for mutual gain that are highly unethical, sometimes even criminal.

Admittedly, all business unionists can not be lumped together in the same pot; there is a considerable difference in the integrity of the best as compared with the worst. But as A. H. Raskin points out, they are both caught in the same trap. If there is nothing wrong in the profit system or in exaggerated money-consciousness, then what can be wrong with a union official selling motion-picture projectors to theater owners with whom he negotiates, or helping an employers' association enforce higher prices to the public? This is at one and the same time the dilemma of business unionism and the cause of its decline in public esteem.

Since the end of the nineteenth century a whole catalogue of practices have been devised by business agents and employers acting in concert, for mutual gain. Among these are:

1. "Soft," or "sweetheart" contracts.
2. Backdoor deals
3. Concealed bribery
4. Joint enforcement of higher prices or of trade practices
5. Implicit or explicit understandings to organize only a section of the labor force, leaving the rest nonunion.
6. Business partnerships

The "soft," or "sweetheart," contract is what the term implies, granting the employer terms and conditions that are substandard—far below what might be gained if the union's full bargaining power were put to work. In the twenties and thirties "sweetheart" deals were often arranged in order to undermine a militant faction in the union that threatened to win the rank and file to its side. Back in 1922 after a protracted strike, John L. Lewis signed an agreement for the bituminous-field coal miners, in which he failed to cover 75,000 strikers who worked for the U. S. Steel mines in western Pennsylvania but who were not then in the union. This large group of miners was left to fend for itself and continue nonunion for almost two more decades because Lewis didn't want to push too far. One of his biographers, Cecil Carnes, commenting on this incident, noted: "He could not, as a business unionist, risk a good contract by insisting upon 'too much.' " When the bituminous men had gone back to work, 155,000 anthracite miners continued striking for a few weeks until Lewis negotiated a contract at the old scale, with no increases.

In February, 1926, Lewis signed a five-year pact for the anthracite miners which gave the union the check-off of dues but left the wage scale unchanged. These are perhaps typical samples of soft contracts made to weaken the opposition. Lewis in this period was plagued by factions of socialists and communists trying to unseat him. The soft contract was a device in this struggle for control. The 1926 pact, which yielded no benefits to the men, did yield the check-off for the union officialdom, and under this check-off Lewis could collect not only dues but assessments and fines as well. This was a potent weapon in the hands of a willful man like Lewis. In the five-year period from January 1, 1919, to January 1, 1924, miners of District 12 of the United Mine Workers paid some $107,000 in fines for striking "illegally" and for loading dirty coal. These fines were divided equally between the union and the Illinois Bituminous Coal Operators' Association.

Another historical example of the "sweetheart" contract was the one agreed to between "Big Bill" Hutcheson, president of the carpenters, and the New York employers in 1916. Hutcheson had been head of the Carpenters' Union only eleven months when 17,000 unionists voted four to one to seek a fifty-cent-a-day raise. Construction was booming and wage scales had been unchanged since 1907. After prolonged negotiations with various employers, the union was able to secure its demand for 14,000 members, but the other 3,000 were faced with the alternative of either striking or accepting defeat. They chose to strike and victory seemed imminent, when Hutcheson canceled the walkout. Hurrying to New York he signed an agreement not only freezing the wages of the 3,000 men on strike but canceling the fifty-cent raise for the 14,000 who had already won it. Here again, internal politics were a primary cause for a "sweetheart" deal. The New York carpenters who opposed Hutcheson denounced the agreement as a "betrayal" and a "corrupt bargain," but Hutcheson retaliated by expelling sixty-five of their locals. What was at stake for Hutcheson was his alliance with a crooked unionist named Robert P. Brindell. The soft contract and the expulsions helped consolidate Hutcheson's and Brindell's hold over the union; and Brindell received $85,000 or a major share thereof for this piece of chicanery.

The Senate Rackets Committee charged in May, 1958, that the A & P food chain had entered into a five-year collusive agreement with Max Block, head of two meat cutters' unions, to freeze out two other unions. Charles T. Douds, former regional director of the National Labor Relations Board in New York, testified that the grocery chain had forced its grocery clerks to join Block's union while two rival unions were in the process of organizing them and one had a case pending before the Board. The company recognized the meat cutters without an election, and probably made itself millions of dollars as a consequence of this "sweetheart" arrangement, the Senate committee charged. While A & P competitors were working forty hours a week, A & P employees labored forty-five hours for approximately the same pay. The savings amounted to perhaps $300 or $400 a year per employee.

Collaboration between employers and business agents to settle for moderate increases, rather than using the full economic power of the union, are not too infrequent. A $2-a-week wage increase for 1,000 employees will cost an employer $104,000 a year. If management can settle for a $3-a-week raise instead of, say $5, the savings will amount to a tidy sum—even if the employer has to make a gift to the union leader of perhaps $10,000. He will still be $94,000 ahead. What is more, the union leader himself will be in no real danger. He has a fine talking point for keeping the wrath of the rank and file within bounds—he has gained something for them too, although not nearly so much as if the full bargaining power of the union had been utilized.

Twenty candy jobbers in a large Eastern city were approached by a business agent in the 1940's and told that the $40-a-week existing pay rate would have to be doubled to $80. This militancy, of course, was synthetic, a mere bargaining point. Eventually the unionist took a bribe of $2,500 and settled for a $50-a-week scale. The workers involved may have felt there was something wrong with the high-handed manner in which their union was conducted, but they were probably satisfied with the $10 raise. The strategy of the opportunist is not to barter away all of the bargaining power of his men, but merely a part of it, saving just enough to make a passable showing for the membership. In this instance a bribe was involved; in hundreds more the union leader gets nothing but peace and quiet from a "sweetheart" transaction. This too is like money in the bank, because without strikes, union treasuries build up rapidly, and, as they pyramid, the business unionist can push through raises in salary, expenses, and other benefits for himself.

VII

A variation of the "sweetheart" contract is the backdoor pact. Here the business unionist undercuts a militant union outside his ranks, rather than a faction inside. This technique came into full flower after the Committee for Industrial Organization was formed in 1935. Employers who bitterly contested unionization for decades were now faced with the prospect of imminent organization by a fiery brand of radicals and militants in the new CIO. In their fear, they sought arrangements with the moderate old-line unionists as a lesser evil. Not a few AFL unions waxed rich on this parasitic practice. Without a single member enrolled and without consulting a single worker, they would meet with the employer, sign a soft agreement, and start collecting dues. When it was all over the employer would either call a meeting of the men in the shop to inform them of the pact and to introduce their made-to-order union leaders, or merely advise them by posting a notice on the bulletin board.

"Organizing the employer" rather than the employee became a widespread practice. There are obviously no statistics on this matter, but it is so well known in labor circles, it needs no voluminous documentation. Hundreds of thousands of workers undoubtedly were enrolled this way. On the West Coast, Dave Beck of the teamsters became a great power, in part, at least, by waving the picture of radical Harry Bridges in front of petrified employers, in order to force quick backdoor deals. Not a few AFL officials considered this a major strategy in their fight with the CIO. Here, for instance, is a letter sent out by President A. O. Wharton of the Machinists' Union to his affiliates on April 20, 1937:

Since the Supreme Court decision upholding the Wagner Labor Act many employers now realize that it is the Law of our Country and they are prepared to deal with labor organizations.

These employers have expressed a preference to deal with A.F. of L. organizations rather than Lewis, Hillman, Dubinsky, Howard and their gang of sluggers, communists, radicals and soap box artists, professional bums, expelled members of labor unions, outright scabs and the Jewish organizations with all their red affiliates.

We have conferred with several such employers and arranged for conferences later when we get the plants organized. The purpose of this is to direct all officers and all representatives to contact employers in your locality as a preliminary to organizing the shops and factories.

With best wishes, I am fraternally yours. . . .

It should be noted that the machinists tripled their membership in six years, and are today one of the five largest unions in the country. This policy of backdoor deals undoubtedly accounts for a good share of that gain. Although Wharton's letter asks officials to arrange for conferences "when we get the plants organized," it must be obvious that a friendly employer, who has a "preference to deal with A.F. of L. organizations rather than Lewis, Hillman, Dubinsky, Howard," is not going to be squeamish about the number of men actually enrolled.

Many AFL unions in the 1930's grew as rapidly as the CIO partially by making backdoor deals. The practice persists to this very day. In the Midwest a few years ago, a group of 330 Negro workers joined a legitimate union almost to a man, only to have the company attorney show up with a "recognition contract" presumably signed six months before with another union. When asked why the workers weren't aware of this other union, the attorney said that management was thinking of moving its plant and had therefore withheld the information until it knew who was going to be taken to the new plant and who wasn't. No worker had ever received a circular from the so-called other union, nor paid a cent in dues to it. Its existence was completely unknown until after

280 employees had signed application cards with the legitimate organization.

(Parenthetically we might note that the National Labor Relations Board is an unwitting accessory to these backdoor deals. All an employer has to do is produce an existing contract, backdoor or not, and the Board will refuse to order an election. The Board does not investigate to see whether the contract was predated, whether the members knew about it or whether they voted on it. The mere exhibition of signatures to a document is usually considered sufficient for the NLRB to hold that it is a "bar" to an election for two years.)

Not too long ago, an AFL union official attempted to organize an optical firm. When he had signed up 60 per cent of the workers he sat down with management to bargain for recognition—a preliminary understanding that the company will negotiate with no other union. Unfortunately bargaining was protracted and fruitless. The company offered this unionist a bribe to get out of the picture but he turned it down. While he procrastinated as to whether to strike, management took some countermeasures and the membership deserted the union. The campaign ended in defeat. A few months later another union, again a legitimate organization, tried once more. After the first leaflet, six workers returned signed cards. Anyone who has had any experience with this kind of technique will testify that this is an excellent beginning in a plant of 100 or 150 workers. But just as the campaign was ready to gain momentum the company attorneys called the union to advise it that a union-shop contract already existed with another AFL union. How was it signed? Who negotiated it? The men in the plant did not know. But the instrument was duly signed by both parties and there was nothing that the legitimate union official could do.

A variation of the backdoor technique has developed where the old AFL chartered company-dominated unions in order to avoid CIO organization. Many of these company unions were legitimate and evolved in a healthy fashion, but not a few remained vassals of management and continued to sign "sweetheart" deals.

VIII

Still another device of accommodation between business unionists and businessmen has been the *concealed* bribe. The union official becomes rich by either selling a service or a commodity to employers. Joseph G. Fay, formerly vice-president of the Operating Engineers, before he was convicted in 1945 of extorting $368,000 from contractors, became wealthy by renting hoisting equipment to the employers he dealt with. Sam Kaplan, once head of Motion Picture Operators Local 306 in New York, operated a *nonunion* projection-equipment company on the side. At that time Local 306 had a system whereby permit men worked for $45 or $50 a week while "card" men earned $85. In designating how many permit men could be used in each theater (at a saving of $35 a week) and how many card men, Kaplan was decisively influenced by where the theater purchased its supplies. Those who purchased from the Kaplan Supply Company found they could use one card man and four permit men; those who didn't had to use all card men, at an additional cost of $160 a week.

A Chicago union leader had already amassed a fortune of a half million dollars by 1915, by selling his equipment to employers he bargained with. The unionist in each of these instances used his power to cut off or turn on the supply of labor as a factor in forcing purchase of his equipment. This may or may not skirt the brim of the law, but it is hardly more than a concealed bribe.

A refinement of this technique—a direct bribe—came to light a few years ago when five St. Louis unionists received ten- to twelve-year prison terms for fictitious deals. The men were accused by the government of setting up dummy corporations which billed contractors for nonexistent welding supplies and other equipment. Judge Rubey M. Hulen, in sentencing the five extortionists, made a few pertinent remarks concerning this whole problem of accommodation between union leaders and businessmen. The judge noted that there was a "glaring indifference" on the part of the business agents to the welfare of their workmen after the contractors began to do business with them. "None of the defendants," he said, "had anything to do with the welfare of the workers from the time the payoffs began. If a contractor wanted a worker fired he was fired with no inquiry as to cause. If the worker was right, where was his union representative after the extortion agreement was made? There is no evidence that any of these defendants had any interest in the treatment of labor by employers after that time."

IX

Probably the most flagrant area of collaboration between business unionists and employers is in price-fixing and policing trade practices. The story of virtual alliance is monotonously similar through the decades. In each instance the unionist gets something, and gives something in return. As a result of an agreement between the teamsters and a coal association in Chicago in 1902, the owners were able to raise the coal-cartage costs from $1.40 to $2 a load. Any employer who refused to follow the association price policy faced a strike. The union leadership was so solicitous of the welfare of the coal association, in fact, that it drove a whole competitive industry—the natural-gas industry—out of the city. By threatening to withhold coal from the large office buildings in the winter the union officials forced the companies to cancel their gas contracts, thus breaking the foothold gained by this industry.

In the late forties, just to illustrate the continuance of such tactics, three men were convicted of racketeering in the Dock Street produce section of Philadelphia. Two were union officials and the third the head of two employer associations. Fred Schlein of the employer groups testified before a congressional committee in 1947 that his associations fought in every instance against the issuance by the public utility commission of certificates to new haulers. Competition was to be restricted to as small a number of haulers as possible. The associations also enforced a rule against "kickback." It passed laws on "package limits" and other trade practices which sought to achieve stability in the industry and raise profits. Testimony showed that the alliance of employers and union officials helped raise prices, and that in a number of instances —aided by a bribe—the allies were able to resolve wage disputes at favorable terms to employers. The instrument for enforcing all these rules and understandings was, of course, the union officials who called strikes against those employers who refused to join the associations or those who refused to abide by their rules. Some who preferred sharp competition to oppressive stability were driven out of business.

A small repair association in the Midwest and a union leader combined to assign each contractor work in a certain area, rather than compete unrestrictedly. A local union in the East, some years ago, called its members off jobs where their employers were trying to cut the price of bread. Similar practices prevail in many fields. Milk unions on occasion have helped milk companies enforce price levels. In many cities you can't change your linen-supply house because there is a compact between union official and employers' association to "stabilize" the industry. What the union leaders actually do in these cases is help employers in decentralized, highly competitive industries establish what amounts to a monopoly.

Under such circumstances, the employers do not need low wages, they can afford to pay decent rates. The employers gain, the union workers gain, the union official gains something. Labor as a whole loses public face for such practices, but the individual union leader hardly cares.

The devices of accommodation between business unionists and employers are as varied as the human imagination. In each case the goal is mutual benefit. A union official agrees to organize only the skilled workers in an establishment and leave the unskilled alone. In return he gains a decent contract for a smaller group of men—and peace. Here and there union officials form partnerships with employers. If the books of some companies were opened it would be found that union leaders and the employers they deal with were stockholders in the same enterprise.

One such instance, involving the aforementioned Max Block, then vice-president of the Amalgamated Meat Cutters and Butcher Workmen's Union, came to light when a Senate Rackets Committee investigator charged that the Food Fair Properties, which operated 280 stores in eight Eastern states, had permitted Block and others to buy stock worth $4 a share for $1. Paul Lafayette, who held a post similar to that of Block in the Retail Clerks' Union, had similarly profited from this practice, according to the investigators. The position of power gained by business agents through their control of collective bargaining is a salable commodity, and not infrequently it *is* sold. Not a few union leaders have had testimonial dinners in their honor, in which employers have bought tickets at $50 or $100 a plate and in which the official is given a personal gift of $10,000 to $50,000 from the proceeds.

Of late, the health and welfare funds established between unions and employers have become a feeding trough for business unionists. The commissions they take, perhaps legal in themselves (though those of the flagrant racketeers obviously are not), are nonetheless ethical only if you consider the role of a union official as a middleman between labor and capital rather than as an agent of the collective union membership. Whatever accrues to the union leader as a result of his agency ought by right to be returned to the membership. Unfortunately, in many instances, there are sticky fingers which let none of these sums pass through.

"I run my union," Dave Beck was wont to say, "like a business. We deal in one commodity—labor." This exposition is classic. Business unionism superimposes the business mentality on the union movement. It adopts that whole admixture of slogans, clichés, and aphorisms which have made American business what it is: "Take care of yourself, devil take the hindmost"; "Number one comes first"; "You scratch my back, I'll scratch yours."

5
Trojan Horse

ONE OF THE UNIQUE FEATURES OF THE AMERICAN LABOR MOVE-
ment is the marriage of business unionism and crime,
known as labor racketeering. Its size has been exaggerated
because newspaper editors are prone to highlight stories of
evil in the house of labor. Yet the fact that racketeering
exists at all is a stigma on labor which cannot be dismissed
lightly. The average citizen is at a loss to understand how a
movement which professes such noble ideals can tolerate
in its ranks criminals who have records of extortion, dealing
in narcotics, burglary, even murder.

The exposés of the Select Committee on Improper Activities in the Labor or Management Field of the United States
Senate in 1957-1958 made the term "racketeer" a byword.
The activity of the McClellan Committee, as it was popularly known, drew more public attention than any other
item of domestic politics. The mass of revelations was so
great, and its publicity so constant, that in many minds the

whole labor movement became suspect. What was lacking, unfortunately, was an over-all insight into the problem of labor racketeering. Where does the racketeer come from? What are his goals? How is he protected?

The answer to these questions are not quite as simple as they sound. What distinguishes the labor racketeer from the average business unionist is not only a greater degree of materialism, but, (1) a willingness to use violence and terror in achieving his personal ends; and (2) connections with and protection from businessmen, politicians, and the national crime syndicate.

In the most glaring cases the labor racketeer is an actual member of the crime syndicate; in others he is a "fellow traveler" who tolerates its activities. Always he performs a service for someone or some force *outside* the labor movement—usually an employer or the crime syndicate, or both. Without such connections labor racketeering could not exist. It is part of the corrupting influence of trustified crime and unethical business practices that corrodes moral standards throughout society itself.

Perhaps the case histories of Dave Beck, former president of the Teamsters' Union, and William E. Maloney, former president of the Operating Engineers' Union, both of whom were forced out of the house of labor as a result of the McClellan hearings, can illustrate these interlinkages.

II

Dave Beck, once a humble laundry driver in Seattle, made a fortune running into seven figures by using his union post as a means of gaining business opportunities. Through his connections with the Anheuser-Busch Company, with whom he had dealt as a union leader, he secured beer distribution franchises for his family and relatives. Through his connec-

tions with Nathan Shefferman, who represented 300 employers, including Sears Roebuck & Company and Whirlpool, he
profited from a whole series of financial ventures. The Senate
Rackets Committee asserted that Beck had taken a $22,500
loan from Shefferman, had shared in the profits from the
sale of bookkeeping equipment, filing systems, furniture,
decorations, and toy trucks, all sold to the union. Shefferman's Union Merchandising Company and its two subsidiaries netted more than $200,000 in 1953-1956, the largest
single share going to one of its inactive shareholders, Norman Gessert, a cousin of Beck's wife. Beck also took a cut
from Shefferman when the latter purchased land for the
union's headquarters in Washington, as well as from the sale
of furnishings for the building.

The full story of Beck's finances has not been told, but
what did come to light indicates that union funds were not
infrequently used for his own business. Beck admitted to the
McClellan committee that he had borrowed $370,000 interest-free from the union. The AFL-CIO Ethical Practices
Committee concluded from its investigations that Beck
"used union funds as if they were his private funds, that no
records were kept of the transactions and no instruments
of indebtedness were signed by him . . . all of the evidence
indicates there was initially no intention to repay." When
in need of funds, Beck did not hesitate to borrow $200,000
from a trucking-company owner. He prevailed on his union
executive board, which he controlled, to purchase his own
$162,000 Seattle home and then turn it back to him to live
in rent-free.

Such financial peculations could hardly result in anything but "sweetheart" relations with employers and employer representatives on the one hand, and tolerance of
criminals who have burrowed into the Teamsters' Union on
the other.

The investigations brought out that Shefferman had purchased $94,000 worth of such merchandise as shirts, diapers, carpets, gardening supplies, from Sears Roebuck for his friend Dave Beck. The items, secured at a discount, were paid for by the Western Conference of Teamsters. When Wallace Tudor, a vice-president of Sears, was asked to explain these strange deals by the industrial relations representative of his firm, he replied: "Mr. Shefferman convinced those involved (at Sears) that it was important that he kept himself informed as to what is going on in the labor movement and at the same time I am certain that we thought that it was important that the top union officials know what Sears stands for so that they would know about the rates of pay in our company, our benefit program. . . ."

Beck must have been impressed by the Sears "wages" and "benefits" because with Beck's help, Shefferman was able to smash an organizing drive by the Retail Clerks' Union at Sears' Boston stores. According to Daniel Bell, former labor editor of *Fortune*, writing in that magazine in February, 1958, "The Shefferman technique has paid off for Sears. Of 205,000 workers in Sears Roebuck, only 14,000 are organized, and of these 7,000 belong to the Teamsters. Strange to say, or not so strange to say, the Teamsters have not yet mounted a really effective organizing drive."

Under the circumstances it is not at all surprising that Beck tolerated other materialists in his ranks, some of whom were convicted criminals. By his ethical standards they were doing much the same as he was, except that their efforts were on a smaller scale, and often less subtle. When Sidney L. Brennan, a teamster vice-president in Minneapolis, and three of his associates were convicted of taking a $5,000 bribe to break a strike, Beck permitted Brennan to remain on as an officer of the union. Such a "minor" crime as strikebreaking didn't seem to disqualify him. "We cannot conceive," said the AFL-CIO report on Beck, "of a greater dereliction of duty." The former teamster head also refused to act against Johnny Dio, a convicted extortionist who represented employers through his Equitable Research Association, and workers through his seven Teamsters' Union locals. Dio had a criminal record and most questionable connections. Yet Beck not only gave him charters in the organization but failed to lift them when the matter came to public attention.

Many others of similarly materialist and criminal bent found sanctuary under Beck's umbrella. At one time Beck argued that he could take no disciplinary measures against the ne'er-do-wells in teamster ranks until the courts convicted them. But in case after case, even after conviction, he permitted them to remain in their posts. Beck himself probably had no direct connections with the criminal gangs; but neither did he have enough aversion to them to throw their associates out of his union. AFL-CIO President George Meany, evidently referring to Beck, told the AFL-CIO Industrial Union Department:

We thought we knew a few things about trade union corruption, but we didn't know the half of it, one-tenth of it, or the one-hundredth of it. We didn't know, for instance, that we had unions where a criminal record was almost a prerequisite to holding office under the national union.

We didn't know that we had top trade union leaders who made it a practice to secretly borrow the funds of their union. We didn't know that there were top trade union leaders who used the funds for phony real estate deals in which the victims of their fraud were their own members.

And we didn't know that there were trade union leaders who charged to the union treasury such items as speed boats, perfume, silk stockings, brassieres, color TV, refrigerators and everything else under the sun.

The story of William E. Maloney is, if anything, even more lurid than that of Beck. Maloney began his career in Chicago as a pauper and retired at the age of seventy-two, under pressure by the Senate Rackets Committee and the

AFL-CIO, with the wealth of a king. By that time he owned a huge estate at Elk Grove, Illinois, complete with colonial house, swimming pools, and stables. He had at his disposal a $35,000 yacht supplied by the union and maintained at a cost of more than $120,000, three Cadillacs and one Chrysler Imperial, paid for by the Operating Engineers, and a Washington apartment in addition to his own mansion. The union was so solicitous of his welfare that it picked up the bill for a $14,000 trip to Europe for himself and his wife, paid his dues at the race tracks, and gave him a variety of minor gifts. Amongst them were a $1,250 diamond-and-platinum wrist watch, a $585 television set, a $386 air-conditioner, shoes, shirts, even baked hams.

Maloney's whole labor history is interlinked with gangsters and gangsterism. In his climb to power he was aided by hoodlums such as "Three-Fingered" Jack White, Charles Fischetti, George "Red" Barker, and similar people. With their help he was able to form Local 150 in Chicago, terrorize its dissidents, and keep the local under trusteeship to him for twenty-nine years. Those who opposed him were, according to the Senate Rackets Commitee, "either killed or frightened out of office." Dennis Bruce Zeigler, an honest unionist who fought the terror, was shot to death in front of his home a few days after being threatened by Maloney and one of his friends. The former president of the union, Arthur M. Huddel, died in a hospital of pneumonia after being shot.

Some power bigger than Maloney himself protected him at every stage in his career. At one point the members of Local 569, for whom he had been a business agent, voted 268 to 0 to oust him from office, but the international union overruled this action. The secret must lie in his associates. One of them was Joseph G. Fay, former sixth vice-president, who himself grew affluent as a result of his criminal connections. In 1940, during the convention sessions of the AFL in New Orleans, Fay slugged David Dubinsky, president of the International Ladies' Garment Workers, because he called for action against racketeers. An opponent of Fay's in the Building Trades Council was unceremoniously murdered. Members of Local 542 in Philadelphia, under trusteeship to him, were brutally beaten and sent to the hospital. In 1948, Fay was sent to jail for seven and a half to fifteen years for extorting $368,000 from employers on the Delaware aqueduct water-supply project. While he was in jail his wife was put on the union payroll as an "adviser," and between them they received approximately $100,000. But none of this seemed to offend President Maloney. None of it stirred him to action. Neither did the activities of similar unsavory men ensconced in other segments of his union, such as William De Koening of Local 138.

As one studies the record of Maloney, the conclusion is inescapable that he could not have stayed in power long without support from employers and the crime syndicate.

III

Historically, violence was introduced into labor-management relations by the employer. During the last half of the nineteenth century, employers hired so-called detectives—the Pinkertons were the most famous—to break strikes, spy on employees, and disrupt organization. According to Louis Adamic, these detective agencies "sent thieves and murderers to the scenes of labor disputes, where employers appointed them 'guards,' with duties to protect property and scabs, to shoot down and slug strike pickets, provoke riots, commit, and incite strikers to commit outrages which later were blamed entirely on the workers." Against such violence the rank-and-file unionist improvised his own forms of reprisal and defense—but he didn't hire any counter-criminals to defend him.

But by 1909 there were many unions, especially in the needle trades, with a large percentage of women. During the big strikes of this period the women were helpless to defend themselves from employer thugs hired to disrupt their picket lines. The unions thereupon took to hiring their own muscle men, men like "Big Jack" Zelig, "Joe the Greaser" Rosensweig, "Dopey Benny" Fein, and others with equally colorful names. "Dopey Benny," after the murder of some of his associates, became the first prominent labor gangster. He formed alliances with other gangs and placed his activities on a businesslike basis. Dividing the city into sections, each of his gangs wrecked shops, slugged scabs, and committed similar acts for which they were paid $7.50 a day per man and $12 for the gang leader. For wrecking a small nonunion plant they received $150. For shooting a man in the leg or breaking an arm the rates were adjusted accordingly, with the understanding that if the thug were put in jail he would receive $25 a week for the whole period of his incarceration. In this period the relationship between gangsters and unions was still simple. The hoodlum, in most instances, did his slugging, took his pay, and that ended the relationship. They did not attempt to dominate the unions themselves. But by 1920 the gangsters had learned that it was possible to pursue the racket further. The men who came to dinner decided to stay on. They muscled themselves into a few local unions as partners.

The next stage in labor racketeering was a broader offensive by the gangs, a more serious effort not only to take over key local unions but international unions as well. In New York, the gambler Arnold Rothstein not only supplied thugs to the furriers and garment unions but bribed police not to molest pickets. His successors, after he was murdered, Louis "Lepke" Buchalter and "Charlie the Gurrah" Shapiro built this busniess into a fortune with reputed incomes of $5 million a year. With a strong-arm squad of 250 men they terrorized the New York painting, flour-trucking, baking, fur, and motion-picture industries for ten years. Lepke and Gurrah—L & G as they were known—supplied their men impartially to both sides of the labor-management conflict. In the 1927 painters' strike, L & G assigned the warriors for labor, while a former associate, "Little Augie" Orgen, supplied them to management for $50,000. As a result of the strike, in which "Little Augie" himself was killed, Lepke and Gurrah gained control of the Brooklyn Painters' Union for a full decade. From this venture the gangster team expanded into the management field, organizing associations of employers in those industries where it controlled the unions, such as in flour trucking. With the true impartiality of middlemen, Lepke and Gurrah represented many local unions on the one hand, and employers, such as the furriers, on the other. But their major effort to dominate a national union—Sidney Hillman's Amalgamated Clothing Workers—ended in failure, and the needle-trades unions, though constantly plagued by racketeers, were able to reassert mastery in their own house.

In Chicago, Al Capone, in Detroit the "Purple Gang," and in other cities other gangs, muscled into the movement in approximately the same way. The hoodlums discovered early the pivotal significance of transportation in modern industry. By controlling key teamster unions they could dominate small, decentralized industries with relative ease. Capone, for instance, organized the Master Cleaners and Dyers Employers' Association as part of a combine that included a cleaners', dyers', and pressers' local union as well as the teamsters in this field. With these three points of power it was a simple matter to assign each cleaner and dyer to a particular master cleaner, and to fix prices. Any shopowner who refused to follow Association dictate soon found a picket line in front of his establishment and might be forced out of business. One sixty-seven-year-old cleaner, whose shop had always been union, balked at the price-fixing of the Association only to find his workers on strike. On appealing to the Association he was told he could remedy the situation by paying $5,000 for a membership; and since he couldn't raise the money he sold his shop. When he wanted to return to business he appealed to the Association as well as the state's attorney, but these efforts ended in failure. The little businessman could only resolve his problem by a short talk with Al Capone himself, cutting the Capone syndicate into his operations.

Entering into the labor field from the outside, and playing both sides of the fence, the gangsters took over key bastions —scores of local unions—that helped them consolidate the power of their business associations. During the prohibition era this aspect of their operation was relatively small, but after the Eighteenth Amendment was repealed the gangs moved into this area of operations with greater vigor. By now they had accumulated great fortunes from their bootlegging and they were looking for new investments. The entrepreneurial wars between hoodlums for this lush field is a disgraceful chapter in American history. It is, however, closely linked with the corrupt political machines of the big cities, Mayor William Hale Thompson's organization in Chicago, Tammany Hall in New York, and similar machines elsewhere. The crime syndicate intermeshed with politics, corrupt police, judges, law-enforcement officers, mayors, and lesser officials to secure immunity from prosecution. Between 1911 and 1923 there were twenty-four labor killings in Chicago alone. In the 1930's this figure was far eclipsed. Gangsters drove up to a union office, displayed a few machine guns or sawed-off shotguns and just took over. In his revealing book, *Labor Czars*, Harold Seidman tells of one mob that invaded a union office to announce, "We are taking over the place for the day," only to be ousted by a rival gang a few days later. At one time in Chicago there were seven labor bombings in two days.

On the eve of World War II, however, it looked as if the gangsters had reached the end of the road. Thomas E. Dewey, then a district attorney in New York, sent Lepke, Gurrah and others to the electric chair. Al Capone was packed off by the federal government for income-tax evasions, and other lesser lights were similarly put away. Ed Lahey wrote in the *New Republic*, September, 1943, that "the worst of the problem is now solved." Unfortunately he was wrong. The crime syndicate had more vitality—and more flexibility—than he imagined. Slowly and methodically it became a centralized empire, rather than a warring group of gangs. Its interests, instead of being 90 per cent illegal and only 10 per cent legal, shifted to a greater emphasis on legitimate business ventures in real estate, breweries, and other fields. Mob murders declined appreciably, but the power of the syndicate pyramided far beyond what anyone thought possible at the end of the thirties.

Virgil C. Peterson, operating director of the Chicago Crime Commission and an authority on the "syndicate," says in his book, *Barbarians in Our Midst*:

In virtually every section of the country the underworld has become part and parcel of political organizations that rule over cities and sometimes states. . . . [It is] a power which enables criminal groups to elevate men of their choosing to governorships, to the mayor's chair in some of our largest cities. . . . It is a power which in many places has made it possible for law violators to control the law enforcers and to formulate law-enforcement policies.

The picture that Peterson draws of the syndicate's power is a terrifying one. Through its hold on the saloons, on gambling, on racketeering of all kinds, it pays the piper not only for the campaigns of dishonest politicians but of honest ones as well. "The power of the underworld stems from the fact that the racketeering element has become an integral part of the political machinery which places men, *both honest and dishonest,* in public office."

Even more ominous a picture of the syndicate is drawn by Paul W. Williams, United States district attorney in New York. "This invisible government has millions of dollars at its disposal. It issues its own edicts. It enforces its own decrees. It carries out its own executions. It includes the major criminals of the country, and has as its allies some public officials tempted by the lure of money and power, as well as shortsighted business and labor leaders." Years ago, according to Williams, prostitution was the syndicate's main source of income, then prohibition, and now gambling, racketeering and other illicit traffic. "This concentration of power at the disposal of the criminal syndicate," Williams concludes, "represents the most serious aspect of the threat to the country. This power is primarily employed to infiltrate legitimate business and labor unions, to purchase respectability, and to influence and buy elected public officials and law enforcement agencies. The danger of organized crime to the country is grave and if organized crime advances in the next twenty years as it has from 1920 to 1958, I do not wish to visualize the consequences."

                                    IV

To put labor racketeering in its proper context it is essential first to grasp the scope of the syndicate's operations, its octopus-like interests. Labor racketeering is not only a source of income for the syndicate but a means of rounding out its empire; it is a not-too-hidden persuader, an integral part of a criminal trust that stretches across many fields. If the syndicate controls a distillery workers' union it is not only for the purpose of extortion and welfare fund profits at the union level, but to help the syndicate sell its own whisky and its own beer. After prohibition was repealed, syndicate bootleggers invested large sums in legitimate breweries and distilleries. Controlling a union in this field, therefore, became a means of "gently urging" wholesalers and saloonkeepers to buy the syndicate's brands. If they refused they might be subject to strikes and other harassment; if they cooperated they would be assured labor peace. The interests of the workers in the union were decidedly secondary to these higher purposes. It should come as no surprise, therefore, that the distillery union was adjudged corrupt and racket-infested by the AFL-CIO in 1957-1958.

Adding the weight of a labor union to the rest of the syndicate empire makes for a compact source of power. A saloonkeeper who is visited by the head of an association of saloonkeepers and told he must pay $2 or $3 a month, usually will pay up without making too much of a fuss. He knows instinctively that he must depend on the syndicate for little favors with the police or a "fix" for petty violations of the law. But if he balks, there is always the bartenders' union—if it is mob-controlled—that can withhold bartenders from him, or put a picket line around his premises that will stop deliveries. If a restaurant or ice-cream parlor refuses to put in a syndicate juke-box, there is always the electricians' union—again, if the syndicate has an alliance with one of its business agents—to refuse repairs or installation, or to refuse to work on some of its other equipment.

A few years ago the New York City Anti-Crime Committee, under the chairmanship of Spruille Braden, former Assistant Secretary of State, made an interesting study of a garbage-hauling racket in the metropolitan area. The evidence indicated that a garbage-trucking union spent its main energies to steer all the garbage business to a company headed by gangster Frank Costello. Those firms that complained that Costello's company was too expensive found themselves with strikes on their hands.

V

What is so dangerous about the modern labor racketeer is his deep roots. The friendships and connections gained through the crime syndicate not only give him a considerable immunity from prosecution but make it possible for him to re-enter the labor movement if he is forced to quit one post or is sent to jail.

The same men, exposed by investigating committees or imprisoned for extortion, turn up once again in a new capacity with the old union or with some other union. Many of the former members of the Lepke-Gurrah gang are now dress manufacturers in Pennsylvania where they practically control one small city. Johnny Dio, sent to jail for extortion, returns to the labor movement by way of paper charters issued to him by Anthony Doria, former secretary-treasurer of the Allied Industrial Workers' Union. When the AIW—under severe internal pressure—insisted that these charters be revoked, Dio was able to move over to the Teamsters' Union.

The periodic clean-up of certain organizations is often, therefore, only skin deep. One or two men are removed, the corruption underneath continues unchecked.

In 1948, Joseph S. Fay of the Operating Engineers went to jail for extorting $368,000. Ten years later the Operating Engineers were shown by the Senate Rackets Committee to be still racket-infested. The infestation was, if anything, worse. Fay, who once had himself elected as a business agent of Local 825 for life, continued collecting his pay while in jail, and was now selling automobiles to the very union which presumably should have had its fill of him.

The man who took William Maloney's place as president of the Operating Engineers' Union was Joseph Delaney, himself with a cloud over his head for welfare-fund manipulations. He and an associate took $400 a week as "consultants" from the racket-milked welfare fund of Tommy Lewis, union head of the Yonkers raceway.

Max Caldwell, who defrauded a union of grocery clerks in Chicago of $910,000 and was thrown out by a group of rebels in June, 1941, showed up in Miami Beach a year or two later, still connected with the labor movement, but in another international union. On February 18, 1948, Irv Kupcinet of the *Chicago Sun-Times* noted that Caldwell was now in a fight for control of the American Guild of Variety Artists. To the day of his death Caldwell remained in the labor movement in one capacity or another.

George Scalise, deposed president of the Building Service Employees' Union, who spent a decade in jail after being prosecuted by Thomas E. Dewey, pleaded guilty in April, 1957, of looting union welfare funds together with Sol Cilento, secretary-treasurer of the Distillery, Rectifying and Wine Workers' International Union.

In former times the labor extortionist was a one-time loser; after being convicted he seldom penetrated the movement again. Now he is part of a network of crime, of which labor racketeering is only a segment, and he has protection and security.

VI

Associated with every important labor racketeer, in addition to the crime syndicate, are businessmen and politicians. They seldom go to jail with the racketeer but they are part of the conspiracy and equally culpable. Harold Seidman, author of a history of labor racketeering, published in

1938, concluded that "no New York labor czar since Sam Parks has lacked the backing of Tammany." The camaraderie between politicians and labor racketeers is most revealing. When Robert P. Brindell, the New York building trades crook, was on trial, his lawyers turned out to be a Tammany assemblyman and a commissioner of public works. The lawyer who received $428,000 in fees from racketeer leaders of an electrical union was a former assistant district attorney. When convicted extortionists Charley Gioe, Paul Ricca, and Louis Campagna were released on parole during the Truman Administration, it was found that their "friends" were politicians who had used their influence all the way up to White House advisers to secure their freedom.

The employers' role is more sanctimonious but equally hypocritical. Thomas E. Dewey, when he was district attorney, spoke disparagingly of those employers who "invite the racketeers to organize their industries to increase their profits at the public's expense." Gordon L. Hostetter, secretary of the Chicago Employers' Association, is quoted in Harold Seidman's book as saying: "Employers in increasing numbers and in many departments of business activity have seized upon this type of labor union leadership and utilized it through rackets and racketeering to the selfsame ends which half a century ago brought capitalism to a position of general disrepute." During the 1958 hearings into the Chicago restaurant unions, in which the Senate Rackets Committee uncovered many links to gangland, chief counsel Robert F. Kennedy of the Committee told the Chicago Restaurant Association leaders that their position was "no better than the union's." To gain labor peace and low pay scales they had knowingly hired, for $125,000, lawyers associated with the crime syndicate.

The employer always makes a profit from the racketeer's activities on his behalf. In New York, Local 229 of the United Textile Workers (formerly AFL), headed by one of

Tony (Ducks) Corallo's friends, had agreements with the
J. Radley Metzger Company for five and a half years. According to the Senate Rackets Committee these pacts provided for no wage increases. When the minimum-wage law
was raised to $1 an hour in March, 1957, the employer had
to raise the wages of some workers earning less than $1; but
other than that he lived in the security of a "sweetheart"
contract. Under the pressure of the racket hearings the
workers rebelled and sought sanctuary in a clean organization, the International Union of Electrical Workers. To gain
their point they had to strike. But the employer refused to
recognize the legitimate union. He insisted he must honor
his contract with the shady organization and struck a false
pose as victim in the conflicts between two unions.

Two rackets that recur repeatedly in the headlines are
those in the garment and waterfront industries. In both instances, any impartial study must conclude that the root of
the evil is the greed of businessmen. The International
Longshoremen's Association, formerly headed by Joseph
Ryan, was a creature of management to secure low-wage contracts, to free itself from grievance machinery, and other
legitimate union objectives. In the words of A. H. Raskin,
New York Times reporter, writing in *Commentary*:

The sordid story of employer collaboration in the degradation
of the International Longshoremen's Association is . . . a quar-
ter-century in the making and it wound up in the transformation
of what had been a union into an amalgamation of gangs so
powerful that the insurance companies and the police joined
with the shipping lines and the stevedores in acknowledging and
confirming their supremacy. The ILA was a Frankenstein monster of the employers' own fabrication. They subverted the union
over the years; they kept its president, Joseph P. Ryan, in automobiles and expensive clothes, right down to the pajamas he
wore to bed at night; they subsidized the hooligans Ryan recruited from Sing Sing to hold the rank and file in subjection.

When the rank and file could stand this no longer and began to challenge Ryan, "Tough Tony" Anastasia, and other gangsters, the employers refused to rise to the defense of their employees. "At no time," says Raskin, "even when its investments in 'harmonious labor relations' ceased to pay any dividends, did the shipping industry undertake any discernible role of leadership in the campaign to dislodge the ILA from its dominant position on the piers. On the contrary, the employers took sanctuary in the pious defense that the law required them to be 'neutral' in union affairs."

Ryan was no enemy of the employers, he was their ally and friend. When Harry Bridges organized the West Coast longshoremen, the employers called on their friend Ryan to sign a secret contract with them. Ryan flew West to sign such a pact, but the situation was already out of hand; the longshoremen broke with his ILA and set up their own CIO union which brought them benefits far beyond those on the East Coast. In Ryan's own territory the workers continued to work under below-standard conditions. Not only were their wages lower but they were the victims of an infamous hiring practice known as the "shape-up." Each day they lined up on the piers and were chosen for work by the hiring bosses like so many cattle and sheep. The oversupply of labor was so chronic that in 1953-1954 there were 35,000 dockworkers in New York, while on the busiest days perhaps 15,000 were needed. The surplus labor made for competition between the workers, and provided an opportunity for additional dues, and for firm control. In October, 1945, the longshoremen finally rebelled against Ryan's soft contracts and went out on a wildcat strike. Ryan, as usual, rent the skies with cries of "communist conspiracy," and mobilized enough criminal cohorts to break the strike within eighteen days. Three years later the men rebelled again. On the West Coast the Bridges union had settled for a fifteen-cents-an-hour raise; Ryan, whose wage scales were inferior to begin with, accepted ten cents. This time, however, the men were not to be by-passed. They struck again and finally forced Ryan to settle for three cents an hour more than he had originally bargained for, plus a few other concessions.

In return for the "sweetheart" deals Ryan and his gangsters not only received bribes and presents, but were permitted to run large-scale gambling, receive kickbacks from employees, and pirate merchandise running into many millions of dollars.

It is naïve to assume that the fine details of this racket were unknown. Labor reporters in New York spoke about them freely for years before Ryan's empire began to crumble. The waterfront racket served a financial purpose not only for the labor racketeers but for the businessmen and politicians as well. The statement once made by Ryan that the labor movement in New York was "Tammany first and labor afterwards" was no idle cliché; it had real meaning.

Eventually the longshoremen rebelled once again and the stench of the waterfront clogged the nostrils of New York's better citizens. New laws were passed, a waterfront commission was set up to register longshoremen and reduce the number of men competing for jobs, and the union-appointed hiring bosses were eliminated. Ryan himself, elected for life, resigned to make way for a more tolerable president, Captain William Bradley. But Anastasia and other gangsters are still around, and their employer-protectors as well as the politicians have never been publicly rebuked.

VII

The racket in the garment industry also pivots around profits and "sweetheart" contracts, but in a somewhat different way. On the waterfront a whole union was corrupted by the racket, and a whole industry benefited from it—at least on the East Coast. In the garment industry the union has been, except for its truckers Local 102, a model of cleanliness. David Dubinsky, president of the union, has been the most outspoken critic of racketeering in the top echelons of the labor movement. What the racket has concentrated on, therefore, is gaining and keeping a foothold in the hopes that someday this foothold can be widened.

That foothold, according to Dubinsky, covers 10 per cent of New York's billion-dollar-a-year industry. That is "less than one-quarter," he says, what it was twenty years ago in the heyday of Lepke and Gurrah. The industry is ideally suited for racketeering—if only the union were susceptible to racketeer blandishments. It is highly competitive, with 9,000 apparel firms clustered in one small section on Manhattan's west side, each trying to produce the most popular dress at the lowest cost. From 1949 to 1958, according to Charles S. Zimmerman, president of the Joint Dress Board of the International Ladies' Garment Workers' Union, a total of 949 new companies entered the field, but only thirty-nine survived. The turnover among workers is 10 to 15 per cent a year. A couple of pennies saved in the sewing of a dress can mean the difference between profit and bankruptcy.

The union has, in a sense, been the stabilizing factor in the garment industry. Since the vast majority of shops are organized, they pay the same wage scales, eliminating some of the cutthroat aspects of competition. But here and there an employer tries to break out of the wage strictures and gain a quick advantage. The amount of money needed to go into business is relatively small. For a few thousand dollars a former cutter or presser can equip his own plant in Connecticut or Pennsylvania, away from the center, and try to operate nonunion. With the right connections he may be able to avoid unionization even in New York.

That is where the crime syndicate enters the picture. Through its control of truckers and trucker unions it makes arrangements between a unionized manufacturer in New York to have his garments sewn by a nonunion subcontractor in Pennsylvania. If the savings are ten cents or fifteen cents a dress they are sufficient to turn red ink into black, even if the trucker gets a two cents or three cents additional commission for his effort.

What the syndicate has done in the garment industry is turn from extortion to more simple forms of enterprise. The remnants of Lepke's old mob are now "respectable" factory owners, truckers, or union officials, plying this new type of racket. The late Albert Anastasia became an owner of trucks and factories. Harry Stasser, with a record of two convictions for dope peddling, owns fifty-five trucks. James Plumeri, another Lepke graduate, is also a manufacturer. Harry Rosen, a convicted narcotics smuggler, owns a plant in Pennsylvania. Other shops are the property of Russell Bufalino and Gaetano "Three-Fingers Brown" Luchese. The syndicate men, with money bulging out of their pockets, are becoming businessmen on a big scale, but they carry over with them some of the habits of the past: the use of violence and terror to make an extra dollar.

Periodically the union is forced to take stern action to check the hoodlums and their businessmen friends. It makes a special effort to organize the nonunion shops, and then the fur begins to fly. In 1949, a number of union officials were hospitalized and pickets severely beaten by paid hoodlums, just as in the old days of "Little Augie" Orgen. On May 9 of that year a union organizer named William Lurye was stabbed to death in a telephone booth on West 35th Street in New York. Grillings by the police of a cigar-stand concessionaire and a pair of bookies brought forth identification of Benedict Macri and John Giusto as the assailants. Macri was an associate of a man who owned both a trucking company and a nonunion dress house that Lurye was trying to organize. By the time Macri and Giusto were apprehended a year later, the witnesses no longer could make a positive identification. One of them admitted he had been approached by a racketeer union official and given $100 to forget his identification. The racketeer—George (Muscles) Futterman—was convicted of subornation of perjury and bribery, but no one was ever convicted for the murder of Lurye.

In 1958, the garment workers' union took the offensive again and called an East Coast walkout involving 105,000, in large measure to fight off the racket. Although wages were an issue, the union sought assurance from primary manufacturers that they wouldn't contract work with lower-paying nonunion firms in Pennsylvania and elsewhere, either owned by hoodlums or serviced by them. In New York the strike was over quickly, but in Pennsylvania, the gangster garment stronghold, it lasted much longer.

One of the countermeasures taken by the union was a $2-million union-label campaign, beginning January 1, 1959. The unionized employers agreed to sew labels into their dresses and the union agreed to promote an advertising campaign appealing to American women to buy only union dresses. In this way it is hoped the nonunion racketeer will be isolated. Whether this will achieve its purpose remains to be seen. The racketeers are strongly entrenched. Dubinsky notes that he has dismissed seventy-five union leaders in the twenty-five years he has been president of the union— seven of them in 1957—for unethical practices, yet the racket still persists.

VIII

Two further examples of the interrelationship between the rackets and industry are perhaps classic. One involved the movie industry, the other the grocery industry in Chicago. In neither case did public stigma ever attach to the employers, but in both they were involved neck-deep. It was their desire for profit that set the wheels of racketeering in motion.

Willie Bioff, a direct link of the crime syndicate, serving as official of the International Alliance of Theatrical Stage Employees, and George E. Browne, president of that union, were both eventually convicted of conspiring to extort $550,000 from four of the largest movie companies. But before they fell out with the movie magnates, or the magnates with them, they were friends and allies working for a common objective—mutual gain.

In 1933, the IATSE was involved in a jurisdictional fight and lost its foothold on the West Coast. By 1936, the union still had only thirty-three dues-paying members in its Hollywood local. Suddenly, however, Bioff and Browne showed up in the movie city and signed a closed-shop contract requiring that 12,000 workers join IATSE or lose their jobs. The companies were concerned about the recent upsurge of unionism throughout the country and were evidently fearful their employees might join a bonafide union which would cost them more money than Bioff and Browne's union.

In 1937, after almost two years of this closed-shop arrangement, a hundred members of Local 37, Bioff's organization, protested that no meetings had been held in this period, that the organization had no autonomy, and that they were forced to pay an assessment of 2 per cent of their weekly wages, which was to be turned over to Browne to be spent as he saw fit. Two of the workers, at the suggestion of Carey McWilliams, now the editor of the *Nation*, filed suit. Both were immediately fired by Twentieth Century-Fox. Another worker, who paid his assessment under protest, was fired the next day by Warner Brothers after a telephone call by Bioff. The assessment brought $2 million into the Browne-Bioff-Capone coffers, on which no accounting was ever made. McWilliams, speaking for the hundred workers, protested to the California legislature as early as 1937 but the committee on capital and labor refused to act. A charge before the National Labor Relations Board that this union was company-dominated also came to naught. It became known that the nephew of movie-man Joseph Schenck had given Bioff $100,000, but the Board never entered a decision as to whether or not this made Bioff's union company-controlled.

Through the years, relations between the movie magnates and the gangsters were more than lukewarm. Charles Moscowitz, head of the Loew's chain in New York, admitted that in the summer of 1935, when the rank and file of the New York Movie Operators' Union began to throw off the bonds of racketeering and fought against a wage cut, Moscowitz called on Browne and paid off $150,000 to end the strike. Moscowitz and Joseph Schenck were later convicted of income-tax frauds. McWilliams says that the producers used Bioff and Browne "to force a settlement with the Screen Actors' Guild . . . to break the strike of the Federation of Motion Picture Crafts in 1937 . . . to raid the Studio Utility Employees the same year," and to threaten Walt Disney employees who were on strike. Harry Warner of Warner Brothers admitted on the witness stand that he had visited Bioff's farm near his own ranch in San Francisco and was quite friendly with him. Mrs. Warner called him "Willie."

This was hardly the setting of antagonists. While it lasted, for four years, it was a profitable arrangement on both sides. Why it terminated is anyone's guess. Perhaps the companies felt they didn't need the protection any longer, perhaps they were afraid that the lid was about to blow off anyway, perhaps the price was too high. But one thing is evident: Bioff and Browne were not bogeymen to the movie industry; they were equal participants in an undertaking for mutual profit. It is inconceivable that the movie magnates, with all the resources at their command, didn't know of Bioff's association with the Capone syndicate. They certainly knew he had only thirty-three members when they signed a contract for 12,000 employees. The bland cry that they were "victimized" hardly rings true.

The same may be said of the Chicago grocery industry, which for four years sponsored a known hoodlum, sent him liquor and other gifts in return for "sweetheart" contracts, but never was meted public opprobrium. The gangster was a syndicate member named Max Caldwell, who seems to have carried a lucky star with him, because he totally escaped punishment. Despite the searing hostility of the influential *Chicago Tribune*, despite the fact that only $62 was left when the union safe was opened, despite the fact that he had counseled the secretary-treasurer of the union to hide while the Draft Board was looking for him, Caldwell spent the rest of his life, until he died a few years ago, outside prison bars in the warm climate of Miami where he burrowed into other unions.

In 1937, a group of workers in a large grocery-chain warehouse became weary of an existing company union and decided to organize a legitimate one. They began as an independent organization but soon negotiated a CIO charter and enrolled 600 employees of the warehouse.

Management, however, refused to recognize the group. It was a period when the legality of the National Labor Relations Board had not yet been fully tested nor had com-

pany unions been completely outlawed. The only alternative for the warehousemen was to strike. While it lasted, almost six months, it was one of the most bitter strikes in the
area. For a few weeks the strikers shut the warehouse with
mass picket lines. Soon, however, the company union reap-
peared with an AFL charter and signed a contract. With
AFL help the company was able to hire hundreds of new
employees and the CIO union was smashed. (Long afterward, the National Labor Relations Board reinstated 150
of its members with $51,000 in back pay; but the contract
between the company and the AFL was not revoked.) To
strengthen its position the striking union had begun to
picket the.company retail outlets, and much to its surprise
a few hundred clerks asked to join their union.

At this point Max Caldwell enters the picture to sell his
"insurance" against legitimate unionism. Caldwell was the
son-in-law of the advertising manager of the local AFL
paper and evidently was able to get a charter with his help.
It is strongly rumored that C. C. Coulter, secretary-treasurer
of the Retail Clerks' Union at the time, had some misgivings about Caldwell and came to Chicago to investigate, but
was met by a few hoodlums of the syndicate and politely es-
corted back to union headquarters in Lafayette, Indiana. In
prohibition days Caldwell had owned a night club and was
frequently in the clutches of the police. In 1925, he was sen-
tenced to six months on a liquor-violation charge, but some-
how never served his term. In 1932, he insinuated himself
into the local waiters' union but his plans were evidently
unsuccessful. An attempt to organize hat-check girls also
failed. In 1934, Caldwell was indicted with two officers of
the waiters' union on the charge of trying to extort $10,000
from the owners of the French Casino; this time he was ac-
quitted.

Despite this unsavory record, undoubtedly known to the
grocery firm and certainly verifiable by a simple check with

the police, the company signed a contract with Caldwell for all its employees. It must be remembered that Caldwell didn't have a single worker enrolled in his union when he made this agreement, nor did the grocery workers even know he was negotiating on their behalf. Subsequently two other big grocery chains, all told covering perhaps 6,000 employees, also signed pacts with the gangster. It was too good an arrangement to pass up. The contracts, never shown to the membership nor voted on, had two clauses: a closed shop, requiring everyone to belong to the union, and a provision that wages were to remain the same for two years. Both clauses were automatically renewable for additional two-year periods and remained in effect for almost five years until a group of young workers in one of the chains led a revolt which unseated Caldwell.

When he was finally removed, partly as a result of the publicity of the *Chicago Tribune*, which at the time was warring against the syndicate, it was found that $910,000 had slipped through his hands. Though he testified that he was broke when he formed this union and had no other income except his union salary of $100 a week, he managed to buy a $45,000 home from the Capone gang leader, Frank Nitti, and in four short years had raised his status to one of affluence.

The companies all pleaded innocent of coddling the criminal. They claimed his record was a surprise to them. Yet they benefited many more times than even he did. Assuming that they saved themselves a $1 a week raise for each employee for each of the four years, the total comes to the sum of $3 million. Both in Los Angeles and in New York, where legitimate grocery unions grew in this period, wages were, and are, far higher for this type of work. The alliance of business and racketeer, under the aegis of the crime syndicate and protected by local politicians, was highly profitable all around.

IX

After World War I the Lockwood Committee in New York and the Dailey Commission in Illinois both put the legislative spotlight on racketeering. A few men went to jail. Many recommendations for a clean-up were made. The labor history books were offered material on the depredations of the Sam Parkses, "Skinny" Maddens, Robert P. Brindells. But as one witness testified before the Lockwood Commission: "What's the use? If it ain't Brindell it will be someone else."

In the 1930's, District Attorney Dewey in New York sent a number of top criminals to jail, and the federal government caught a few labor racketeers in the net of income-tax evasion and sent them to federal prisons. The forties were years in which America was occupied with the war and with postwar world-wide reconstruction, so that the issue of racketeering tended to stay in the background. But in the fifties, more investigations brought to light more alliances between crime and politics. The Kefauver Committee, then the Douglas Committee, and finally the McClellan Committee all exposed new facets of racketeering.

Senator Paul Douglas of Illinois brought out in 1953 that a new form of profit-making had become widespread—mulcting the welfare funds. Beginning in 1948 the labor movement had won important new concessions from management. Nine or ten million workers soon were covered by health and welfare funds, and auxiliary pension benefits to supplement federal social security. In New York alone there were 600 welfare funds by 1953, insuring 1,115,000 employees and their 1,785,000 dependents. This was a historic advance for labor. The overwhelming majority of these funds were undoubtedly well-administered and honestly run. But the crime syndicate, ever alert to new areas of endeavor, saw in it a new field for plunder. Corrupt unionists could make millions through kickbacks, commissions, welfare-fund salaries, and just plain stealing.

They could and, as Senator Douglas illustrated, they did. The mob cut itself in. In one such welfare fund alone, more than $900,000 disappeared without trace. In Teamster Local 805, New York, it was found by the New York State Insurance Department that the fund was empty even though it collected $250,000 a year through employer contributions. The former vice-president of the union, Abe Gordon, was the fund's administrator. For his labors he received not less than 10 per cent of the annual payments, plus 2 per cent for expenses. Out of the fund he paid $55,000 for some land in the Catskills, which the local tax assessor insisted was worth only $25,000. Perhaps the disparity is explained by the fact that the land was bought from Gordon's cousin. Altogether it cost about 30 per cent to administer this fund whereas another teamster local, better run, did the same thing for 3.2 per cent.

In Local 1115, Restaurant, Luncheonette and Soft Drink Employees CIO, administration costs ran to 34 per cent for the three years ending December 31, 1953. Two officials received $16,380 a year each, spent the winters in Florida and summers in the Catskills, used union cars for both, all at the expense of the fund. Another welfare fund, that of the United Culinary, Bar and Grill Employees' Local 923, paid its two union administrators almost as much in salaries as in benefit payments to union members.

The ingenuity of the syndicate racketeers is boundless— so long as politicians wink at their crimes and businessmen are willing to go along for a profit. As a result of the McClellan and Douglas hearings there will no doubt be laws to

tighten up on welfare-fund administration. But labor racketeering is not a phenomenon of the labor movement; it is
unfortunately merely an offshoot of a bigger and more per-
nicious racketeering. The roots lie in the American concepts
of morality, in business ethics, in the abhorrently low level
of local politics, in the apathy of the citizenry. So long as
these exist the struggle against labor racketeering can only
be limited, and the syndicate can be expected to find ever
new and more clever methods of "making a buck."

If there is any real hope to end the practice of labor racketeering it lies not in passing new laws (though some good
laws might be helpful), but in two historic developments:
the changing social attitudes toward the crime syndicate,
and the changing patterns of collective bargaining. There
is reason to believe that the syndicate has outlived its historic welcome. Most of its leaders are now old men and
quite wealthy. Increasingly they turn to legitimate enterprise such as manufacture or investment. Many yearn for
respectability, particularly for their children and grand-
children. The corruption of local government, while still
rampant, also becomes more difficult with each passing year.
Countervailing forces such as the labor movement, and liberal organizations such as the Americans for Democratic Action have tended to make the politicians more wary. Many
of the big city machines have been purged to an extent.
Furthermore, the federal government has, of late, shown a
new concern about the syndicate. The Attorney General's
office announced a campaign against the hundred leaders of
the crime syndicate. Paul Ricca—imprisoned with Bioff and
Browne—was placed on trial for income-tax evasion early in
1958 and convicted. The combination of these two factors,
the changes in the syndicate itself and government offensive,
may whittle the power of trustified crime to the point where
the labor racketeers lose their protector and their connections.

Of even greater significance, not only in eliminating racketeering but in modifying business unionism, is the changing pattern of collective bargaining. Racketeering tends to flourish in the decentralized industries where many employers compete against each other. Its locale of operations is usually in one city. Because of the syndicate's connections with the corrupt city machines the racketeers can function relatively unimpeded. But of late, collective bargaining has been expanding beyond city or state borders at a rapid tempo. Jimmy Hoffa, president of the teamsters, boasts of his new single contracts which cover the trucking industry of twelve and twenty-three states respectively. Measures are being taken in most of the old-line unions to establish some logic to their wage patterns from city to city and state to state. Each of these steps away from localized collective bargaining isolates the racketeer and cuts his roots.

Welfare and pension funds too are being centralized. The teamsters in a number of cities have set up a common welfare fund for all their employers. Soon there will no doubt be regional and perhaps eventually national welfare funds, with common rules, central administration, and far less opportunity for lush commissions or stealing.

The AFL-CIO, responding to the new social and economic requirements, has taken the offensive with unexpected vigor. Under the leadership of George Meany it expelled three national unions for corruption—the teamsters, bakery workers, and laundry workers—and forced other organizations such as the distillery union, the former AFL textile union, the Operating Engineers, and the Allied Industrial Workers' Union to make important changes in personnel—or face expulsion too.

It is possible that the combination of all these factors may seriously reduce labor racketeering. This will be particularly true if the socially minded unionists in the labor

movement gain the upper hand against the more materialistic members of the hierarchy.

For the moment, however, the evil runs deep, a source of
worry not only for honest citizens and crusading unionists,
but above all—because of its interlinkings—for society itself.

6
Hoffa and Reuther

THE VICTORY OF MATERIALISM IN THE HOUSE OF LABOR WAS
hardly won by default. Nor does it remain unchallenged
even today. At every step it was defied by crusading unionists
who denounced the business unionists as "labor fakers" and
"pie cards," led innumerable strikes of unskilled workers,
and preached ceaselessly the message of industrial unionism
and class struggle versus craft unionism and class collaboration. The AFL was newly established when Daniel De Leon,
head of the Socialist Labor party, formed the Socialist
Trade and Labor Alliance in 1895 to fight it. Eugene V.
Debs, who was later to play so prominent a role in the Socialist party, organized the ill-fated American Railway Union in
1893 and a year later led what Professor Selig Perlman
called "a revolutionary strike on the continental European
model." Neither of these organizations lasted long or caught
fire, but they were to be forerunners of a more effective radical unionism. Both dissolved in 1905 into the colorful Indus-

133

trial Workers of the World. The I.W.W. at its height probably never had more than 120,000 members, but for two decades it led hundreds of important strikes and innumerable
free-speech struggles involving many hundreds of thousands of workers; and it produced some of the most fiery
radical leaders in American labor history, "Big Bill" Hay-
wood, Vincent St. John, Elizabeth Gurley Flynn, William
Trautmann, Joseph Ettor, Arturo Giovannitti, and many
others.

Even within the AFL the voice of radical opposition never
stilled. At the 1912 convention the socialist minority
reached peak strength. Its candidate for president and its
resolution on industrial unionism polled one-third of the
vote. World War I gave a new impetus to radicalism within
the AFL. John Fitzpatrick, president of the Chicago Federation of Labor, attempted—together with William Z. Foster,
later to become head of the Communist party—to organize
the packinghouse and steelworkers on an industrial-union
basis. The 1919 national steel strike was one of the most bitter in labor history. Fitzpatrick also took many steps to help
create an independent labor party, including a campaign
in 1918 as the mayoral candidate for the Chicago Labor
party. In February, 1922, a sizable group of socialist unionists from fifty national unions, together with friends in
farm, cooperative, church, liberal, and other organizations,
set up the Conference for Progressive Political Action to
pursue a more leftist course in politics than that of the business unionists around Gompers. During the 1920's, too, the
Communist party sank roots in the labor movement. Its
Trade Union Educational League, formed in 1920, won surprising support for a time on the question of "amalgamation"—industrial unionism—and independent political action. Amongst the needle trades, miners, railroad workers,
steelworkers, and others it gained enough converts so that
Foster could claim—probably exaggerated but impressive

nonetheless—that "under our leadership, fully half of the whole labor movement demanded an amalgamation."

In the 1930's a new type of challenge plagued business unionism—the CIO. Composed of radical socialists, communists, Trotskyists, and the like, as well as middle-of-the-roaders such as Sidney Hillman and John L. Lewis, the CIO was so formidable an opponent of old-line unionism that many an observer predicted it would wipe the older federation off the map. "It is inevitable," wrote the novelist Sinclair Lewis, "that the Committee for Industrial Organization will do to the American Federation of Labor what the Federation did to the Knights of Labor." Sinclair Lewis was wrong; the AFL not only recovered from the first blows of the CIO but more than tripled its membership in the following two decades. Yet the challenge to business unionism persists. Today it is no longer led by radical socialists or communist or syndicalists, but by a new—and again, a special American—type of unionists, what we have called the "social unionists."

To illustrate the scope of this challenge, as well as the shifting grounds between the antagonists, it is perhaps well to explore the personalities of their leading advocates.

II

The symbols of conflict in the house of labor today are two dynamic devotees of Big Labor, each operating at opposite poles of union philosophy: James R. Hoffa, president of the million-and-a-half Teamsters' Union, and Walter P. Reuther, president of the million-plus United Auto Workers. The final result of this conflict obviously does not rest on two men, nor is it certain that these particular two men will be the contenders when the decision is reached. It is entirely possible that Walter Reuther may find himself in the role of Sidney Hillman in 1935—somewhere in the center, with new radical forces forming to the left. It is also possible that Hoffa, currently surrounded by a group of ex-socialists, may drift away from his past associations; or his meteoric career may end quickly if he is sent to jail or if further exposés make his position untenable. All sorts of shifts and realignments are possible in the labor movement, but Reuther and Hoffa typify "social unionism" on the one hand and business unionism on the other.

The two men, different in so many fundamental respects, nevertheless have important points of similarity. Both Reuther and Hoffa head big unions, each highly centralized, and each with assets in the tens of millions. Yet it is significant that most of the Auto Workers' money is earmarked for strike benefits—some $24 million out of $35 million; while teamster assets of $41 million are not differentiated. The Auto Workers' headquarters in Detroit, Solidarity House, is a comfortable workshop, big but not lavish. The teamster $5-million home in Washington is complete with auditorium, solarium, and other symbols of opulence.

Both Reuther and Hoffa are determinedly ambitious, beyond any other two men in the labor movement; but for Reuther, power must serve some social end, while for Hoffa it seems to be power for power's sake. Reuther would undoubtedly deny it, but he must certainly have thought about the possibility of running for President of the United States. He knows that if labor should ever form an independent political party, he is the logical choice for its standard-bearer. Hoffa would never think in such terms. He may visualize himself someday as the president of a federation of all labor, but his sights do not reach beyond that. On money matters, it is hardly conceivable that Walter Reuther would ever go into business or invest large sums in a business venture; but Hoffa has made a small fortune in such enterprises, some of them seriously open to question, and sees nothing wrong with it.

Both men are of impeccable personal habits, solid family men, who do not smoke, drink, or "run around." In their relations with others both are distant, but Reuther, because he is an intellectual, wins his point through the sheer force of logic; Hoffa wins it because he is purposeful, single-minded, dynamic. As president of Teamster Local 299 in Detroit, Hoffa's office door was always open to any rank-and-file member who wanted to see him—no matter how involved Hoffa might be in the broader affairs of the union. Yet this was not the closeness that comes from rapport or mutual warmth, but a relationship of unequals in which Hoffa could do favors and revel in his power. Reuther is the diplomat. He knows everyone's name. He greets union officials in the hallways of Solidarity House with a friendly remark and a businesslike inquiry about mutual problems, but he cannot bring himself to the camaraderie of an accomplished extrovert. Despite their bombastic personalities, both men are geniuses at waiting. Reuther became president of the United Auto Workers by careful biding of his time to replace a man he at first supported, R. J. Thomas. Hoffa first helped Dave Beck to the presidency of the teamsters, then helped retire him in 1957 when the McClellan Committee had besmirched his reputation beyond redemption. Both men work ten, twelve, and eighteen hours a day, sometimes seven days a week.

Beyond these superficial similarities, however, the two men have little in common; they revolve in and around entirely different worlds. Reuther has a well-oiled machine, but the men near him are, like himself, men who read books, are highly literate, social-minded, capable. A staff member of the UAW can take issue with Reuther privately. He can disagree fundamentally with Reuther's philosophy, without fear of being fired. It is only when he "breaks discipline" or goes to the public over Reuther's head that he is in jeopardy. Hoffa's associates, except for new ones such as his executive vice-president Harold Gibbons, the president of the Toledo teamsters' council, Lawrence Steinberg, and a few others, are of a different caliber. They are neither book readers, polished orators, nor "eggheads." Few of them would question one of Jimmy's decisions, either privately or in public. Hoffa will listen and listen carefully, to glean knowledge and ideas from other people, but the decision is always more of a one-man operation than is the case with Reuther.

For Walter Reuther the labor movement was the natural outlet of a socialist philosophy, the finest goal he could achieve. For Jimmy Hoffa it was a field he stumbled into by accident, unrelated to his personal *Weltanschauung*—assuming he has ever had any.

III

Jimmy Hoffa's is a typical American success story—with philosophy or lack of philosophy to match. One of a family of four children, whose father died when he was four, Hoffa lived in dire poverty during his formative years. At eighteen he became a warehouseman for the Kroger company in Detroit, and in 1932, chafing against a stretch-out system which required him to be in the warehouse twelve or fifteen hours to get only seven or eight hours of work, he organized a highly successful one-hour strike. No social attitudes underlay this or any other act in his life. It was purely a personal revolt by a tough young fellow against an oppressive situation. "I got interested in unions," he says, "because we were getting kicked around." Shrewdly he waited until a load of strawberries came to the warehouse, and then presented management with a bargaining request at the strategic moment when it must either face the rotting of its strawberries or recognize the makeshift union that Hoffa and four others had fashioned. This combination of toughness and shrewdness is Hoffa's trademark. He would undoubtedly be lost in a conversation about Keynesian economics or Sorel's theories on violence, but he is exceedingly capable in the economics of union negotiations or in the organization of a solid picket line.

From this small beginning Hoffa formed an independent union, affiliated it first with the AFL directly as a federal local, then secured a charter in the Teamsters' Union. A year later this charter was merged with another, that of Local 299, and this became his base of operations until he moved to wider pastures. By 1940 he was made the negotiating chairman of the Central States Drivers' Council, for whom he negotiates pacts for drivers of twelve states. In 1942, he helped form the Michigan Conference of Teamsters of which he was elected president, and in 1946 he became president of the Teamsters' Joint Council 43 in Detroit. In 1952, Hoffa momentarily hitched his star to that of Dave Beck, who gently eased old Daniel Tobin into retirement. Five years later the Detroit teamster leader, having consolidated his position as the president of the Central Conference of Teamsters and as the man behind the scenes for the Eastern and Southern conferences, similarly eased Beck into retirement.

In themselves these bare facts, like all bare facts, tell little of Jimmy Hoffa's rise to power. What he contributed to the Teamsters' Union in this period was both muscle and organizational ability. One cannot conceive of Hoffa's running away from any kind of a fight. Though he is only five feet five and a half inches tall he engaged in literally hundreds of pitched battles on and off picket lines to build his union. The employers, says Hoffa, "hired thugs who were out to get us, and brother, your life was in your hands every day. There was only one way to survive—fight back. And we used to slug it out on the strikes. They found out we didn't scare. The police were no help. The police would beat your brains in for even talking union. The cops harassed us every day. If you went on strike, you got your head broken." On one occasion Hoffa was arrested eighteen times in a twenty-four hour period; each time, after bail was put up, he returned to the picket line to be arrested again.

Violence is deplorable, not only in the labor movement but in all social intercourse. It is an undeniable fact, however, that violence has been a feature of American life, particularly on the frontier, ever since the country was settled. Since the first union was formed American workers have had to defend themselves with their two bare fists, on thousands of occasions, from company thugs and police. Hoffa's antics on the picket line, and off, are thus no different from those of many thousands of other unionists. Perhaps in the more placid labor-management atmosphere of post-World War II it is easy to forget the bitter battles of the union movement to gain recognition, and the scores of deaths and shootings. But in the thirties violence was routine, and Jimmy Hoffa was not atypical. In the same period there were many tough boys in the Auto Workers, similarly involved in scores of fights with police and strikebreakers. It seems to be a general rule that in the formative days of all union movements, violence, particularly in self-defense, is inevitable.

In that respect Hoffa's early career differs little from that of many other unionists who were tough but whose toughness eventually was tempered by social consciousness. By way of example: a young worker in a Chicago foundry was told by co-workers he would have to join the union. Being gregarious, though unversed in union matters, he joined. A few days later, he in turn approached a burly athletic chap and asked him to join, but was refused. In anger he challenged the bigger man to a fight, beat him up, and then became the hero of the plant. Soon he was elected shop steward, then president of the local, and today he is the head of a department in the Auto Workers. In his case, however, he began to read about the theory and history of unionism, and to educate himself in many fields of knowledge. His toughness eventually mellowed and was transformed by his social consciousness.

In Hoffa's case toughness is a way of life, rather than a necessary evil. He is no egghead, tied to the labor movement because of any theories of social progress. He is still the harried young man being kicked around and who kicks back. For him the union is an extension of his own personality, rather than part of a social struggle. What Hoffa wants is success, not crusades; and to be successful he believes one must be tough. Thus, in his relationship with rank-and-file workers, he is kindly and helpful; but let any group of workers challenge him and they are in trouble. The union for Hoffa is an army where each man must obey, rather than a cooperative venture in which all men are equal. A warehouseman, member of Hoffa's Local 299, told reporters in 1957 that on one occasion he got up to raise a point of order. "The guy up front told me to sit down or I'd get fined $25. I kept standing and one of my buddies pulled me down in my seat. I guess he saved me $25." Hoffa insisted to these reporters that no one was actually fined, but the threats are made at meetings because "you have to have discipline."

Success is the motivating force of Hoffa's life, but success is defined in terms of the same goals as those of a businessman. As long as you get results, that's all that counts. Hoffa has worked with unsavory men like Johnny Dio and the leaders of the independent longshoremen's union. The Senate Rackets Committee charged that he "runs a hoodlum empire, the members of which are steeped in iniquity and dedicated to the proposition that no thug need starve if there is a teamster payroll handy." But Hoffa also associates with high-caliber intellectuals like Harold Gibbons, Richard Kavner, Lawrence Steinberg, Sam Baron, and a few others.

In all cases it is not any preconceived philosophy that motivates his association, but success. Hoffa insists on dynamic people, men who "carry their weight," and he doesn't care much whether they are hoodlums or socially minded thinkers, so long as they produce results. Thus in St. Louis Hoffa helped Gibbons throw out the gangsters in the Teamsters' Union. One telephone call from Hoffa probably saved Gibbons' life and put him at the head of the joint council of teamsters in that area. Similarly in Toledo, Hoffa helped Lawrence Steinberg throw the racketeer elements out and become president of the teamsters' council there. But in New York Hoffa has supported for the leadership of the teamsters' council a man of the opposite type, Thomas O'Rourke.

To get results Hoffa is guided by no preconceived principles. Many charges have been made against him that he bribes political officials and that he has opponents beaten up. Edward Chevlin, a dissident teamster in Kansas City, testified that Hoffa once beat him over the back with iron chains. A 1954 congressional hearing that began looking into Hoffa's affairs ended abruptly. One congressman, Wint Smith, Republican of Kansas, said: "Pressure came from so high that I can't even discuss it." But neither these facts nor his associations are a full measure of the man. For whatever Hoffa does meshes with the individualistic and materialistic point of view that plagues society generally. By a process of social osmosis he has absorbed them, and he believes in them fervently.

Hoffa is the rugged individualist, and like many another rugged individualist he does not ask anyone to do what he is not willing to do himself. Prior to becoming the president of the Teamsters' Union in 1957, he boasted that he had never missed a picket line of any group in his Detroit organization. "What right," he asked, "have I to send my men out on the picket line, if I don't go out too?" Yet his militancy on the picket line is not reflected in his philosophy.

Speaking to the St. Louis Advertising Club in August, 1956, he noted that "there is nothing more important to the Teamsters' Union than prosperous business." Victor Schaeffner, counsel for the Michigan Cartagemen's Association, told *Time* magazine: "Hoffa knows the trucking business better than probably 99 per cent of the owners. He knows what he wants, and he knows what he can get. That's why his demands are never out of line with what the industry can pay." Another businessman, who negotiates with him, noted that "you don't go into negotiations thinking you are going to be enemies from the word go. Hoffa is a businessman. He's trying to build up that impression. He's not a crusader, not like Reuther." Still another labor-relations man claims that "when you finish negotiations with Jimmy Hoffa, you can sleep well that night. When you finish with Walter Reuther, the trouble is often just beginning."

Hoffa doesn't want to change the business world; he wants to accommodate himself within it. "I'll admit," he told two reporters, "we were tough when we were organizing in the early days. We had to be. We still are if our contracts aren't lived up to. But we're not like Reuther. He spent ten million at the Kohler Company, four million at General Motors of Canada and a million and a half at Perfect Circle. We don't do that. Long strikes you can't win are too expensive." Speaking to a group of teamster stewards in Toledo in 1958, he made his point even more strongly: "We have won and will continue to win wage increases for you that are better than any international in the world. And I want to point out that we have and will continue to do it without the costly strikes that wear out our members and our union. Unlike some unions, who lead their members to destruction through strike action, we know the industry and we know the problems. We can win our demands without strikes."

Being friendly with business and modeling himself on business ethics is not considered wrong by Jimmy Hoffa. His sixty-five business agents in Detroit drive around in Cadillacs, just like the employer class they deal with, earning about $200 a week plus fringe benefits worth another $100. Hoffa himself has borrowed money and lent money to businessmen with careless abandon. He borrowed $5,000 from a labor-relations adviser named Jack Bushkin with whom the teamsters negotiate agreements; $5,000 in cash from a truck owner, J. L. Keeshin; $25,000 from a real-estate promoter. In 1956, one of Hoffa's welfare funds lent $200,000 to a department store that was being struck by the Retail Clerks' Union. "The strike," Hoffa told a reporter, "had nothing to do with the loan one way or the other. This was strictly an investment." It didn't seem wrong to him to be investing money in an anti-union company that was busy fighting a rival union.

Nor has it seemed wrong to Hoffa to form a variety of businesses in the same areas in which the Teamsters' Union operates. One of these was a truck-leasing company organized for him and his lieutenant, Bert Brennan, by Albert and Carney Matheson, lawyers for large trucking companies. The stock was transferred to the wives of the two unionists, under their maiden names, and brought them $62,000 over a period of four years for no ostensible work. The firm rented hauling equipment to freight carriers in which the Mathesons owned substantial stock and with whom Hoffa dealt as a union official. Hoffa was also associated with these same men in a brewery, in a freight terminal, and in a loan-and-investment company. After he became president of the teamsters he divested himself of such business interests. But it is doubtful that Hoffa considers such associations wrong in principle. In clarifying his views to a magazine writer Hoffa said: "I don't object to my men having businesses outside of the union as long as it doesn't interfere with the union activities. That way they get to understand the employer's problem as well as the employee's problem."

When a testimonial dinner was given for him in Detroit on April 20, 1956, the chairman of the sponsors' committee was a department-store owner of Chicago, Joel Goldblatt. Among the other sponsors were officials of the Norwalk Truck Line, Pioneer Motor Service, Southwest Freight Lines, Michigan Mortgage Company, Cartage Employers Management Association, Better Brands, Inc., and General Linen Supply Company. The general manager of the Highway Carriers Employers Association sent him a message "in recognition of your contributions to the stability and progress of the industry."

Such solicitous friendship from the employers does not cut Hoffa off from his members. Many admire him for having improved their lot, for getting results. One Detroit teamster told reporters: "We have to pay $5 a month dues anyway and we don't care what's done with it. We got the best contracts anywhere."

To Hoffa the union is a business in which the members are his beloved customers and he is the paternalistic boss. "I'm not worried about my staff men," he says. "They're my men. I pay good wages, have good working conditions, and I've never lost a man. If a promotion comes along, I give it to the man most entitled to it. He may not be the smartest guy, but if he knows the business and has been loyal, he gets promoted up." The idea that the union is "mine" or that promotions are "my" sole discretion puts it in the class of a business in which decisions are made from the top down, rather than the traditional form of labor organization in which matters of pay and promotion are supposed to be democratically decided by the membership. When Hoffa speaks of "loyalty" he means loyalty to himself, rather than to labor as a whole. He expects it from his organizers and, in turn, he has an intense loyalty to them as well.

Between 1954 and 1957 Hoffa distributed through the Detroit Joint Council's Good and Welfare Fund a total of $85,489 to the wives of four officials of the Pontiac Michigan local who were convicted of extortion. Legal fees for these four, plus William Bufalino, president of a Detroit juke-box local, came to some $30,000. Another $54,381 was spent defending Gerald Connelly of Minneapolis Local 548, convicted of extortion and dynamiting. When his men were released from jail, Hoffa usually gave them their jobs back. The four Pontiac men convicted in 1953 for taking bribes from employers were all kept on the payroll of this local while indicted. Time after time he has put back in key positions men who obviously betrayed the interests of the rank and file by taking bribes or other such acts. Once, he secured a charter in the hotel and restaurant union for Sam Feldman, a safecracker who had served three years in jail. When asked for an explanation, he said, "Feldman is my friend. I believe the issuance of the charters is proper because independent unions can make a lot of trouble, especially with teamsters' unions, who become involved whenever there are picket lines." When asked why he had put Connelly back to work for Local 548 after Connelly had been questioned by a House special subcommittee about possible involvement in a Florida murder, Hoffa said: "Jerry isn't as young as he used to be. He had to run out of Florida. He can't keep on running forever. If he doesn't stay in Minneapolis, he'll have to move and it isn't so easy to start again." The question of possible murder or bribe-taking didn't seem to be as significant as loyalty.

Combined with this theme of loyalty and benevolence is a passionate patriotism for the Teamsters' Union. "My

friends in the labor 'business' are mostly all teamsters,"
Hoffa says. "The rest you gotta watch with both eyes." Speaking to the city-wide conference of Local 688 in St. Louis in
February, 1956, he opened with the bombast that "we'll fight
anyone who fights the teamsters." In his acceptance speech
for president at the teamsters' convention a year and a half
later, he again struck the chauvinistic note. "We shall go
forward. We are teamsters. We are brother unionists. As
brothers, we may disagree among ourselves. But we shall
present a united front against any attack from the outside
and we shall never surrender our birthright . . . to fight
against all odds in the service of our Brotherhood."

Everything about Hoffa bespeaks rugged individualism,
the temper of an empire builder. "I learned a long time
ago," he says, "that whatever you can do to me, I can do to
you, only more." His devotion to his empire is as great as
that of any other man of power. Hoffa loves his union as
much as Walter Reuther loves his, but his vistas are limited
to this one union rather than to labor as a whole or to labor
as a class. "What we want," Hoffa proclaims, "we try to get.
What we get we keep." It is this overpowering devotion to
success for success' sake that explains why Hoffa will grant
a paper charter to men like Johnny Dio or seek out alliances
with the longshoremen's union. That explains why, on the
other side, he has thrown some gangsters out of the Teamsters' Union. What attracts Hoffa is dynamism, ability, success; its moral content seems to be irrelevant.

In the search for success Hoffa has been as responsive to
the growing integration of our economy as Walter Reuther,
perhaps more. Unlike Reuther, he has not concentrated on
new social themes, but rather on structural changes in his
union to meet the challenge of centralized industry. Under
Hoffa's prodding, Dave Beck set up three sectional conferences, the Central States, Eastern, and Southern, in addition
to the one functioning for years in the West. Fifteen national

trade divisions were formed: automotive, bakery, brewery and soft drinks, building materials and construction, cannery, chauffeurs and taxicabs, dairy, municipal employees, produce, laundry, over-the-road, truckway, newspaper drivers, warehouse, and miscellaneous. Each of these seeks uniform contracts on an area-wide basis—soon perhaps on a nation-wide basis. In 1955, Hoffa signed contracts covering not only highway truckers in twenty-three states but city truckers in twelve states. The local cartage agreement covered 14,000 employers and in some cases it brought local drivers up from ninety-five cents an hour to $2.24 in the short period of only thirty months, while reducing their work week from as much as sixty hours to forty. Bringing scores of local unions together and thousands of employers was no mean organizational achievement.

The center of gravity in the teamsters has shifted away from the city councils of teamsters, often run like stagnant feudal empires, to the trade divisions, conferences, and the national office. The new motif is centralization. In the past, a local teamsters' union might shut down one warehouse in one city, but the employer could shift the work load to one of a dozen other warehouses he owned in other parts of the country. The new trade divisions and the coordinated efforts by various locals now make that impossible: the teamsters can close down a whole chain from Maine to California with one signal. Such centralization makes for further control and further reduction of rank-and-file participation. But it gives the union and above all its leadership an economic potential never before wielded by a single union or even by a group of unions in America.

As a further step to match economic power with management, Hoffa and Beck signed mutual assistance pacts with a selected group of other unions: machinists, flight engineers, butchers, bakery and confectionery workers, carpenters, operating engineers, laborers, laundry workers. Hoffa felt these pacts would lead to sustained joint organizing drives that would scoop hundreds of thousands if not millions of new members into the teamster orbit. So far, however, the results have been meager. In August, 1958, the AFL-CIO instructed its affiliates to break relations with the Teamsters' Union. If formal relations are severed, however, informal ones to the same end may very well continue. Hoffa's theme is centralization of economic power, and there is no doubt that he will continue pushing in this direction.

Centralization in industrial relations seems to be inevitable. With Hoffa, however, the question is how he will implement it. Will the unions in alliance with him become satellites, or can they remain relatively independent? Since the teamsters are the most vital part of the alliance, the smaller unions must play the role of vassals unless the alliance is based on belief in labor solidarity as a firm principle. Hitherto the teamsters have operated on a "pick and choose" concept of solidarity. They rewarded their friends in the labor movement by respecting their picket lines, and punished their enemies by driving through. On many occasions they walked through the lines of the Retail Clerks' Union with whom they were feuding. Will this change now? Is Hoffa accepting a broader view of labor solidarity than his predecessors and many of his present associates? The time has been too short to tell.

For the first year of his tenure in office Hoffa has operated under a cloud of legal prosecutions, investigations by the McClellan Committee, and a barrage of newspaper hostility such as few unionists have ever faced. Yet the Teamsters' Union itself, far from losing members, reached the highest numerical peak in its history by mid-1958: 1,600,000. Hoffa himself was evidently more firmly entrenched than ever before. Neither of the two candidates who ran against him in 1957 intended to challenge his position again. The campaign manager of one, Peter Hoban of Chicago, wrote a five-page letter to Counsel Robert F. Kennedy of the McClellan Committee rebuking the Committee for the attacks on Hoffa. Of the 104 unions under trusteeship when Hoffa took office, sixty-three were returned to their memberships, and similar action was pending in other cases. The July, 1958 executive board meeting of the union reinstated nine members and one local officer who were suspended by subordinate bodies. Samuel Feldman, business agent for Local 929, was removed from office; and Anthony ("Ducks") Corallo, a New York hoodlum who controlled three local unions, was persuaded to sever connections with the teamsters. All of this was far too little and too slow to influence the attitude of the AFL-CIO or the investigators, but there was refreshing evidence that the Teamsters' Union was on its best behavior. When Hoffa signed a five-year pact with the Montgomery Ward Company he insisted that the Retail Clerks' Union, which was conducting a hopeless strike and boycott at sixty-two locations of the company, be offered a similar agreement. Teamster locals were respecting picket lines of AFL-CIO unions to an extent not evident hitherto.

Is Hoffa shifting with the winds? Will the Teamsters' Union modify its course and purge its malefactors under his leadership? Or is all this merely a momentary concession to public opinion and pressure?

IV

One of the strange features of Hoffa's ascent to power has been his alliance with Harold J. Gibbons of St. Louis. Hoffa has leaned heavily on this ex-socialist who has been identified with dozens of liberal causes. He carried Gibbons to the very pinnacle of the Teamsters' Union in 1957 when he helped elect him vice-president, and then appointed him his chief administrative assistant. As a result of his association,

Gibbons has been put under the McClellan Committee microscope much as was Hoffa and was charged with using violence in strikes, "purchasing" the union he now heads, and other unethical practices. A reading of the record in less emotional times will no doubt indicate that the accusations were out of context. In rebuttal, Gibbons stated that his union was involved in violence only in ten of 250 strikes and that, far from "purchasing" his present union when his independent organization of warehousemen amalgamated with a teamster local in 1949, he merely kept the teamster officials on his payroll until their regular terms of office expired. Despite intense search the Committee could find no evidence that Gibbons had misappropriated funds or that he had been associated in any business ventures with employers with whom he dealt. He had no record of arrests or convictions, except for contempt of court in 1954 when he refused to turn over his books to a grand jury. The grand jury, however, found no evidence of wrongdoing once the books were brought before it.

Gibbons is as different from Hoffa in background, personal habits, and philosophy as it is possible for two men to be. He has no business interests; he is a spendthrift who will probably die poor; he is well-read, highly literate, socially minded, and his own union, Local 688 in St. Louis, is run along entirely different lines from that of Hoffa's Local 299.

Gibbons is certainly not an apostle of business unionism —anymore than is the United Auto Workers' Union. His concern with social problems and democratic expression for the rank and file is exemplary by present American standards. Local 688, before it became affiliated with the teamsters (it used to be in the CIO retail union), was one of the first groups to establish a health center for its members, and its Labor Health Institute is still considered one of the two or three best in the country. Local 688's stewards meet monthly and have a veto power over anything done by Gibbons or the other officers. The union's political and community program is unique and highly effective. In each St. Louis ward the union has its "community stewards," who function much as the shop steward does in the shop. These men handle community grievances involving street lighting, traffic, public transportation, playgrounds, sanitation, safety standards. In a number of wards the union has set up headquarters where it offers "free community services" to all citizens. "We have broader concerns," says Gibbons, "than the eight hours we spend at labor. Our wives, our children, our homes, indeed, our leisure hours, mean that we also have a stake in the neighborhood and the community in which we live."

Where Hoffa's background has been with tough musclemen, Gibbons' has been with socialists and liberals. He has been associated with the Americans for Democratic Action, is on the advisory committee of the Congress of Racial Equality, supports such organizations as the Workers' Defense League, the National Association for the Advancement of Colored People, and has been a fighter for civil rights throughout his career. None of Gibbons' organizers, nor he himself, drive Cadillacs. Few are known for their "muscle." Many are ex-socialists.

An annual conference of elected delegates is the highest body of Local 688. Each unit of the organization meets once a month and has the determining voice in its own affairs. At one time Gibbons was holding hundreds of meetings monthly of groups of twenty-five workers each so as to increase membership participation. He operates a smooth, high-gear machine in this 9,000-man organization, but the rank and file is not ordered about. It has a means of expressing itself without reprisal. Gibbons has faced opposition for office on a number of occasions.

It is interesting to speculate on why Hoffa has worked so closely with Gibbons. Is it because he needs the polish, ideas, and articulateness that Gibbons has to offer and is momentarily "using" him? Or is it, as Gibbons would like to believe, that Hoffa is shifting gears to a more progressive type of unionism? In an interview with Robert Lewin of the *Chicago Daily News,* Gibbons said of his associate Hoffa: "Jimmy had a bad past—and all of those things exposed by the McClellan Committee and the AFL-CIO executive council. Jimmy is willing to change. He's got to change. He's got to find new friends. He's got to live by new practices."

Historically there have been a number of business unionists, even racketeers, who have altered their ways. The Machinists' Union, which in the 1930's called on its affiliates to sign "backdoor" contracts, is run along more socially oriented lines today under A. J. Hayes. There is a small coterie of men in their fifties, sixties, and seventies in New York and Chicago who were once associated with the crime syndicate, who now run legitimate organizations without any semblance of criminal ties. By way of example, there used to be a union office in the 1930's which was a cover for a bookie joint. The union "leaders" were unconcerned with the problems of the few members they had under contract; the big operation was bookmaking. At the back of the small "union" office there was a door leading to a large bookie parlor. One day, as part of a gang war, a group of rival gangsters invaded the office, killing the heads of this racketeering union. The only man left of the operation was an office boy who handled odd errands for the hoodlums. After the shooting he found himself suddenly with a union on his hands. Instead of just walking out he decided to build it up into a legitimate organization. Today it is a clean union, with good wages and quite a few social benefits for its members.

Is Hoffa traveling in this direction? Will he slowly break with some of his past associates? The pressures of his past are no doubt great; they may be decisive. It may be that once his power is fully consolidated and the legal attacks

against him abate, Hoffa may break with the new associates
like Gibbons who have been such useful allies in his climb
to the top. The relationship may be only a temporary one.
On the other hand, there are pressures of another kind on
Hoffa, pressures of the changing world. The sands of time
are running out on business unionism as America continues
to become more centralized and government plays so vital
a role in economics. Some union leaders will no doubt stay
mired in the past. But a man like Hoffa, who worships success, can bend with the wind. Other men did this in the
1880's and again in the 1930's as American capitalism itself
reached important turning points. The John L. Lewis of the
Roosevelt era was decidedly different from the John L.
Lewis of Coolidge days. It can happen again.

V

The man who is most strategically placed to give leadership to a better type of labor movement in America is Hoffa's
inexorable rival, Walter P. Reuther, president of the most
dynamic organization in the house of labor, the United Auto
Workers. Reuther is the symbol of a new philosophy of unionism which is perhaps best described as "social unionism."
It is not social*ist*, because Reuther, like Hoffa, though with
many more reservations, endorses the free-enterprise system. But neither is it business unionism. Reuther himself
calls it "pragmatic idealism," indicating the dichotomy that
exists in his own mind, as well as its hybrid character—an
admixture of social reformism with power-politics realism.

Walter Reuther is the man in the middle guarding labor's
left gate. One of the vice-presidents of his union, Duane
(Pat) Greathouse, has popularized a phrase which ideally
fits Reuther. "No one," says Greathouse, "turns his left end."
No one can be more radical when the occasion demands.

Reuther is a weathervane, he shifts with the political climate. He can be radical when need be, and quite moderate
when the pendulum swings the other way. When he gets off
the plane in London or Calcutta he speaks like a fervid socialist; it would be difficult to convince a British or an Indian
union leader that Walter Reuther subscribes to a free-enterprise philosophy. But back in Detroit he is again the pragmatic idealist. Because of such shifting behavior he has been
called an "unfinished personality." But it is more proper
to say that Reuther has adapted his radicalism to an America in the age of unparalleled prosperity. This compromise
in goals is for him no transgression in principle but an adap-
tation to a specific historical moment when the sights of
American workers do not focus on panaceas. He still guards
the left, he will permit no one to turn his left end, but he
guards it from a point closer to the middle than he would
have twenty years ago. For Walter Reuther is no ideologue,
no heavy theorist, no deep thinker. He is, rather, a brilliant
strategist who feels that without power the vision of a beautiful tomorrow is meaningless. Many of the bold plans that
he has dramatized, such as the "escalator clause" and the
"guaranteed annual wage," did not originate with him, but
he has the knack—the feel—for picking out ideas and making them living realities.

What distinguishes Reuther from Hoffa is that he will not
sacrifice vision for power. He does not seek power for power's sake, but only in the service of what he believes to be a
better world. He has no monetary ambitions whatsoever, and
far from trying to ape the business world or adopt its ethic,
he constantly heaps scorn on it. Even the McClellan Committee paid tribute to his personal integrity. It reported that
his sole income since April 30, 1936—with minor exceptions
—has been his salary. The $13,000 earned in speeches and
articles since 1951 he turned over to a Reuther Labor Foun-
dation. On the occasions when the AFL-CIO paid him $50

a day for expenses in attending a meeting or other duties, he turned in the $50 to his own union and accepted the regular UAW $7.50 to $12 per diem instead. The Auto Workers' Union, under his guidance, audits its books so carefully, according to the McClellan Committee, that on one occasion when Reuther charged it $1.50 valet service, the charge was stricken off and he had to pay it personally. In 1948, he bought the only stock he ever owned, $1,000 worth of Nash-Kelvinator; eight years later he sold it at a total profit of $1.26.

Reuther drives no Cadillac, owns no stocks or businesses, and if he ever had a kind word to say for an employer it was hedged with a thousand misgivings. Excessive wealth and conspicuous consumption are not virtues for Reuther, but shameful vices. Speaking at the special convention of the UAW, early in 1958, he was remorseless in his criticism of the auto magnates.

"Now what," he asked, "have they been doing with [their profits]? Well, they have been doing a lot of things. I noticed in the paper the other day that Mr. Kanzler . . . this Ford executive, is reported in the society section of the *Detroit Free Press* to be building another house. I don't ordinarily read the society section, but on January 13, the big headlines said, 'They will have four homes from here to France.' It went on to say that Mr. Kanzler and his wife were a very happy couple flitting from one home in Grosse Point to one up in Maine, from the one in Maine to the one in Miami Beach and now Mr. Kanzler is going to leave . . . for Southern France where he is building his fourth estate. Now, ain't that just ducky?"

Continuing in the same vein he quoted another society squib: "Speaking of the Fords, we hear that Mr. and Mrs. Benson Ford are having a yacht built in Nassau and will christen it with a party in June. . . . Our source told us also that guests from Detroit and Europe will be flown in for the party." A delegate from the floor, at this point, re-marked that the auto workers were paying for part of these luxuries. Whereupon Reuther answered sarcastically: "We are paying for all of it. What do you mean, a part of it?"

Reuther no longer believes in the theory of the class strug-gle. Testifying before the McClellan Committee, he said that the class-struggle concept was merely a device for "di-viding up scarcity." But neither, evidently, does he believe in the theory of class peace, or of harmony of interests. Some-time around 1938, he decided that socialism had no immedi-ate future in the United States, but when he retreated from it he withdrew, not to a pro-business attitude, but to the next bastion where he can still guard the left gate but be closer to the center.

This is the heart of Reuther's strategy of leadership. He is not tough like Jimmy Hoffa. Not that he has ever flinched from danger: in 1937 he was brutally beaten while giving out circulars to the Ford workers; a year later, hoodlums broke into his home and assaulted him; in 1948 hired thugs shot and seriously maimed him in an attempted assassina-tion. Yet it is not in Reuther's character to be a physical bully or to pick a physical fight. He is tough and strong-willed in the intellectual, rather than physical sense. Nor is he a leader by virtue of his personal warmth. Hundreds of thousands of auto workers literally idolize Reuther. "You've got to get up early to beat him," they boast. They look upon him as clean-cut, impeccably honest. Yet no one calls him "Walt" or "Wally" or "Red"; he is not that sort of a person. He holds his followers by the brilliance of his in-sights, by the power of his logic, and by his sincerity. Busi-nessmen don't like Reuther, but they don't dislike him enough to try to destroy him either. Neither Phil Murray, the late president of CIO, nor George Meany, president of the merged federation of labor, had or has any deep affec-tion for him. But he has been able to work closely with both.

Reuther knows how to bob and weave, how to take ground and give it, how to advance a few steps then retreat, how to blend visionary aims with practical necessities.

Walter Reuther and his brothers—two of whom, Victor and Roy, are leaders of the Auto Workers in their own right —were born to the labor movement. Their father, Valentine Reuther, a German emigré, was a socialist and a friend of Eugene V. Debs. Socialism was the daily ideological fare of the Reuther household, and to be a labor leader a high ideal. In recent years Reuther has frequently introduced his father to UAW, and previously to CIO, conventions as a source of pride: he has made good on the image of a good life he learned at his father's table. The elder Reuther, like his sons, was a young prodigy in the labor movement. At the age of twenty-three he was already president of the Ohio Valley Trades and Labor Assembly. Once, he ran for Congress on the Socialist ticket.

The sons, weaned on this radical philosophy, were magnetized to the labor movement. Forced to quit high school to help support the family, Walter went to work as an apprentice toolmaker at Wheeling Steel's corrugating plant. There he tried to organize the men against Sunday work, but was fired before he could complete the task. Hoffa, it should be recalled, was immediately successful in his first union venture; whether he would have remained in the movement otherwise is open to question. But Reuther failed not only on this occasion but for the first two or three years after he moved to Detroit. Yet, such was the pull of his radicalism that it was inevitable he would continue trying.

A few years after the Wheeling debacle he drifted to Detroit where he worked for Briggs, Ford, and other companies as a skilled tool-and-die maker. When he was fired by Ford in 1933 he and his brother, Victor, made an extended trip around the world. For sixteen months they worked in a Russian auto plant near Gorki and were undoubtedly sympathetic, like many radical young men of the period, to the Soviet experiment. Reuther underplays this phase of his life as well as his associations with the Socialist party, but it is known that he campaigned for Norman Thomas for President in 1932 and remained in the party until 1938 when he disagreed with the Socialists over their refusal to support New Deal Democrats in electoral campaigns.

On return to Detroit from his world trip, Reuther once again devoted himself to organizing the auto workers. The mid-thirties were a turbulent period in the auto city. Socialists, Lovestoneites, communists, Trotskyists, Wobblies, Proletarian party members* (scores of whom, now ex-socialists, ex-Lovestoneites, etc., are still in the UAW hierarchy) were busily engaged in the CIO organizing drive. Blacklisted by the companies, Reuther nonetheless united dozens of shops into the large West Side Local 174, which in one year grew from seventy-eight to 30,000 members. Active in the sit-down strikes of the period, quick-witted, he became a figure in the UAW early, rose to the executive board, then to the vice-presidency, and in 1946, after a bitter factional fight with the communists and their supporters, became the president of UAW by a mere 104 votes. A year later he carried his whole slate with him and has ruled, with only minor opposition, ever since.

Reuther's appeal to the union as well as to the public has been in the broad sweep of his ideas. Unlike Hoffa who thinks only in terms of the Teamsters' Union and the teamster industry, Reuther thinks of his union role as subordinate

---

* The Proletarian party was a communist group, formed shortly after the Russian Revolution, that refused to merge with the official Communist party. It maintained an independent existence for many years, then went out of business. "Wobblies" was the popular nickname for the members of the syndicalist Industrial Workers of the World. The Lovestoneites were a rightist split from the Communist party who called themselves by various names. Their leader was Jay Lovestone, former secretary of the Communist party and now closely associated with George Meany in the formulation of foreign policy for the AFL-CIO.

to his social role. In 1940 he publicized an elaborate plan to use idle auto capacity to produce 500 planes a day. The auto companies were to pool equipment and manpower into a central organization, with labor and government participating in the direction of the combined industry. This was more than a year before Pearl Harbor and the auto companies loosed a barrage of ridicule on the proposal. But when war broke out, the industry was forced to accept a watered-down version of the plan.

During the war, Reuther was one of the men who propounded the theme of "equality of sacrifice." Though it was not his own exclusively, it had that same quality of viewing an immediate problem in total perspective. "Equality of sacrifice" meant ending all war profits, stopping rising costs and inflation, rationing of all food, clothing, housing and other necessities, abolishing luxury consumption, adjusting wages to meet increasing living costs, declaring a moratorium on debts, involving labor in production planning, and preparing economic and social blueprints for the postwar period. It was this "equality of sacrifice" program which for a while made the wartime no-strike pledge palatable to the rank and file of auto. When in 1943 they began to feel that there was no true equality of sacrifice and insisted that the no-strike pledge be abrogated, Reuther shifted to a middle course. He proposed that the government take over plants "where management is not bargaining in good faith." A year later, when the pressure mounted still more, and 37 per cent of the convention insisted on revoking the no-strike pledge, Reuther proposed that it be abrogated only in those plants not producing for the war. This was one moment in his life when a substantial number of people, including Emil Mazey, now secretary-treasurer of the UAW, did turn Reuther's left end. But a year or two later he quickly returned to his role as defender of the left gate.

Following the war, with his socialism a receding memory,

Reuther evolved a peculiar strategy of interlinking bargaining demands with social issues. In the first round of negotiations with General Motors at the end of 1945 he presented a novel—and old leftist—proposal that the corporation open its books to the union. The implication of this demand was that the full story of profits was being withheld from the public. Coupled with it was an even more radical demand that the auto corporations pledge in advance that they would not raise prices even though they raised wages. General Motors refused to accede to either suggestion and the Auto Workers went through a bitter 113-day strike before they settled for a compromise eighteen-and-a-half-cents-an-hour raise—without the pledge of "no price increases." Reuther was forced to drop the idea because he could muster no support from Philip Murray, president of the Steelworkers, then also on strike, or from the United Electrical Workers' Union which bargained for 30,000 G. M. unionists. In an oblique reference to Murray, Reuther stated at a meeting of his supporters: "The torch we lit during the General Motors strike was not picked up by the steelworkers." Yet the boldness of Reuther's two proposals won him many friends amongst the secondary leadership of the auto union and helped plummet him into the presidency of the organization in 1946.

In successive years the same pattern was followed. Each bargaining proposal was encased in a social objective. It was as if, having dropped the idea of an independent labor party or a socialist party, Reuther was trying to achieve a political goal through economic action. In European countries, the labor movement fights against inflation through its political arm—the Labour party in Britain, the Social Democratic party in Germany, the Labor party in Norway. But Reuther tried to achieve the same goal through collective bargaining. In 1948 he introduced the "escalator" clause and annual improvement raises into American collective bargaining on a wide scale. Each three months there is a review of the cost of living, based on the United States Department of Labor Cost of Living Index, and if the cost has gone up, wages are increased accordingly. If it goes down, wages too fall, but not below the base wages at the beginning of the contract. Each year, to improve their living standards, there is also an annual improvement raise—now about seven cents per hour— that theoretically compensates for productivity advances. This was Reuther's answer to inflation, a bold—though limited—attempt to redistribute income as productivity rose, and to protect the real value of wages.

Another social objective for Reuther was to improve federal social security. The Social Security Act, passed during the New Deal, granted retiring workers a small sum of $30 a month. In the course of time, inflation had eroded much of the purchasing power of this $30, and it was Reuther's plan to bring it back to its original level or higher. If labor had its own political party in the United States the obvious means of doing this would be to introduce legislation in Congress; but since labor had no such party and since its liberal friends in Congress could not carry the project, Reuther devised another tactic—to have the political head wagged by the economic tail. If a higher pension could be won for the Auto Workers, he reasoned, it would soon be accepted in other mass-production industries, and the employers in their own self-interests would lobby for higher federal pensions. Since they were required to pay only the difference between a federal pension and their own, raising social-security levels would benefit the employers financially. In this instance, Reuther's strategy worked. In 1950, he won the supplemental pensions at G. M. and Ford without too much trouble, and at Chrysler, which refused to follow pattern, after a 104-day strike. As he had visualized, Congress soon raised social-security payments so that today it is four times—in dollars, not purchasing value—what it was during the New Deal.

The same happy fate did not, however, crown Reuther's

efforts in the health and welfare field. Here again, Reuther pioneered in bringing medical insurance to workers in mass-production industries. Thousands of corporations signed pacts with new health and welfare plans, but there was no rush to introduce a national health insurance program as in Britain or Germany. There is still no such plan.

Perhaps one of the best barometers of Reuthter's character is the "living document" theory he evolved in 1953, in the midst of a five-year pact with the major auto companies. Workers were restless over the long-term contract and demanded some concessions. Though there was no provision for reopening the agreements, Reuther evolved the theory that a labor contract was a "living document" that had to be modified under extraordinary circumstances. He convinced the auto companies to deal with him and make some significant improvements.

In 1955, Reuther once again put forth a social objective in economic terms: the Guaranteed Annual Wage. In the two decades since the New Deal had introduced unemployment compensation, inflation had shrunk the money received by the jobless from two-thirds of their take-home pay to only one-third. Reuther's objective was to repair this disparity. Since he had little faith that it could be done in the halls of Congress, he began his offensive at the bargaining table, hoping that the spirit would catch on. As it was finally worked out, the Supplemental Unemployment Benefits Plan guaranteed the auto worker about two-thirds his take-home pay rather than 80 per cent as asked for, and for a period of twenty-six weeks rather than a full year. Even at that, it was a major step forward. But though the Steelworkers soon won a fifty-two week plan, the victories in auto and steel have not yet resulted in a new approach by government on unemployment compensation benefits generally.

An interesting sidelight to the 1955 negotiations was the method Reuther used in pigeonholing the demand for a shorter work week. Carl Stellato, president of the largest UAW local, 600, at Ford's River Rouge plant, called for a concerted campaign for the thirty-hour week with forty hours' pay. Reuther did not entirely reject the idea, but he relegated it to the future, insisting that the Guaranteed Annual Wage must come first. Nineteen fifty-five was a year of prosperity, and like a true weathervane, Reuther knew that the rank and file was not thinking of the dire prospect of unemployment. He promised to make it an objective at the next negotiations in 1958. But when 1958 rolled around—a recession year with more than five million out of work—Reuther suddenly scuttled the shorter-work-week proposal which had been ballyhooed throughout the union for the better part of a year, in favor of another dramatic proposal: profit-sharing.

This plan too was aimed at a social star: the curbing of a monopolistic practice. The three recessions that followed World War II were distinguished from other American recessions by the fact that prices continued to rise during periods of slump. Reuther and the whole labor movement believe that this is the result of "administered" prices, whereby the large corporations in auto, steel, and other industries are able to circumvent the law of supply and demand. Despite a drop in demand the big companies can raise prices by administrative fiat if they work together. To reverse this trend, and pump purchasing power into the economy, Reuther proposed giving each automobile purchaser a rebate and each worker a share from the profits of the corporations. Beyond 10 per cent profit on investment, each company would be required to give 25 per cent of the remainder to its customers in the form of a rebate and 25 per cent to its workers in the form of a year-end bonus. The remaining 50 per cent would stay with the corporation.

The plan was full of loopholes. Based on 1957 figures,

profit-sharing would have meant a twenty-nine-cents-per-hour raise at General Motors, which earns the highest level of profits, but might mean nothing to workers at companies like Studebaker-Packard, which either lose money or earn very little. Reuther, however, had tested the pulse of his membership and concluded that this was not the year for so drastic a struggle as for the shorter work week. The men in the shops were far less concerned with their unemployed brothers than had been assumed. A backlog of 900,000 automobiles in dealers' showrooms stood as the greatest glut on the market in history. It was, therefore, necessary to make an orderly retreat to a less spectacular demand.

It is noteworthy of Reuther's genius that in retreating he makes his position seem more aggressive. To the people in the "middle"—to the consumers and to liberals—profit-sharing and consumer rebate seemed like a sensible, fair-minded proposal. To the radicals and socialists in his ranks, Reuther offered three bones of appeasement: first, that the shorter-work-week demand was not being given up, merely being postponed; second, that the union would be more aggressive in helping its local unions gain their specific local demands; and third, he let the more radical elements console themselves that profit-sharing, achieved through collective bargaining, was really a major step toward codetermination of industry. This last point was particularly attractive to some socialists in Reuther's union. If the employer gives you profit-sharing, went the argument, the union will have a voice in how profits are to be determined, how amortization shall be figured, the rates of bonuses to executives, and similar matters that affect profits. It will mean, in effect, that labor has a decisive voice in management. Socialists on the auto-worker payroll were impressed enough with this argument to give him the same kind of support as right-wing delegates who were fearful of putting forth too radical a demand. Some 10 per cent of the convention delegates voted against his proposal but once again no decisive force had turned Reuther's left end.

By the time a three-year contract was agreed to in September, 1958, after almost a half year of bargaining, the profit-sharing proposal had long since been dropped and the economic gains were the smallest in the UAW's postwar history. "For the first time in a decade," wrote Edwin L. Dale, Jr., in *The New York Times,* "a major auto settlement did not establish a new principle of benefits, such as company-financed pensions, supplemental unemployment benefits, cost-of-living escalators or annual 'improvement factor' wage increases." The same annual improvement and escalator raises as the companies had originally offered in May, 1958, were continued, but management agreed to raise pensions, increase supplemental unemployment benefits to thirty-nine weeks instead of twenty-six, and grant an additional raise up to eight cents per hour to skilled workers. The only new idea was a small severance-pay provision, but this had none of the drama of former Reuther victories. Reuther's retreat was obvious. Sensing the mood of a recession period and the sickness of the industry, he had refused to plow new social fields. He had dropped the shorter-work-week proposal in favor of profit-sharing, and then dropped this as well in favor of more mundane concessions. As usual Reuther was the pragmatic idealist rather than the revolutionary attempting to storm new citadels.

Anyone who seeks for consistency in Reuther's position will not find it in his individual proposals, but only in his socially motivated attitudes. Every proposal must have a social objective, but it must never be so radical that it alienates him irretrievably from the American people. Some years ago Reuther published a pamphlet called *A Total Peace Offensive.* In it he outlined a bold plan for foreign aid of $13 billion a year, for a hundred years, to help industrialize the underdeveloped countries. Once formulated, however, the plan has never been pushed. Like many other Reuther suggestions, it lies dormant until a propitious moment when he feels it can be "sold" to the American people.

Reuther does not crowd history. He waits for what he considers to be the correct time. In 1946, when there was considerable agitation in his union for forming a labor party, he summarized his views as follows:

"A party serving the true interests of the common people cannot be declared into existence; it must grow. The time must be ripe, the people must be ready. Labor's political responsibility is neither to close its eyes to the necessity of new alignments nor to surrender to doctrinaire moves to launch a new party prematurely on a too-narrow base. It is rather to recognize the transitional, stop-gap nature of its present political activity, to reach out into the community for natural alliances with farm and progressive middle class groups, and to lay the organizational and programmatic groundwork for a people's party."

This is an interesting statement. It pays homage to the wish of many rank and filers for a people's party; it also postpones action until the time is ripe and the people ready. With someone else this might be simple demagogy; with Reuther it is unquestionably sincere. His training, his instinct, and his logic all turn him toward a labor party, but his practical mind shows him it is not yet on the agenda. As a "pragmatic idealist" he marks time by forging alliances with liberals like Senators Hubert Humphrey, Paul Douglas, Wayne Morse, Richard Neuberger, and Governor G. Mennen Williams. When the time comes for the liberal wing of the Democratic party to split from the Dixiecrats, Reuther will be in the forefront of this effort. And if the economic situation should deteriorate to the point where there are new moves toward a labor party, Reuther will be in the forefront of that too. His ability is so outstanding and his record so unmarred by materialism or scandal that he is the logical choice for guiding labor in any new political direction.

In the meantime Reuther bobs and weaves, marks time, consolidates his apparatus, caters to the middle classes at the center, but never takes his eye off the left gate. Testifying at the McClellan Committee hearings on the four-year-old Kohler strike, Reuther deplored the mass picketing of his union at the outset of this conflict. Old-time unionists could hardly believe their ears—this display of moderation by a man who has been in, and led, many mass picket lines. But Reuther evidently has put his finger to the wind and found that this is a moment for appeasing the center. When he dropped the thirty-hour week demand in 1958, he attributed it at first to the fact that the Russians had launched their first sputniks and that the nation was therefore in too much of a crisis to undertake a shorter work week. This time he evidently measured the winds wrong, because at the convention which officially jettisoned the shorter-hour demand Reuther dropped the sputnik argument; he recognized quickly that the ranks were not thinking of sputnik in this way. With Walter Reuther there is nothing devious or personally opportunist about such maneuvers. As a pragmatic idealist his first concern is to end the long Kohler strike and put some of his members back to work. As a pragmatic idealist he feels he must not show his union's weakness publicly when he makes a retreat, so he fastens on some international event as the camouflage for that retreat.

The men around Walter Reuther, the cornerstone of his apparatus, are like him, ex-socialists, capable, literate, devoted, visionary. They include Emil Mazey, secretary-treasurer, and Leonard Woodcock, vice-president, either of whom would replace Reuther if he stepped up to the presidency of AFL-CIO or some other position; Jack Conway, his top administrative assistant; his brothers Victor and Roy, who are a shade more radical than Reuther on many issues;

"Pat" Greathouse, another vice-president; Martin Gerber, executive board member from New York, and literally scores and scores of international representatives, educational directors, and research men.

In its operations the UAW is a dynamic and democratic organization. It spends perhaps a million dollars a year on education conferences, seminars, literature. It publishes a monthly paper, *Solidarity,* runs a radio station, conducts an excellent radio program each morning called "Eye Opener," makes films, operates training schools, extension classes, cooperatives, and welfare programs.

Reuther's machine in the UAW is, after eleven years, fairly institutionalized. The 750 men on the international staff (trimmed by 1959 to 580) are all Reutherites and pay $5 every two weeks into a "flower fund" which is actually a caucus fund. Being put on the staff of the UAW today amounts to a promotion in economic status of about 150 per cent. An auto worker in the shop earns perhaps $100 a week, while a staff member (before the 5 per cent cut in 1959) received $153, plus $35 tax-free expense money, plus about $100 a month for an automobile, plus a contribution by the union of approximately $15 a week to a severance pay fund, plus medical insurance and other benefits—a total of perhaps $12,500 a year. Once on the staff, the representative stops functioning independently. He can state his opinions in private, but if he openly opposes the top leadership on any issue or in any election the chances are he will be dismissed. On the other hand, Reuther also has a functioning Reuther caucus of perhaps 400 rank-and-file workers from the shops all over the country who pass on every major issue before Reuther presents it to the membership as a whole.

With this kind of machine the factional conflicts that marked the formative period of the union from 1935 to 1947 are no longer evident. The communists have been reduced to impotence. Carl Stellato, of Local 600, and a few others

continue to oppose Reuther on issues but they cannot challenge his hold over the union. The channels of democracy
are still wide open. Conventions are held every two years,
with large educational conferences in the off years. Three
thousand delegates or more attend, and Reuther religiously
sees to it that all points of view are heard. National officers
and full-time members of the staff are prohibited by tradition from being convention delegates. This is in sharp contrast to such unions as the Teamsters' where most of the
delegates are either paid officials or hand-picked by the paid
officials. Any signs of criminality or undemocratic practice
are dealt with ruthlessly by the auto union. On a number of
occasions Reuther has removed officers and committeemen
of local unions because they were making book.

There are no repressive trusteeships. Members who feel
abused can now appeal over the heads of their union leaders
to a public-review board of seven prominent men, whose decisions in matters of discipline supersede those of the union
itself. In one important instance recently, where members
took a case to court and were disciplined for it, the review
board overruled Reuther. Yet despite these democratic safeguards and the notable efforts to involve the rank and file,
effective opposition to the Reuther leadership is no longer a
realistic possibility. It would take a major schism in the national executive board to challenge that leadership. The
pages of the union paper, *Solidarity,* no longer carry letters
and articles on union disputes as they did in the days when
Reuther himself was fighting the then incumbent, R. J.
Thomas.

The United Auto Workers, like the labor movement generally, has lost some of its idealism over the last two decades.
Particularly disturbing have been the separatist tendencies
of the skilled-trades workers, who have demanded better
treatment than the unskilled and semiskilled get, on threat
of seceding. Reuther has yielded a bit to this separatism by

permitting the skilled workers a special vote on items that affect them exclusively. This is, in a sense, a worrisome breach of industrial unionism. Nor is the fighting spirit of the UAW, especially in the regions outside Detroit and Flint where the union was born in a flurry of sitdown strikes back in 1936-1937, as intense as it has been.

Yet if business unionism is to be effectively challenged in America it will be done in part at least by men like Reuther and by unions like the Auto Workers. The *dramatis personae* may change, someone may in fact turn Reuther's left end and rise to top prominence in the labor movement just as he himself did in 1946, but it will be around the wider interpretation of the labor movement that Reuther suggests that they will rally. For, in essence, what Reuther seeks is a broader role for labor in society, rather than the narrow one of business unionism. That is the pivot of his philosophy and it stands 180 degrees opposed to the old-line unionism. The two may live together for some time, particularly if the economic storms are mild, but they cannot do so permanently.

7

Radical Interlude

LOOKING BACK OVER THE YEARS, DAVID DUBINSKY, COLORFUL president of the International Ladies' Garment Workers' Union, was trying to explain in 1944 the evolution of his attitude to socialism. "When I resigned from the Socialist party in 1936," he said, "it was for purely political reasons. We . . . wanted Roosevelt re-elected. But since that time I have come to the conclusion that socialism, certainly of the orthodox variety, will never work. Trade unionism needs capitalism like a fish needs water. Democracy is possible only in a society of free enterprise, and trade unionism can only live in a democracy."

One of the unique aspects of the American labor movement is the conversion of its radicals, time after time, from a leftist to a moderate philosophy. Dubinsky had been a socialist all his life. His union, like the other needle-trades organizations, was avowedly of the same political bent, and its leaders either members of the Socialist party or fervid

172

sympathizers. In 1932, at the height of the depression, with millions walking the streets or selling apples on street corners, they helped socialist Norman Thomas garner a respectable 884,781 votes. Four years later their ardor cooled, but they still felt that by supporting Roosevelt they were paving the way for socialism. After another eight years, however, Dubinsky could record his total rejection of socialism in favor of free enterprise.

The political evolution of Dubinsky differs only minutely from that of tens of thousands of other radicals in the labor movement who have been drawn away from their revolutionary principles to more tepid—usually capitalist—philosophies. The late Sidney Hillman, once a socialist fairly friendly to the Soviet Union (in its early days), finally became enough of a Democrat for Franklin Roosevelt to advise the 1944 convention delegates, seeking a vice-presidential nominee, to "clear it with Sidney." Walter Reuther left the Socialist party in 1938. Innumerable socialists, communists, Trotskyists, Lovestoneites, Wobblies, who joined the CIO after 1935 because they thought the new unionism would speed the social revolution in America, were soon liberal Democrats in the Americans for Democratic Action or had forgotten about politics entirely.

There is in all this something reminiscent of the first years of the AFL, when socialists of an older generation, one after the other, deserted their radical cause. Many times in American life, when capitalism seemed hopeless, the nation witnessed a surge of radicalism; but as the economic ship righted itself to push toward an ever-spiraling prosperity, the leftists sought shelter in less controversial philosophies. Prosperity altered the sights of such men, away from panaceas to "pragmatic idealism"—or just to pragmatism without idealism. What distinguishes the ex-socialist and ex-communist unionists of the 1930's is the road they traveled away from their radicalism. The earlier socialists converted into simple, and "business" unionists. In a milieu of laissez-faire capitalism and rugged individualism, that was the inevitable form of the institutionalization of their movement; but in the current period of controlled capitalism, in the era of the mass man and mass conformity, the ex-radical seldom becomes a business unionist. Institutionalization of his union takes on the hybrid form of "social unionism." For better or for worse, accommodation between labor and capital modified union philosophy one way when unions were based on the decentralized industries, and a different way when their *locus operandi* was in the mass-production industries.

Unions are a natural habitat for leftists. An instrument of "partial revolt" against the status quo must inevitably attract those who want a total revolt, a total change. So long as there are underprivileged workers, so long as there are pockets of poverty, there must be leftists in the labor movement. When there is stability and prosperity, radicalism is reduced to a minimum, confined to the secondary echelons of labor; when there is depression and instability, leftism grows.

The process of radicalization and de-radicalization is continuous in the labor movement. Not every union leader is a business unionist, pure and simple; nor a radical, pure and simple. Most are in the process of moving to one pole or the other, subject to the pressures of many sorts for moderation on the one hand and radicalism on the other. Yesterday's radicals in America have been whittled down to the reformer level; on occasion to business unionism. But there are always present those militant workers whose "sights" are raised toward radicalism. In periods of prosperity the would-be radical subdues his radicalism because the ranks are not receptive; but in periods of recession and depression, as the restive rank and file begins to look for panaceas, the voice of radicalism becomes more articulate.

II

As America faced its third great historical challenge in the 1930's this familiar pattern of radicalization and de-radicalization repeated itself. The generation into which Jimmy Hoffa and Walter Reuther were born was a generation of depression, malaise, restiveness. Looking back on it from the placid terrain of the 1950's, it is difficult to capture the drama and the hopelessness, the strife and the fervor of that period. But for ten or twelve years America shook with crisis and stoked the fires of radicalism, until World War II finally put the unemployed back to work and fashioned a synthetic prosperity based on military production. The pendulum swung at first sharply to the left, with leftists burrowing into unemployed organizations, hundreds of new industrial unions, student groups, veterans' movements. Then the reins were quietly but forcefully pulled back by the reforms of the New Deal on the one hand, and the middle-of-the-road leadership of the CIO—around John L. Lewis and Sidney Hillman—on the other. Out of the depression era of 1929 evolved a stubborn wave of radicalism. Out of that radicalism was born the CIO. And out of the CIO, moderated by the New Deal, by Lewis and Hillman, and by two decades of unparalleled prosperity, evolved the type of social unionism now symbolized by Walter Reuther.

In later years Franklin Roosevelt boasted he had saved America from revolution, and he was probably right. Before his election, the mood of the country was bitter. On March 6, 1930, hundreds of thousands of unemployed demonstrated in New York, Detroit, and other cities. In 1931 and 1932 hundreds of thousands more were involved in two national hunger marches. The disillusioned veterans, seeking their government bonus, set up bivouacs in Washington for three

months in 1932, only to be surrounded by the army and
forcibly evacuated—leaving two men dead and a number
wounded. Farmers improvised militant tactics for defending
their land. With guns in hand they would stop a foreclosure
of one of their neighbor's farms, or they would hold the bid-
ding down to some ridiculous sum like $1 or $5, so that the
farm could be returned to its owner. Mass demonstrations
prevented eviction of many hundreds of tenants, often years
behind in their rent. The Pennsylvania Unemployed League
in 1934 "auctioned off" a constable and sent him to the hospital when he attempted to evict a needy family. Students,
more socially conscious than they have been ever since, organized youth movements and held hundreds of demonstrations against war, fascism, and depression. Many smuggled
themselves into Spain to fight in the civil war against Franco.

America was at a historical impasse similar to the one of
the 1770's and the 1860's. It either had to meet the challenge
of the most serious depression in its history or decline into a
second-rate power.

What Roosevelt did was to renovate the whole theory of
American government. A man of great personal charm, lacking any clear ideology, but strategically flexible and highly
sensitive to the pent-up emotions of his time, he tossed the
theories of laissez-faire to the winds and refashioned the nation along lines of *controlled* capitalism. The great British
economist John Maynard Keynes visited Roosevelt in 1934
and came away painfully disappointed: "I supposed," he
said, "the President was more literate, economically speaking." Yet the New Deal did remake America in the Keynesian image. Up to that time it had been assumed that capitalism was a self-regulating mechanism, having its ups and
downs, but with the built-in stabilizer of the free market, always ready to bring it back from depressions to new heights
of prosperity. A depression was no source for worry, it would
correct itself just as it had so many times before, provided the

government kept its hands out of the economy. The New Deal, however, debunked this notion: capitalism would *not* stabilize itself without government help. Henceforth the state was not only going to mix in the economy, it was going to be its most important regulator. Roosevelt did not succeed in putting all the unemployed back to work—until wartime —nor did he ever fundamentally alter the plight of the "one-third of the nation" that he said was "ill-fed, ill-clothed and ill-housed." As late as 1939 there were still nine and a half million jobless, 17 per cent of the work force. But he took the sting out of the depression, he gave the nation some hope.

Almost before he had settled in office Roosevelt was spending $3.3 billion for a large-scale public-works program, and had made 300,000 jobs for unemployed youth through the Civilian Conservation Corps. Instead of sitting by like his predecessor while the hungry starved waiting for private charity, Roosevelt made available large sums to the various states to pay relief. In 1935 he initiated a Works Progress Administration (WPA) which was to spend $10½ billion before it disappeared from the scene, and which was to be the butt of thousands of jokes, but which nonetheless put people to work and pumped purchasing power into the economy. By 1936 the government was building roads, bridges, airports, sewer systems, and parks; erecting schools; clearing slums on a large scale. It was making work for some 3.8 million people, many of whom hadn't worked for two, three, and four years.

The government intervened everywhere. To raise agricultural prices, it gave farmers subsidies to cut production. Grain was plowed under, hogs were destroyed, oranges were burned in California, but the price of farm commodities went up as planned. The government openly encouraged monopoly action by businessmen—to regulate trade practices and fix prices—so that the cutthroat competition of the 1929-

1933 period could be checked. Hundreds of NRA (National Recovery Administration) codes of "fair competition" were entered into by various industries. In the first four years of the New Deal, $14 billion was "pump-primed" into the stream of purchasing power to stimulate consumption, and through consumption, production. The government passed a number of social reforms which are today, a generation later, generally accepted, but which then met bitter opposition from old-line conservatives: measures such as unemployment compensation, public housing, social security. Laissez-faire capitalism, so impotent in the four years of Herbert Hoover, died a quick death under Roosevelt—never to be revived.

When America was finally embroiled in war in December, 1941, the state towered over the economy like an implacable giant. It set prices through OPA, controlled wages through a War Labor Board, froze manpower so that workers in "war industry" could not move from job to job without government permission, allocated raw materials, built billions of dollars' worth of factories for timid corporations which couldn't or wouldn't invest their own money, and planned the national product to an extent never envisioned prior to that period by anyone but a socialist or communist.

A decade and a half after the end of the war, state influence is still a major force in our economy. Various controls have been abolished, such as those over prices and wages, but the federal government still spends one of every six dollars of the total gross national product. It manipulates interest rates, pays out billions in social security and unemployment compensation, subsidizes housing, farming, the airplane industry, and other facets of the economy. If it should curtail its spending even $5 billion or $6 billion it could precipitate a small depression; if it increases it a few billion, millions of men go back to work. During the recession of 1957-1958 there no longer was a question as to whether the state should intervene, only how much and where; the Republicans as well as the Democrats agreed on that. No responsible government official can be found anymore who insists that capitalism can regulate itself automatically, that the "free market" is all that is needed. Controlled capitalism is now an accepted way of life.

III

Parallel to the change in capitalism back in the thirties—in fact, preceding and prodding it—was an inexorable shift in the house of labor from the conservative business unionism of the AFL toward radicalism. The number of organized communists, socialists, and other leftists was never more than 150,000. Inside the unions it was only a few thousand. Yet such was the boundless energy and the skill of these men that they became the driving force of the period. Just a handful of socialists or communists strategically placed in a union of many thousands would soon control it. And though the left was numerically small by comparison with the established parties, its influence on liberals was so great that leftist ideas penetrated everywhere.

The left filled a vacuum that needed filling. By 1930 the AFL had been thoroughly discredited—inflexible, rockbound, old, stagnant. It could not meet the challenge of a new era. Built around the skilled worker, it would not or could not organize the unskilled in the mass-production industries. An industrialist, Gerard Swope, president of General Electric, once asked William Green if the AFL wouldn't consider organizing GE workers into one union rather than fifteen warring craft groups. He was told that it couldn't. Of a nonagricultural labor force of thirty-six million, only three million carried AFL cards; only 8,600 steelworkers were unionized out of a half million; and only 10,000 auto workers out of 300,000. As late as 1934 the boilermakers had only 14,-

000 members (today 151,000), the hod carriers 44,000 (today 400,000), bridge workers 16,000 (today 138,000), operating engineers 35,000 (today 200,000), carpenters 200,000 (today 750,000), bricklayers 45,000 (today 120,000), plumbers 45,000 (today 200,000).

Having developed a close rapport with employers, the AFL leadership was incapable of matching the radical temper of a depression era. Though a fourth of the working class was unemployed in 1933, the AFL never made an effort to set up some organization for them; it left the job to the radicals —the communists, socialists, and A. J. Muste's American Workers party. At its convention in 1931 it rejected unemployment compensation in the same terminology that President Herbert Hoover had used; it called it a "dole." One of its arguments, typical of its narrow view of social problems, was that if union men were out of work they might have to accept jobs alongside nonunion workers or lose their unemployment benefits. A year later the Federation was forced to change its position, but it never propounded any program against the depression that had the fire of a crusade. It appealed to no one. In the 1932 elections it could not bring itself to choose between Hoover and Roosevelt—or Norman Thomas. It was "neutral," immobilized. Its leaders were old, set in their ways, monarchs of little empires, fearful that the millions of unorganized workers clamoring for the doors to be opened would topple those empires. It could look in only one direction: back. America stood at a great historical turning point, but the AFL leadership was incapable of turning with it.

The vacuum was occupied by the radical left. Hundreds and hundreds of unions were forming spontaneously. Workers would suddenly be confronted with a grievance—a wage cut, the discharge of one of their members, speed-up—and a union would form quickly, perhaps conduct a short strike. Some applied for a federal charter in the AFL, many stayed independent. It seemed that every plant had a militant old miner in it, who had been through the strikes of the 1920's in coal, or a young socialist or communist who knew just what to do in these moments. "The country is full of spontaneous strikes," wrote Benjamin Stolberg in December, 1933. "Wherever one goes one sees picket lines." The number of strikers in 1930 was 158,000; in 1933, 812,000; and in 1934, 1,353,608. More often than not the strikes were defeated and the unions reduced to a baker's dozen. But that baker's dozen were usually a small nucleus of men who looked upon unionism not merely as a means of bettering their own wages and working conditions, but as the chosen vehicle for the assault on capitalism itself. They always returned to organize new unions and new strikes.

Four hundred and seventy-five thousand textile workers up and down the eastern seaboard were out on the picket line in 1934—under socialist leadership. A. J. Muste's American Workers party (later that year to merge with the Trotskyists) guided the Auto-Lite strikers in Toledo to victory, after the courts had issued injunctions against picketing and the situation looked hopeless. The victory gained here played no small part in the future growth of the United Auto Workers. The Trotskyists in Minneapolis, through Farrell Dobbs and Vincent Dunne, organized the teamsters in a general strike and then became the hub of a virile organizational drive both in Minneapolis and nationally. The communists organized the longshoremen up and down the West Coast and led them in one strike after another, including a general strike in San Francisco. Wherever one turned, radicals were at the head of picket lines, at Briggs, Motor Products, Hudson, among seamen in the Pacific Coast area, leading the rubber workers in Akron, the electrical workers at General Electric, and the seamen on the East Coast.

Just how significant were these efforts can perhaps be illustrated by the role of the Trotskyists in Minneapolis.

Though they were eventually thrown out of the Teamsters' Union they were a serious threat to business unionism for a few years; but for a few strokes of bad fortune and strategical mistakes they might have altered the course of this union decisively.

In 1934, the Teamsters' Union was a relatively small organization, with only 95,000 members, limited to a few metropolitan areas, sluggish and unimaginative in its organizing drives. Each of its local and city organizations was a "feudal barony," powerful perhaps in its own right, but hardly effective in any national or broader sense. The small Trotskyist group in Minneapolis finally perfected the weapon which made teamster growth possible. In a series of three strikes in 1934, Farrell Dobbs and Vincent Dunne came off with a sensational victory, winning recognition and other benefits for the truckers. Afterward they mounted a campaign throughout the Midwest and nationally to enroll the over-the-road trucker, and their efforts were so successful that at one point Dan Tobin, the late president of the union, pleaded with Dobbs to take a top national position in the union. The Trotskyists were the first to understand the power that could be generated by using the organized truck driver as a lever for further unionization. Using the technique of "leap-frogging," they saw to it that every driver that came to a unionized terminal had to wear a union button. The newly unionized men in one city became the wedge to organize terminals in other cities. The over-the-road driver helped to organize local drivers, and local drivers in turn helped further to organize not only other long-distance haulers but warehousemen, cannery workers, fruit pickers, florists, auto salesmen, miscellaneous factory workers, retail stores, dairy farmers, and many others.

The radicals were ever vigilant to perfect an old or utilize a new technique—the sitdown strike, use of the unemployed to help the employed, spreading a single strike until

it became a general strike in a city or an industry, mass picketing, and the like. Their pressure on the AFL was so persistent that a schism in Federation ranks became inevitable.
After a few years, a confluence of the left and center merged
—in 1935—to combat the right within the old Federation.
The center, around John L. Lewis, Sidney Hillman, David
Dubinsky, Charles P. Howard, supplied the generals and the
money for the new organization; the left supplied its ser-
geants and lieutenants, and leadership for its strikes and
picket battles. The Committee for Industrial Organization,
formed in 1935 when the AFL refused to accept Lewis' resolution on industrial organization, was the vehicle for left-
center unity.

Unlike William Green, John L. Lewis recognized early
that the mood of the times could not be ignored. After the
passage of Section 7a of the National Industrial Recovery
Act, which gave unions legal protection in organizing, he
had gambled the union's $75,000 treasury in a campaign to
rebuild his own Mine Workers' Union. In a blitzkrieg drive
he increased the miners' membership from 150,000 to a half
million in a few boisterous months. The same could be done
in steel, in auto, and elsewhere, he felt, if the new unions
could be organized industrially—and above all under "safe
leadership." Like Green, he didn't want the young radicals
to dominate the new organizations; he had fought—and expelled—the communists and socialists from his own union
in many battles during the twenties. But Lewis was a realist.
The radicals were becoming entrenched. They could not be
removed by a frontal attack; they could only be outflanked.
Furthermore, in the initial organizing stages they were in-
valuable, the best organizers he could find. Lewis even hired
for the new CIO some of the men he had driven out of the
Miners' Union, men like Powers Hapgood, a left socialist,
Adolph Germer, another socialist, and John Brophy. Leo
Krzycki, of the Amalgamated Clothing Workers' Union and

the chairman of the Socialist party, was also added to the staff in a leading position. When asked once why he permitted so many socialists and communists on his CIO payroll, Lewis quipped: "Who gets the bird, the hunter or the dog?"

In this uneasy alliance of left and center the center always exhibited a troubled concern about the left. Charles P. Howard, president of the International Typographical Union, and an associate of Lewis in forming CIO, stated this concern at the 1935 AFL convention:

"Now let me say to you that the workers of this country are going to organize, and if they are not permitted to organize under the banner of the American Federation of Labor they are going to organize under some other leadership or are going to organize without leadership. And if either of these conditions should eventuate, I submit to you that it would be a far more serious problem for our government, for the people of this country and for the American Federation itself than if our organization should be so molded that we can organize them and bring them under the leadership of this organization. . . . I don't know . . . how many workers have been organized into independent unions, company unions and associations that may have some affiliation with subversive influences during the past few years. However, I am inclined to believe that the number in these classes of organization is far greater than any one of us would grant."

In his own dramatic way Lewis told the same convention: "I stand here and plead for a policy . . . that will protect our form of government against the isms and the philosophies of foreign lands that now seem to be rampant in high and low places throughout the country."

IV

In the new CIO, Lewis let the reins out a little, gave the radicals some leeway; always, however, keeping firm control in his own hands. In the end the "hunter" got the bird. Wherever he could, Lewis set up organizing committees instead of autonomous international unions. Thus the Steel Workers' Organizing Committee was headed by the vice-president of Lewis' own union, Philip Murray. The Packinghouse Workers' Organizing Committee was headed by another miner, Van Bittner. Similar committees were set up in textile, oil, and elsewhere. Lewis and Hillman saw to it that these committees were generously supplied with funds. The SWOC, for instance, had 433 full-time and part-time organizers, paid for out of monies contributed by the miners and the two needle-trades unions. But the organizing-committee unions had no rights of their own. Their members could not decide policy, negotiate contracts, call strikes or vote on any issue without the approval of the Lewis-dominated organizing committee. Control for Lewis and Hillman was of the essence if there was to be an "orderly" campaign.

Another feature of the Lewis strategy was to avoid strikes by dealing directly with the big-corporation officials. He sought no backdoor contracts as Green did; he didn't have to because CIO was enrolling new members almost faster than it could tally them. But he tried in informal, often secret, sessions with company officials to arrive at an understanding without involving rank-and-file committees. In March, 1937, Lewis and Murray signed a recognition agreement with Myron C. Taylor, chairman of the board of directors of U. S. Steel, after three months of secret negotiations. Lewis' praise of Taylor for his "farseeing vision and industrial statesmanship" was in sharp contrast to the attitudes of the radicals in auto and rubber. On their side the employers were usually highly impressed with Lewis' moderation. The *New York World-Telegram* reported that "two financiers closely identified with Morgan interests [said] they had only praise and admiration for Mr. Lewis. Supplementing each other's statements but apparently thoroughly in accord on the main theme that complete industrial organization was inevitable, they hinted that other industrial leaders may be just as receptive to unionization of their plants as is Myron C. Taylor, chief of Big Steel." Walter Lippmann warned businessmen that "the more they treat Mr. Lewis and the CIO leaders as public enemies to be resisted at all costs, the more impossible they make it for Mr. Lewis to develop discipline and a sense of responsibility in the ranks of his young and inexperienced followers. The more they compel Mr. Lewis to lead strikes to obtain recognition for organized labor, the more they compel him to depend upon his most militant followers. . . ."

The radicals, though they worked closely with Lewis and accepted his leadership in decisive moments, nevertheless pursued a strategy decidedly at variance with his. When the Goodyear Company in Akron cut wages and fired 137 workers in 1936, the unionists formed an eleven-mile picket line —longest in history. For most of the young men in their early or mid-twenties this was their first taste at·leading a mass movement, and they were exhilarated by the experience. They were often disappointed as Lewis put the damper on some of their projects, or forced them to leave factories where they were "sitting in" before assurances of full victory. But organizing the unorganized was a worthwhile goal in itself and they had little time for high-level feuds.

Most fortunate for Lewis was the fact that the communists in this period had executed another zigzag in their long history of zigzags—one that was highly favorable to both the New Deal and the center within the CIO. As late as 1934 the communists were still calling the New Deal a "fascist conspiracy," Sidney Hillman an "NRA strikebreaker," the Wagner Act "demagogy" and the whole Roosevelt program a "preparation for imperialist war." In 1929 they had organized a dual-union movement called the Trade Union Unity League, which not only agitated for higher wages but blared forth such slogans as "against imperialist war and for defense of the Soviet Union." This was a period in communist history when they considered the socialists as the "twin" of fascism and the AFL leaders as "agents of Wall Street." But by 1935 the winds of Moscow had shifted; Ambassador Maxim Litvinov had made a pact with Roosevelt, and the Soviets were now embarked on a soft, popular-front line. The American communists thereupon suddenly discovered that the New Deal was not fascist after all but a highly progressive development, and that the unsuccessful dual unions must be liquidated in favor of "work in the AFL," (later the CIO). Working with Lewis became a religious principle with the communists; they didn't fight him, they burrowed into his apparatus all the way up to the top. A communist became Lewis' lawyer, another became the editor of the CIO newspaper, and others filled similarly high positions. At one time, according to Edward Levinson, the communists controlled national unions in the CIO with more than 800,000 members and local unions in other internationals with hundreds of thousands more.

Professors Bernard Karsh and Phillips L. Garman in *Labor and the New Deal* (Derber and Young, editors) estimate that the communists "at minimum . . . controlled unions containing about twenty-five per cent of the CIO's total membership and at maximum they wielded powerful influence in unions having another twenty-five per cent." The third largest union in CIO, the United Electrical Workers, was completely in their hands. The communists were part of the alliance that ruled the UAW, and they exercised considerable influence at the local-union level of the steelworkers, although they were shut out at the top. In addition they ran a large number of the smaller unions—longshoremen; mine, mill and smelter workers; tobacco workers; and office workers.

The alliance of left and center within the CIO remained a relatively peaceful one until World War II; first, because of the popular-front communist line, and second, because the noncommunist radicals were neither well organized nor disposed to fight Lewis during a period of great victories. While the left pursued a militant strategy, Lewis capitalized on the gains from that militancy but waited quietly for it to run its course.

Probably the single greatest cause of the sensational CIO growth in its first two years was the sitdown-strike technique introduced by the leftists in rubber and above all in auto. Instead of picketing in front of a factory, where experience was teaching them bitter lessons of police and company brutality, the radicals decided to sit inside the plant where the terrain was less vulnerable to attack. This technique originated spontaneously but the left was quick to seize on it. Sitdown strikes in the rubber industry were taking place every week. In the nine months between September 1, 1936, and June 1, 1937, no less than 484,711 workers were involved in sitdowns, the most important at the Flint General Motors plants and at Chrysler in Detroit. Most of them were called to secure sole bargaining rights for their union, and though few won the victory immediately, they established an atmosphere of victory that gave the letters C, I, O a magic ring with millions of unorganized. For the first time great corporations like General Motors, Chrysler, Goodyear, and others had been humbled. The auto union grew from 30,000 members to 400,000 in less than one year.

The flavor of this short period is perhaps epitomized by a

song composed by the lawyer for the auto workers, Maurice Sugar:

> When they tie the can to a union man,
>   Sit down! Sit down!
> When they give him the sack they'll take him back,
>   Sit down! Sit down!
> When the speed-up comes, just twiddle your thumbs,
>   Sit down! Sit down!
> When the boss won't talk don't take a walk,
>   Sit down! Sit down!

After the major sitdown strike at General Motors had terminated in 1937, there were eighteen wildcat sitdowns in twenty days. Mindful of this militant mood, *The New York Times* wrote: "One of the questions inherent in the present situation is whether Mr. Lewis does not stand in some danger of losing control of his movement. . . . In the automobile union it is the young hot-heads who have been coming to the fore in recent weeks." Among these "young hot-heads," of course, were the three Reuther boys. When 144 women workers at Yale & Towne in Detroit were on the verge of being evicted by the police in 1937, Walter Reuther climbed into their plant to boost morale. Spontaneously workers from Kelsey-Hayes Wheel Company, Babcock and Bartell, and many other plants shut their lines and came out to support the beleaguered strikers and Reuther. Never in the twentieth century was labor solidarity more fervid.

V

The radical offensive, however, spent itself quickly after two or three years. Slowly but inexorably, Lewis introduced into the movement what he called "responsibility"; he tamed the lion. He discouraged sitdowns (there were no important ones, it should be noted, in the steel industry) and soon agreed to abolish them entirely. The New Deal too produced its moderating effect, as each social reform of the "brain trust" caught the imagination not only of the rank-and-file unionists but of many socialists as well. A new theme began to evolve within the left that Roosevelt was spoon-feeding the nation small doses of socialism. As early as 1936, thousands of intellectuals and unionists who had supported Norman Thomas in the previous election were on the Roosevelt bandwagon. On this second occasion Thomas polled only 187,342 votes—less than one-fourth of his 1932 tally.

The temper of the left, except for isolated groups, became more tranquil. One of its first programmatic casualties was the labor party plank. At the 1935 AFL convention, 104 delegates with approximately five thousand votes (one-sixth of the total), had supported a proposal for a labor party. Among them were delegates from the textile union; ladies' garment workers; hats and caps; hotel and restaurant; fur; auto; and dyers and cleaners. When the CIO was founded it seemed logical to believe that this point would be pursued.

The American Labor party, organized in New York on the initiative of Dubinsky, Hillman, and other socialists, was conceived by some as a forerunner of a national party. Throughout the country at the time, there were groups like the Washington and Oregon Commonwealth federations, the Non-Partisan League in North Dakota, the Minnesota Farmer-Labor party—all looking forward to a national third party. But this never reached fruition. The CIO, unlike the AFL, recognized the need for political action. The end of laissez-faire capitalism meant that labor had a far greater interest in national politics. The government was hiring millions of workers on WPA, was introducing Wagner Acts, social security bills, unemployment compensation, labor boards, works projects—all of which seriously affected the worker and the unions. The narrow apolitical attitude of business unionism could not meet this challenge. But Lewis and his associates stopped short of forming a new party. Though they toyed with the idea for a while, they settled for a hybrid political instrument, a league.

Labor's Non-Partisan League, organized by Lewis in 1936, was a cross between the haphazard politics of William Green and the labor-party sentiments of his more radical allies. Its purpose was to re-elect President Roosevelt and it spent almost a million dollars, and considerable energy, on this task. In Ohio it held 344 political rallies, in Chicago, 109. All told some 35,000 union officials were enlisted in the drive to keep Roosevelt in the White House.

Somewhere between 1936 and 1940 Lewis and Hillman began to quarrel over further support of Roosevelt and the League lapsed into inactivity. After Lewis quit the CIO, Hillman formed another league, the CIO Political Action Committee (PAC). By this time, during the war, the radical elan had spent itself. New Deal reforms plus wartime full employment once again altered the sights of the radical left, as well as those of the rank-and-file workers. For the time being at least, the idea of a labor party was dropped.

This was to be the experience in every phase of union activity. The "revolution" initiated by the CIO was never completed; it stopped in mid-career. Its initial direction was toward radicalism, militancy, labor partyism. But the New Deal social reforms, prodded though they were by the strikes, demonstrations, and marches on Washington, nevertheless created an atmosphere of moderation. In the two decades that followed the formation of the CIO, it lost much of its militancy, its idealistic elan, its sense of venture. The radicals in its ranks, like Reuther, who first looked on CIO as a step to socialism, now accepted the free-enterprise system. But their new "social unionism" reflected their radical past, and gave the CIO a different "tone" from that of the

AFL. The new Federation was deeply conscious of social problems. It was honest, relatively incorruptible, less bureaucratized, and practiced labor solidarity in a way that business unionism could neither understand nor emulate.

Except for the communists, the left began to lose ground seriously in 1938. The Proletarian party, the Lovestone dissident communists, many Trotskyist splinter groups, folded their tents. The Socialist party, which split in 1936 on the issue of supporting the New Deal, among other things, declined into insignificance. By 1956 or 1957 it had only a thousand members. The official Trotskyists split and splintered a number of times and today have less than a thousand members, and little union influence.

The communists showed more staying power, growing at one time to approximately 100,000 members; this was primarily because they identified with the New Deal until the Stalin-Hitler pact of 1939, and later because of the Russian victories in World War II. As usual the Stalinists twisted and turned with each shift of policy from Moscow. From 1935 to 1939 their line was "soft." Earl Browder, then leader of the party, called communism "twentieth-century Americanism" and denounced all opponents of Roosevelt as reactionaries. From 1939 to 1941, in accord with the Stalin-Hitler pact, the communists pursued a "hard" line. The war in Europe was denounced as an "imperialist war" and communist unionists organized vigorous strikes wherever they could. Once Russia was attacked, however, the policy altered again to "soft," and the communists became the most fervid advocates of the "no-strike" pledge. They condemned even the Montgomery Ward strike—called because the company refused to abide by a National Labor Relations Board decision—which had the endorsement of the whole labor movement. One of the unions they controlled, the United Electrical, Radio and Machine Workers, proposed a 15 per cent speed-up by "the direct additional expenditure of energy and effort, over and above such increases as will be effected through improved methods of techniques instituted by our war production councils." After the meeting of Stalin, Roosevelt, and Churchill in Teheran the communists were so enthusiastic about the postwar possibility of cooperation with Russia they even considered offering a permanent no-strike pledge.

But when the cold war erupted in 1947, communist policy shifted again to a synthetic "leftism," and the communists found themselves isolated completely from the CIO leadership and the American people. Their role in organizing the Progressive party and in supporting Henry Wallace for President in 1948, as well as their denunciation of the Marshall Plan, brought about a final break with the CIO. In November, 1949, Philip Murray, president of the CIO, was able to muster the whole organization to expel twelve "communist-dominated" national unions. All but a few soon disintegrated.

Following the death of Stalin and after the Khrushchev revelations at the Twentieth Congress of the Soviet Communist Party, a group of right-wing communists in America tried to achieve a measure of Tito-like independence from Moscow. From 1956 to 1958, a full-scale faction fight raged in the ranks, openly and publicly, but in the end—after perhaps three-quarters of the members had left the party—the Moscow-oriented wing was again in control. The party not only disintegrated further but was reduced to a cipher in the union movement as well. Its former allies, such as Michael Quill of the Transport Workers' Union and Joseph Curran of the National Maritime Union had deserted it more than a decade before. Now most of the leading party unionists themselves quit the party and began searching for new political moorings. At the moment, the communists are down to less than 5,000 members and with fewer sympathizers than at any time since 1930.

For all practical purposes there is no radical left in America today. A few leaders of national unions in the AFL-CIO can still be identified with moderate socialism—men such as A. Philip Randolph of the Sleeping Car Porters' Union and a vice-president of the AFL-CIO, or John Burke of the Paper, Pulp and Sulphite Union. But these are only minor organizations; radicalism today is a negligible force amongst the top labor cadre. The pendulum had swung its full course. Prosperity, New Deal reforms, full employment corroded radical attractiveness. The Communist party helped destroy itself by slavishly following the Moscow line. The left gate Walter Reuther guards is today close to center.

8
The Un-Radicals

BY THE TIME THE CIO REUNITED WITH THE AFL IN DECEMBER, 1955, twenty years after the split, it had traveled a familiar path. First, from 1935 to 1940, there were the harsh battles, militant sitdown strikes, a surge of radicalism. Then, tempers cooled, the new unions gained recognition, there was an intermediate period of more moderate struggles. Finally, though sporadic fighting continued, both sides of the labor-management table were reconciled. Neither one any longer tried to smash the other; each sought merely to limit and confine the other's power. There was relative peace.

During the 1956 national steel strike, the United States Steel Company at its South Works mill in Chicago furnished the picket captain with a desk just inside its gate and ran a power line and water to the union's six trailers. One night it supplied the pickets with beer. In another steel mill, management provided the strikers with perambulating toilets. Republic Steel told its workers to take their vacations during the strike so that they would be ready and fit when the mills stoked up again. The strikers never had it so good. No one was angry. The giant corporations made no effort to start back-to-work movements. John A. Stephens of U. S. Steel had not a single harsh word to say about union president David McDonald or the union itself.

What a sharp contrast to the earlier days of steel organization! At the Carnegie steel mills in Homestead, 1892, seven men were killed when Pinkerton strikebreakers sailed to the mills in barges, like an invading navy. The strikers, fighting against a wage cut, mounted a small brass cannon and set fire to barrels of oil they had poured on the waters near the barges. Under such attack the Pinkertons finally ran up the white flag of surrender as if they were at war. Six days later the state government mobilized 8,000 militiamen and helped run in 2,000 strikebreakers. The strike lasted almost a half year and went down to utter defeat with 3,200 workers losing their jobs. In the national steel strike of 1919, involving 350,000 workers, martial law was declared in many localities, and twenty persons were killed, eighteen of them strikers. This time too the strike was smashed. On Memorial Day, 1937, during the Little Steel strike, Chicago police shot unarmed pickets in the back, killing ten and wounding at least a hundred.

But by 1956 all this had changed. There were no beatings, no arrests, no tear gas, no shootings, no strikebreakers. Labor had "arrived." Not all labor, but a significant segment. The new unions, organized in the strife and turmoil of the turbulent thirties, were entering an era of guarded friendship. It wasn't sinister, based on any collusion between labor and management. It just grew.

There is a compelling parallel between the evolution of the CIO and the saga of the AFL at the end of the nineteenth and beginning of the twentieth centuries. Both had noteworthy achievements to their credit. The first great AFL advance was the eight-hour day. It won the fight against sweatshops. It helped pass legislation for workmen's compensation. It established the principle of collective bargaining; and it raised the wages of its members consistently and substantially.

The CIO's record was even more noteworthy. It finally made labor an accepted force in society. It won, for members and nonmembers both, such benefits as paid vacations, health insurance, higher pensions, pay for holidays, supplemental unemployment benefits. It brought the worker security on the job never before enjoyed—through seniority rights and extensive grievance machinery. It won civil rights for the Negro in thousands of organized factories and it gave the mass production worker a dignity and sense of equality he had never enjoyed before.

Yet the AFL, after its first great victories, arrived at a *modus vivendi* with management, and, as a corollary, bureaucratized its structure. The CIO unions too are following a similar—though not the same—evolution. Most of them still have a dynamic tone and structures that permit of dissent and opposition. But the center of power shifts ever farther away from the rank and file.

The history of the CIO unions is divisible into two periods. From 1935 to 1949, before the communist-dominated unions were expelled, a lively factionalism persisted not only in most national unions but in the CIO itself. Some of the disputes were over opportunistic issues of posts and control, but many were over fundamental policy. International union conventions were held annually, or at most biannually, with the election of delegates a stormy battle of leaflets, speeches, and the inevitable caucus meeting. Union newspapers, such as those in the UAW, many times carried articles by opposing sides, making it possible for discussion to filter to the ranks. The active unionist of this CIO period was almost as wedded to his inner-union caucus as to the union itself. Polemic bulletins ran off the mimeograph machines like torrents.

The second period begins with 1949 and runs to the present. Now the spread between conventions tends to increase; so do the terms of office of the leaders. A single national caucus, instead of two or more, takes the reins in each organization. Dissent is sharply reduced; factionalism either dies or tapers off. The union newspapers become house organs, more and more given to "puffs" of the leaders and with little or no controversy in their pages. The heated discussion during union classes over political and labor theory are replaced by more mundane ones on how to handle a grievance or negotiate a pension plan. The pendulum of power swings more and more to the national officers and to the professional organizers who are beholden to them.

The union leader, too, has "arrived." The young hotheads mellow or are replaced. The new union representatives are no longer the harassed youngsters of the thirties, no longer the evangelists, but more and more the hardheaded professionals, the "organization men"—part of labor's managerial class. In the process of "arriving," social unionism starts along that wide, wide road toward institutionalization.

II

By December, 1941, when America entered World War II, the major battle for union recognition had been won. The Little Steel companies, which had refused to sign union contracts in 1937, in 1941 came to terms or were forced by the War Labor Board to come to terms for their 170,000 employees. The lone major holdout in auto, Ford, not only recognized the United Auto Workers after a short strike the same year, but gave it its first national union shop and check-off of dues. The smaller unions too were filling out. The Packinghouse Union signed master agreements with Armour and Cudahy covering twenty-two plants. The Rubber Workers' Union brought Goodrich into the fold, adding thousands of new members. Even the AFL unions extended their frontiers. In part this was due to backdoor contracts, in part to the government agreement, made through Sidney Hillman, recognizing the AFL building-trades unions on all federal construction projects. But in considerable measure too it was because many of the old unions—e.g., the machinists and teamsters—were opening their doors to industrial unionism and leading legitimate battles for the unskilled worker.

According to economist Sumner Slichter, only one of every fourteen workers outside of agriculture was in a union in 1933; by 1940 it was one out of every four; and by 1950 one out of every two and a half. More than half of those in manufacturing, four-fifths of those in construction and transport, and three-quarters in coal, were union members. This was a phenomenal growth. In one respect it was even more sensational than the statistics themselves indicate because unions, prior to 1933, were strong primarily in peripheral industries; now they were firmly ensconced in the very heart of our economic system, the mass-production industries.

It is possible that if the war hadn't intervened, industry might have caught its breath and taken the offensive against the tenuous younger unions. There were still less than nine million union members in 1940, and few of the organizations were fully consolidated. But the corporations never got their chance. Under the slogan of "national unity," the government enforced a policy of uneasy collaboration between unions and employers. In modern warfare, unlike that of yesteryear, production behind the lines is as important as the military effort itself. President Roosevelt contended, therefore, that there must be no interruption of the war effort through strikes. At his request the whole labor leadership, except for John L. Lewis, yielded labor's primary weapon, the right to strike, for the duration. Instead of strikes, both parties were henceforth to submit their disputes to a War Labor Board, composed of four members each from labor, management and the public. The Board would not only be the final arbiter, but it would set limits on what the parties could negotiate voluntarily. Thus in July, 1942, it evolved the Little Steel formula by which wages were frozen to the estimated rise in the cost of living since January 1, 1941—15 per cent. Employees who had already received 10 per cent in increases, could now bargain only for 5 per cent more. This formula was often stretched as worker resentment mounted, but it put a lid on labor's efforts. On the other hand, insistence by the Board on the fundamental rights of workers to organize and bargain collectively also prevented management from mounting an offensive to destroy unions.

There is little doubt that labor could have gained far more during the war if it hadn't bartered away its right to strike. Its bargaining power was never greater. Production skyrocketed, profits rose, and there was not only full employment but a persistent shortage of labor. Individual workers, despite the federal manpower freeze, found ingenious ways of quitting one job and getting another with much better pay. Employers used all kinds of ruses to wean workers away from competitors at higher rates. The mineworkers under John L. Lewis, who had refused to give a no-strike pledge, fared much better than their wartime brothers wagewise. It is not even certain that the number of strikers would have been greater if labor hadn't pledged not to strike, because with the lush profits of wartime most employers would have yielded without strikes.

But, despite the limitation, the labor movement came out of the war with two significant gains. It added six million members to its rolls from 1940 to 1945—jumping from nine to fifteen million. This was as great an advance as from 1933 to 1940 and it was achieved without strikes, violence, or radicalism. The degree of union allegiance of the new, unseasoned members was less than that of the unionists won to the colors in the 1930's. But as the labor force grew by ten million, unions added members almost automatically. A large share of the increase was in the construction industry where the building-trades unions had closed-shop arrangements, and in manufacturing where the CIO unions were entrenched. When a construction project grew from 500 workers to 2,000 the union grew apace without any additional organizing efforts.

A second advance was in union security. The War Labor Board, as a compromise between labor's demands for a union shop and employers' demands for an open shop, ordered "maintenance of membership" clauses written into union agreements. This provided that every member who already belonged to the union or wished to join had to maintain his membership for the duration of the union contract; he could not resign in that period. Labor had expected to win a full-scale union shop in return for the no-strike pledge, and Philip Murray, president of the CIO, protested vehemently against the compromise. But this was the first step in the direction of further union security. It helped give the new unions stability in their period of consolidation, and it paved the way ultimately for the union-shop agreements that were won in most of the mass-production industries in the fifties.

The war was an important, perhaps decisive, interlude for the new unionism. It was a period of enforced accommodation between labor and management by official decree of the state. The two had either to resolve their disputes peacefully or yield to government boards to make the final decisions. If either of the antagonists balked, the state was ready to take sterner measures. Forty times during the war President Roosevelt used his authority to seize plants because of labor disputes—twenty-three times because employers refused to accept a government order, and twenty-six times when unions refused. (On nine of these occasions, it was because both refused.) The most dramatic of these was in 1944 when soldiers carried Sewell Avery, president of Montgomery Ward, from his office because the large mail-order house would not bargain with the Retail, Wholesale and Department Store Union.

A change from all-out fighting to "getting along" took place in the labor-relations field, without either of the parties necessarily happy about it, but both submitting nonetheless.

III

By the time the war ended the temper of the rank-and-file unionist was at the explosive point. Demands for "action" on the part of the Auto Workers, who had fabricated much of the war materiel, were particularly insistent. Thousands of one-hour and one-day "quickie" strikes were taking place in industry over the restrictive decisions of the WLB on wages and the failure to adjudicate grievances quickly. In 1944 there were almost 5,000 unauthorized "wildcat" stoppages, affecting more than two million workers. The victory of the coal miners after four national walkouts in 1943 added fuel to the fires. The miners, disregarding the no-strike pledge, won "portal to portal" pay—a convenient formula by which the War Labor Board circumvented its own wage freeze—granting Lewis' men pay for the time it took them to arrive at their work station. Pointing to this victory, other unionists demanded similar concessions but were held in check by official AFL and CIO policy.

Once the Germans and Japanese surrendered to the Allies, however, it was inevitable that a rash of strikes would break out. In 1946, four and a half million workers hit the picket lines, a half million more than the previous peak year 1919; and 113 million days of labor were lost in strikes— four times as many in the militant year 1937. In coal, auto, electric, steel, maritime, and the railroads there were nation- wide stoppages. The core of American capitalism—the mass- production industries—was under attack. City-wide stop- pages occurred in at least seven important cities.

But the bigness of the 1945-1946 strike wave belies its basic character. This time there was no attempt to destroy unionism as such; for all practical purposes the strikes were merely a "safety valve" to let off steam. After War I, employ- ers used violence, spies and all manner of measures to smash the steel, packinghouse, and other unions. But after War II there were no such tactics, except in small isolated cases. Management now could *afford* unionism; it had learned to accommodate itself to the "monster" just as management had learned to accommodate itself to the AFL simple union- ists at the beginning of the twentieth century. The "seller's" market and the increasing trend toward "administered" prices made it possible to shift costs of wage hikes onto the backs of the consumers. From the end of the war to 1958 the steel companies raised prices twenty-three times.

Government tax policy also took the sting out of strikes for the employers. Under the "carry back" provision of the tax laws, corporations that lost money after the war could seek re- bates from the government of excess-profit taxes they had paid during the war. The J. I. Case Company, an agricultural- implement manufacturer, was struck for fifteen months at its Racine plant and at Rockford for one full year. Sales fell sharply and the operating profit-and-loss sheet was blotted with red ink. But under the "carry back" provision, the com- pany was able to turn its deficit into a surplus of almost $1½ million. The nation as a whole was subsidizing employers for strike losses.

Fortune magazine pointed out in November, 1946, that:

A variety of factors makes strikes fairly cheap, in the short-range view, for some corporations. The excess profits tax was in force until December 31, 1945; in the first eight months of the year the big war contractors had already made about as much money as they could hope to clear for the whole year; in some cases it was actually more profitable, in terms of the 1945 balance sheet, to shut down toward the end of the year rather than pay higher wages in advance of price relief.

Though the big corporations in 1946 granted a "first round" wage increase of eighteen and a half cents, that increase was usually more than offset by price increases. The steel companies were permitted by the Office of Price Administration to raise prices $5 a ton, which according to the *Chicago Sun* would net them $435 million more income per year, as against increased wage costs of only $185 million.

Fortune summed up the postwar situation well when it said:

The strikes and strike threats of 1945-46 generated violent emotions, but it was an impressive fact that for the first time a wave of strikes stirred up almost no physical violence. The strikers of 1945-46 were not desperate men. On the public platform their leaders sounded off with booming phrases directed at the enemy Capital; but privately they, like the strikers, were calm, cool, even friendly warriors.

Walter Reuther tried to introduce a few new concepts in labor-management relations. He demanded that the companies open their books and pledge not to raise prices. But, as already indicated, his plan was undercut by Philip Murray who, beyond a few platonic words, showed little interest in holding the price line. The all-around relationship between unions and employers in the mass-production industries became more friendly. After letting off steam, the unions got a raise, the corporations were more than indemnified by a price increase, and both were satisfied.

IV

With little modification this pattern has continued to the present. The bitter battles of the thirties are forgotten, replaced by a peculiar type of arms-length accommodation. Unlike the business unionists, the social unionists do not consort with employers nor waste words of praise on them. An exception to the rule was the trip made together by David McDonald of the steel union and Benjamin Fairless of the U. S. Steel Company to the various U. S. Steel mills. But ordinarily the corporations and the mass-industry unions are in a limited but perennial propaganda war. They snipe at each other constantly. During the 1958 recession, for instance, James B. Carey of the Electrical Workers' Union urged the General Motors executives to forego their bonuses until all laid-off workers returned to work. Employers, in turn, asked various unions to forego automatic wage increases provided for by their contracts. Yet despite some long strikes, and a number of important attempts to actually break a big union, such as in the Westinghouse strike of 1955, the temper of labor-management relations has mellowed.

Business Week could record on June 7, 1958, that "as a matter of policy, steelmakers have preferred to bargain with a strong international union able to dominate its locals. The industry on occasion has deliberately done some things to strengthen the command position of the USW [United Steel Workers' Union] leadership, past and present." Nor were the steel companies the only ones to adopt such an attitude. The new strategy in the organized industries called for working with the national, "responsible" union leaders as against the local union "hot-heads." It no longer sought to destroy the union as such, as in the 1930's.

The big corporations, far from suffering under union pressure for more pay, prospered as they never have in American history. They grew ever bigger. In 1957, the Senate Anti-Trust and Monopoly Subcommittee reported that from 1947 to 1954 the fifty largest corporations increased their share of manufacturing production from 17 to 23 per cent of the national total. The share of the largest 200 companies rose from 30 to 37 per cent. Billion-dollar corporations raised their profit rate from 14.9 per cent of assets in the first quarter of 1956 to 16 per cent in the same quarter a year later. The U. S. Steel Company, although it shipped a half million less tons of steel in 1957 than in 1956, earned $419 million in net profits as against $348 million the year before. Despite the wage increases granted to the union in 1956, after the strike, and the automatic increases of 1957, profits more than held their own. The wage bill went up by $180 million but profits rose $71 million over and above that. The same could be said of many other corporate goliaths.

Under the circumstances there was just no reason for the big employers to fight the new unions; no sense to the old policy of hiring thugs or police and sheriffs to shoot strikers.

Instead of a do-or-die conflict at the bargaining table the strategy of industry has changed to a more subtle one of *limiting* labor's power. Over-all management strategy has been to *contain* the labor movement, rather than try to kill it. When the UAW organizes a new Ford plant it meets relatively little resistance from the company. But attempts by small unions or the AFL-CIO itself to penetrate the South or to organize white collar, retail, or agricultural workers have been fought off vigorously. A host of techniques are used to keep the movement hemmed within its present boundaries. Some employers have joined together for strike insurance. The Chicago Restaurant Association, according to McClellan Committee testimony, had a "voluntary fund" which compensated member employers confronted by a picket line. The twenty-six sugar plantations of Hawaii contribute to a strike-insurance fund devised in 1956 when the industry was threatened by a walkout. Similar arrangements no doubt prevail in many industries, particularly where they are relatively unorganized. Management seems to have put up a "so-far-and-no-further" sign, as far as unionization is concerned.

Where labor is weak politically it often confronts serious legislative hurdles to its union drives. Right-to-work laws in nineteen states, which outlaw the union shop, keep tenuous unions off balance. They find it hard to grow, because there is constant disharmony between union members and nonunionists, and they find it hard to build adequate treasuries to defend themselves. Many a local union in a right-to-work state disappears before it can negotiate a contract.

A more serious handicap to labor has been the changes in National Labor Relations Board procedure, both as a result of the Taft-Hartley law and administrative rulings by the Board. The subject is too complex to be dealt with here, but the general effect has been to limit labor from exercising its full potential. The "secondary boycott" provision of the Taft-Hartley Act, for instance, prevents one union from helping another in certain strike situations.

Board procedures generally have changed so drastically that they offer a minimum of protection to the employee trying to organize his shop. The figures of Labor Board election results since 1950 tend to confirm this. In 1950, labor won 73 per cent of all elections; in 1951, 74 per cent; but after that the figure declined steadily so that in 1957 it was only 61 per cent. In 1950, labor won the right to represent 759,038 new workers; by 1956 the figure had declined to 296,983 and by 1957 to 269,050.

In its early days, after the Supreme Court had declared the Wagner Act constitutional in 1937, NLRB decisions were usually friendly to labor. Republic Steel was forced, by Board decision, to rehire hundreds of strikers and to pay millions of dollars in back pay as a result of the Little Steel strike in 1937. Thousands of other workers, fired for union activity, were quickly reinstated with full back pay. The burden of proof fifteen or twenty years ago was equally on management and labor, and decisions came through in a few months. The worker thus lost his fears of employer reprisal, and this was a potent weapon to enroll new plants.

In recent times, however, the Board's concept of proof in discharge cases has become increasingly legalistic and the burden today rests on the union. The period of adjudicating a case takes seven to fifteen months, sometimes years.

By way of example, in the highly publicized Kohler strike which began on April 5, 1954, Labor Board hearings on unfair labor practices did not begin until ten months later —February, 1955; and a decision by the trial examiner was not made until October, 1957—two and a half years later. This is still a long way from resolving the issue, because the Board itself must either uphold or overrule the examiner, and at least two or three years of judicial litigation will follow. Thus, though the examiner held, in a 156-page report, that the company was guilty of refusing to bargain in good faith and of illegally discharging many employees, it will be many years before any of them are reinstated unless the strike is resolved through collective bargaining. Late in 1958 the Labor Board reopened the case for new evidence and many more months of delay are inevitable.

The theme of these and other legal measures has been simple: prevent strong unions from coming to the aid of the weak, prevent the movement itself from spreading into new industries, give employers additional weapons in strikes and in Labor Board elections. For the employing class the results must be viewed as successful since labor's organizing progress has slowed drastically.

The sum of management's efforts, however, have been a flank attack rather than a frontal one. No attempt was made to dislodge the unions from those strongholds where they were already entrenched. And beyond this policy of containment the relationship between the new unions and the large corporations has achieved a level of harmony never anticipated in the thirties.

George Brooks, educational director for the Paper, Pulp and Sulphite Union and one of labor's most competent educators, in a recent speech summed up the new relationship between labor and capital as follows:

When anti-unionism was abandoned in the Forties and Fifties by significant segments of American industry, a new world was created for the unions. For it now turned out that the *imperative* requirements of the union, that regular flow of new members and dues, could be underwritten by the *employer* with considerably more reliability than was possible under earlier arrangements. The employer not only can do it better, he does. Unions were in many cases relieved, almost suddenly, of work that used to occupy 90 per cent of their energies. Even the task of new organizing was simplified. For in our particular expanding economy, most of the expansion is in the form of improved facilities or the building of new plants by already established companies. As long, therefore, as a union stays within its 'jurisdiction,' it is likely to find that the employer is as eager as the union to 'wrap up' each new plant under that set of rules and personal associations which are already sanctified by long usage in other plants of the same company.

V

What have been the effects of this postwar harmony on the social unions?

The first is a dramatic improvement in the living standards of the union membership. Prior to the formation of the CIO, the highly paid craftsmen were referred to as the "aristocracy of labor." After World War II, a second aristocracy of labor has been added to the first. The mass-production union members at first suffered a deterioration of their lot. Hundreds of thousands were downgraded from skilled to semiskilled or unskilled jobs. Overtime was eliminated, and according to the CIO, earnings were cut by about 20 per cent, while prices continued to rise. But the first four rounds of postwar wage increases remedied the situation. Net spendable income, measured in constant dollars, fell slightly from 1945 to 1949; but by 1950 it was back to 1945 levels and from then on it continued to rise steadily. For almost a quarter of a century now, according to Sumner Slichter, average hourly earnings in American industry have increased without break. The records of the Bureau of Labor Statistics indicate that this is the longest unbroken period of rises in money wages since at least 1840. The mass-production workers today are no longer low-paid or brutally exploited. Their lot, to be sure, is far from ideal, but it is a long way from the circumstance of yesteryear. By 1956 the oil refinery worker was averaging $108.39 a week; the steelworker was earning $102.47; the auto worker $95.11; the rubber tire worker $100.30. By contrast the relatively unorganized employee in general-merchandise stores received only $43.40; in laundries only $43.32; in year-round hotels only $42.13; and in banks only $62. Unionism had paid off for the second aristocracy of labor, just as it had for the first.

From every material angle—wages, growth of membership, union security—the new unionism, therefore, has been a success. Two of its unions—auto and steel—had more than a million members each, others were in the respectable 100,-000 to 400,000 class. Their combined annual revenue ran to hundreds of millions of dollars. Their treasuries were substantial and their offices, if not lavish, at least comfortable.

But labor's very successes since the war have also led to its current crisis. Other results of the new-found labor-management harmony have been negative. Joseph F. Collis, president of the small American Newspaper Guild, perhaps pinpointed it when he wrote in his union paper on February 14, 1958: "There was a time when we organized in cellars and back rooms. We have come a long way since then to fruit juice flowing over ice at the Hotel Mayflower. But somewhere along the way the principles on which the American trade union movement was founded have been lost."

Collis wrote in bitterness because the AFL-CIO had refused at the time to recognize a union of its own organizers, the Field Representatives Federation. His point about "lost principles" is overdrawn, because there is—as there always must be—a reservoir of idealism in the labor movement no matter how institutionalized it becomes at the top. But he is rightly concerned over the new bigness, the remoteness, the impersonal, almost corporate quality of so large a sector of the movement. That union organizers should organize against their own "boss," AFL-CIO, is in itself testament to that remoteness. "Somewhere along the way" the rapport between the brass of American labor and its organizer corporals, as well as its rank and file, had been lost.

VI

The transformation of "social unionism" has been subtle but extensive. In both its moral overtones and its intrinsic philosophy it has tended to blend with the very forces of Big Business which it fights so steadily on the narrow economic front. Instead of remaining a maverick force within the social stream, as it has grown older, it has become "responsible," sluggish toward new ideas, practical rather than idealistic, legalistic rather than militant, more conformist than anticonformist.

In its early period the CIO made the greatest contribution to civil rights of our century. It gained for the Negro equality of opportunity in the factories to a degree unheard of in the past. It protected him through seniority rights and the grievance machinery as he was never protected before. The new unions still fight for improvements in civil rights. Almost every one of them has a civil rights department and makes the required lobbying gestures to secure fair employment practices. The sum total of all the individual efforts against discrimination is impressive. But the *fire* is gone. The unions are no longer the leaders in this fight. The initiative for securing further improvements has passed to Gandhians like Martin Luther King and to the National Association for the Advancement of Colored People.

In the struggle for school integration in Little Rock, Arkansas, and other Southern cities, as well as the Montgomery, Alabama, bus boycott, labor was only a sympathetic bystander. It contributed a few dollars here and there, but it did not mobilize its members to help in the struggles. It did not take the initiative in bringing together church, liberal, farm, and other organizations for a crusade on behalf of civil rights. The labor "institutions" could record that the IUE had won a nondiscrimination clause in a contract in Tennessee and that all the Auto Workers' locals below the Mason-Dixon line held unsegregated meetings. All of which was well and good, but this was the progress of an institution which carries out its accepted tasks in routine fashion, by rote, rather than the progress of a missionary force.

The new unionism plays no independent role in foreign policy; with minor points of difference it is part of the bipartisan bloc. Inside the house of labor there is a conflict between Walter Reuther's friends and Jay Lovestone, the guiding spirit on foreign affairs for George Meany. Reuther feels that Lovestone's rabid anticommunism is more of a handicap in fighting the Kremlin than a help. But his own position, and that of other leaders of the social unionists, is little different from that of Senator Hubert Humphrey or Senator Lyndon Johnson or Speaker Sam Rayburn. The new unions sound no clarions for stopping hydrogen-bomb tests or for any new kind of a foreign policy. They speak in the same militarist terms as the public generally, barren of any new approach.

The same is true in the field of civil liberties. The leaders of social unionism were among the last to speak out against McCarthyism—and only after it had been generally discredited—rather than the first. Inside their own ranks there are still vestiges of this undemocratic philosophy. Communists are constitutionally precluded from holding office in most unions; in some, from even holding membership. To its credit the Auto Workers have defended a number of workers who were dismissed as "security risks." But when the auto union attempted to raid the communist-line independent Farm Equipment Union a decade ago its propaganda centered around a vulgar, red-baiting anticommunism, rather than on the obvious superiority of the auto union. For such a transgression of principle the auto union was defeated by the workers at International Harvester who preferred to stay with their old leaders, communist or not. Some years later most of these same groups quietly joined the UAW when a non-red-baiting approach was made to them.

The International Union of Electrical Workers (IUE) engaged in the same kind of red-baiting practices at General Electric. It too suffered defeat in many instances as the price of its folly. A local machinists' union in Chicago has been under trusteeship by international officials for approximately two years because of fear that four socialist-minded (not communist) leaders might assume office.

On these and many other questions the new unions are not

conservative—but neither are they trail-blazers any more. Their pronunciamentos are careful, legalistic documents. During the 1958 recession the ex-CIO unions, like the ex-AFL unions, did their share of lobbying for increased unemployment compensation, for tax cuts, and other antirecession measures. But except for one or two places they organized no demonstrations, formed no unemployed auxiliaries, and took no other action of a more imaginative or fiery nature.

VII

A second negative offshoot of the era of harmony is the widening gap between the rank-and-file member and the collective-bargaining process. Until the 1940's, a good share of bargaining in the mass-production industries was still at the plant level. The rank and file elected committees, voted on the demands, were given daily or weekly reports on the progress of negotiations with management, and ratified the agreements before they went into effect. They *knew* the men who were bargaining for them and had at least a measure of control over them.

But one by one the large corporations agreed to nation-wide *master* contracts. Local unions in most mass-industry organizations no longer do their own bargaining on major issues; the job is assigned to the national officers who bargain directly with their national counterparts in the corporation, and to experts—lawyers, economists, actuaries, research men.

Labor, like society itself, is plagued by "Bigness." In matching economic power with Big Business, a large part of it has become Big Labor. Half of the Auto Workers' membership is employed by three companies: General Motors, Ford, and Chrysler. Seven hundred thousand steel workers are employed by six companies. Rubber, oil, packinghouse all deal with a small group of large employers. The Mine Workers' Union negotiates with many hundreds of corporations, but they belong to two or three associations. The Teamsters in 1955 negotiated a single contract for 180,000 truck drivers in twelve states, superseding 200 previous contracts.

Furthermore, the centralization does not end here. Whatever major gain is won at General Motors is almost always accepted by Ford and Chrysler. Whatever is won at U. S. Steel, the "pattern-maker," automatically is accepted by the other major steel corporations. The rubber union sets patterns in negotiations with the "Big Four," the packinghouse union in negotiations with the "Big Three." Within a major industry collective bargaining is now fully "patternized." After bargaining with the large corporations, the international union insists that other companies, whether or not in the same industry, "follow the pattern." Thus the farm-equipment plants under contract with the auto union followed the supplemental unemployment benefits pattern won in auto in 1955; Reuther declared this a "must" in every contract. Beginning with 1947 the rubber workers required that all locals must "submit their contracts to the General President of the International Union for approval before such agreements were to be signed." This ensured that patterns would be followed.

Bigness has so infected industrial relations that patterns increasingly cross industries. What is won by auto and steel tends to become the pattern for lesser unions. Whatever conditions the Auto Workers win at General Motors automatically applies to the Electrical Workers who have contracts for a small segment of the GM employees. In 1946, when Phil Murray and the steel companies agreed to an eighteen-and-a-half-cent wage increase, this became the pattern for auto, electric, rubber, oil, and many other unions. The miners that year received a larger increase, but they too had to do so within the "eighteen-and-a-half-cent formula"—by stretching it somewhat. The rail workers, likewise, had their fate determined by the over-all eighteen-and-a-half-cent formula. The second round of national wage increases in 1947 resulted in a "fifteen-cent package," with Phil Murray and the steel companies again setting the pattern. The "package" consisted of twelve and a half cents in wage increases and two and a half cents in fringe benefits, including pay for holidays. The auto and rubber workers that year received the same fifteen cents though only eleven and a half cents of it was in direct wage increases. Following this "second round," the pattern-setting became somewhat less rigid, with the auto and steel unions vying to set the pace. In 1948 the auto workers gained the escalator clause and annual improvement raises. Other unions didn't follow "pattern" immediately but by September, 1952, some three and a half million organized workers were covered by similar clauses. In 1949, after a prolonged strike, the Steelworkers won a supplemental pension to increase social security payments for retired workers to $100 a month. The Auto Workers gained the same objective at Ford's around the same time and soon it was "pattern" for the rest of Big Industry. When Chrysler refused to follow suit in 1950 it was subjected to a long 108-day strike.

Pattern-setting carried over even to "fringe issues." Prior to the war, union efforts revolved primarily around wage-and-hour problems. But with the war's end and under the pressure of the social unionists, social issues became an integral part of collective bargaining. In 1949, the courts held that under the Taft-Hartley law, employers were obligated to bargain on health insurance and pensions. By the middle of 1950, seven and a half million workers were covered by such plans, and by 1954 more than eleven million. Holidays, vacations, supplemental unemployment benefits all came within the purview of union demands and all tended to follow pattern in the major bargaining units.

None of this was necessarily automatic. Frequently the big unions shaved their demands slightly for smaller firms. Thus in the first three rounds of postwar wage increases, at least 98 per cent of the steelworkers employed by the "integrated" companies—the basic producers—received identical benefits; but in "nonintegrated" units only 84 per cent in 1946, 82 per cent in 1947, and 70 per cent in 1948 received the "key bargain" increase. Yet the key bargain was the pivot of other collective bargaining in these unions, with each organization paring its demands only moderately and always keeping the pattern in sight.

Rank-and-file involvement in the process of collective bargaining became even further removed beginning with 1948. Up to that time most agreements were for one-year periods. Now the time lag began to increase. In 1948, the auto union signed a pact with General Motors for two years. In 1950, Reuther and General Motors came to terms for a five-year contract. One of the gains of the union in this settlement was the "modified union shop." When the five-year contract expired in 1955, a new three-year agreement was reached, this time calling for supplementary unemployment benefits. Again, other unions followed suit shortly thereafter. The length of agreements tended to grow to three years, with the big unions and big corporations tending to follow pattern as made either by auto or by steel.

Long-term contracts had the side effect of building up union treasuries, because in the interval of peace there was little expenditure for strike benefits. In 1946, 116 million mandays of work were lost through strikes. After that the number declined appreciably and was usually only one-fifth or one-fourth as high, despite the fact that the number of unionized workers increased.

Commenting on long-term contracts, *Fortune* made some pertinent observations:

> Why companies seek long-term contracts is plain enough. They want an end, as one steel executive put it, to the 'guaranteed annual argument.' For somewhat the same reason union leaders like long-term contracts too. The rank-and-file members don't; they dislike being tied up for years—a leader of the Glass Workers admitted, for example, that the union officers 'caught hell' from the members last year for the three-year contract. But many union leaders would welcome a breather from having to 'deliver' each year. Long-term contracts will become more commonplace, particularly in large corporations which believe they can calculate rising productivity and commit themselves to sizeable wage increases three or four years in advance. More important, labor relations continue to grow more bureaucratized, and so will labor itself.

Just as the corporation has had the effect of depriving ownership of decision-making, so Big Labor—though far from the same degree—deprives the rank and file of similar privileges. There is no evil intent behind this; most Big Labor leaders would like to reverse the process. But they are both caught in the maw of capitalist consolidation, and have tasted more than a decade of the pleasant policy of "getting along." It is not an easy situation from which a union leader, even the best, can extricate himself. In these last twenty years the unions have greatly humanized capitalism; intolerable working conditions have been abolished in so many areas. But, in turn, bigness has partly dehumanized the big unions themselves.

VIII

Harmony and centralization have spread a pall over the great unions formed a quarter of a century ago. The inner life has become routine. The local unions, according to

George Brooks of the Paper, Pulp and Sulphite Union, "starve to death simply for lack of things to do." The national unions are institutions with vested interests. Each man has his job, each job has its man. The emphasis is on efficiency, protocol, public relations, rather than evangelism, devil-may-care equality, and propaganda.

Factionalism is again rapidly disappearing, just as it did in the old AFL after the first two decades of its existence. No one has opposed Walter Reuther since he was re-elected in 1947. Carl Stellato sometimes puts up token opposition by running for a vice-presidency of the union, but he seldom marshals more than a tiny percentage of the vote. Reuther is firmly entrenched. Here and there minor conflicts break out in his organization such as a contest for a regional director's post. Almost all the contestants, however, are themselves Reutherites. Since the communist-line unions were expelled from the CIO in 1949, internal conflict has been reduced to the vanishing point. Factionalism wracked the rubber workers from its day of founding until a decade ago. In 1948, L. S. Buckmaster, current president of the union, was elected by the slim margin of 810 to 808 votes. The following year he was removed from office by his general executive board, but was vindicated by the convention and re-elected. He and his slate have remained in office ever since. Perhaps when he retires this year or next there will be a struggle over succession, but this will be a different type of factionalism than that of the '30's and '40's.

Joseph Curran has now headed the National Maritime Union for twenty-one years; O. A. Knight, the oil workers, eighteen years; Joseph Beirne, the communication workers, fifteen years; Michael Quill, the transport workers, twenty-three years; Ralph Helstein, the packinghouse workers, twelve years; Jacob Potofsky, the clothing workers, twelve years. Almost all of these men are elected every two years without opposition. The former CIO unions still hold conventions more frequently than the former AFL unions—the rubber workers every year, the auto workers every two years (with a special educational conference in the off year), the electrical workers every two years, the packinghouse workers every two years. But there are seldom contests for major office any longer.

In the Steelworkers' Union there has been only one race for the presidency in all its history—in February, 1957—and that is an interesting case history of the concept of democracy by at least one of the Big Labor leaders, David McDonald. After McDonald made a trip around the steel mills with the chairman of the board of U. S. Steel, Benjamin Fairless, he was the object of severe criticism. Rank-and-file workers were disoriented by his new line of "mutual trusteeship" with industry. At the union convention in September, 1956, he tried to offset some of this criticism by glowing references to the "lean and hungry" vigor of the early CIO days. Somewhat at odds with this "lean and hungry" look, however, he not only suggested a $2-a-month dues increase for the members, but a $10,000-a-year raise (to $50,000) for himself and the union's other two executive officers. The dues boost evidently angered the delegates because the international union at the time claimed reserves of $21 million and the affiliated locals had assets of nearly $20 million more. On the floor of the convention, international representatives and staff personnel tried to assuage the growing rancor, but it persisted. *The New York Times* reported:

> The debates grew so bitter that Mr. McDonald repeatedly admonished the delegates not to boo. When the dues increase was put to a voice vote, the division was close enough to necessitate a show of hands. This still left the outcome obscure. Mr. McDonald then called on the unionists to record their sentiment by rising to their feet. He pronounced the increase approved by an "overwhelming vote."

When the delegates shouted for a roll-call vote the request was refused. The $5-a-month dues went into effect, but a month later a dues protest committee was organized by Donald C. Rarick, a grievance committeeman at the Irvin Works of U. S. Steel. The committee circulated a petition for a special convention "to amend the constitution to provide that any assessment must be submitted to the membership for approval." The union constitution provides that when 25 per cent of the local unions call for a special convention it must be granted. Rarick's subsequent vote for presidency of the national union, against McDonald—one-third of the total—indicates that the rebels might have mustered this 25 per cent. But on November 28, McDonald ruled the rank-and-file movement "illegal" and "dual unionist," and threatened to expel its leaders. No special convention was ever called.

At the next convention, in 1958, McDonald consolidated his position once more. The delegates, many of whom were members put on the payroll by McDonald, rejected an opposition resolution to have all business agents and organizers elected instead of appointed. In fiery tones, reminiscent of John L. Lewis in the 1920's, McDonald branded the leaders of the dues protest committee "traitors" and called on the convention to "rip this cancer out of your bowels." A novel theory was advanced to the effect that anyone who continues to fight a union position, such as the $5-a-month dues, after a convention has voted on the subject, is guilty of "dual unionism." McDonald himself stated that he favored expelling Rarick and his friends without the formality of a trial, but the convention decided to give the rebels their day in court. Only two delegates—out of 3,500—had the courage to vote against a resolution which made opposition per se a union crime.

Rarick's forces were certainly greater than this vote indicates; one estimate is that 15 to 20 per cent of the delegates

were with him. But the threat of expulsion as "dual unionists" hung over everyone's head. Delegates who came from
divided locals were afraid of being put on trial in their home
organizations. Though Senator John Kennedy praised the
democracy of the convention, McDonald's majority was not
always won by democratic methods. The election of delegates
was a perfunctory matter in many locals with the executive
board nominating itself and having the membership ratify
the act. Unlike the United Auto Workers, where there is a
standard procedure with proper safeguards, and a secret ballot vote, the steelworkers permit each local to decide for itself how to vote. Frequently the poll was taken at a membership meeting, where perhaps 5 or 10 per cent of the workers
are present, rather than in a special election which would involve a far higher percentage. McDonald's apparatus not only
isolated Rarick but created an atmosphere of fear that would
make future opposition difficult as well. Until there is a revolt in the top hierarchy itself, the voice of rank and file and
secondary leaders seems to be effectively muzzled.

No other ex-CIO leader has taken so flagrant a position
on democracy as McDonald. They haven't had to. The wellsprings of inner-union conflict dried up by themselves. The
members of the mass production unions are too distant from
the center of power to be able to influence it much. And the
secondary leaders who could organize opposition are now,
for the most part, on the national union staffs.

IX

The staffs of the younger unions are now hierarchies where
few representatives ever speak their mind publicly. That
holds true of the Auto Workers as well as most of the others.
In the Steelworkers' Union it has always been thus, but in
unions where factions existed until the mid-1940's, interna-

tional representatives had greater leeway of expression. The trend toward involuntary monolithicism eliminates even that. The "reps" speak as one voice with the top leadership. They often pay regular "dues" to their top official's caucus, usually checked off their salaries, and they speak in favor of official "policy" at the meetings of the local unions they service, whether or not they personally agree with it. They are now part of the "team." What this does to a union like the Auto Workers, where most of the capable secondary leaders are on the staff, must be obvious. When the voice of these articulate men is silenced, the pressures of the rank and file themselves become weakened. That rank and file still has democratic avenues of expression open to it, but it is short of leadership, because its leaders are recruited to the staff, where they become immobilized.

The professional representative, necessary though he is under current conditions, develops a whole set of special attitudes. Since he is appointed by the regional directors or top officers rather than elected by the membership, he tends to lose a feeling of responsibility. His post is now a "job," and he is no longer as vitally concerned about pleasing his own sense of mission as in pleasing his regional director, or at least keeping clear of his lash. His own salary and benefits become progressively larger by comparison with the members who still work at the lathe, and his economic stake tends to make him moderate just as the secure doctor or lawyer tends in the same direction. He is now an "organization man." What is a "life-and-death" strike for his members or a serious grievance for the individual worker, is only "work" for him—work that he would like to get out of the way as quickly as possible. More and more he becomes the mediator, the middleman, trying to make acceptable deals between the aggrieved worker and management.

Imperceptibly there has been a decisive change in the caliber of leadership in the mass-production big unions. In the thirties the symbol of the new unionism was the agitator, the fiery fellow in his twenties who damned the boss, capitalism, low wages, the open shop, unemployment, and perhaps fascism and war, as he spoke to the membership. He was a man trained at the soapbox in Chicago's Washington Park Forum or its equivalent in New York, Cleveland, Pittsburgh, and Detroit. He was the dynamo who had cut his eyeteeth on a socialist, communist, Lovestoneite, Trotskyist, or Wobbly dogma and whose barbs blistered with emotion. In that period there was one front: against the employer; and one problem: organizing the unorganized. The rest was a redundant luxury. These young, shirtless, devoted organizers made innumerable and strange sacrifices. In Local 291, Retail and Wholesale Employees, an athletic young man sold his blood each month to earn a few dollars so that he could pay his rent and work full time for his union. In Local 205, UAW, four persons slept in the headquarters each night to save rent, and begged their food from radical sympathizers, so they could work full time for the new local. Hundreds of young people worked without pay, or with sporadic pay, for what they considered to be a noble cause.

The symbol of social unionism today is no longer the zealot flaying his arms against the injustices of the profit system or shouting down the employer at the bargaining table, but the suave professional leader who is as much a diplomat as a soapbox orator. Yesterday's agitator spoke the soothing language of a utopian dream, a world free of exploitation and poverty; today's professional talks the hard language of seniority rights, cold-cash raises, and a good man in Washington.

The newspapers of the new unions and of the AFL-CIO itself also reflect this change. Almost every one of them is a "house organ," which publishes appropriate "puffs" of the leadership, and seldom carries a word of self-criticism or self-analysis. They are lifeless, lacking in controversy or new ideas. Even their attacks on business or government lack the feel of mission. The one newspaper that rose above this level was the national paper published by the Typographical Union, *Labor's Daily*. There was some hope that this would become the daily newspaper of the whole labor movement. In March, 1958, however, after six years of subsidized publication, it quietly lapsed when the big unions failed to come to its aid.

What emerges from bigness and accommodation is "cash register" unionism. The union becomes for the rank-and-file worker little more than an insurance policy, not too different from the one he takes out from the Metropolitan Life Insurance Company. The union is no longer a way of life based on cooperative effort, but a guarantee against management abuse and the rising cost of living. Somewhere along the way—as Joseph Collis puts it—the new unionism, like the old, has lost something.

9
The Alienated Breadwinner

IN ALL THE TALK OF LABOR'S DERELICTIONS, THE RANK
and file unionist is the anonymous hero. Of the millions of
critical words that are written about labor unions, none is critical of the composite man known as the "average member."
He is the victim, not the victimizer, and to be a rank-and-filer
is a badge of honor. "Two straight-talking rank-and-filers" is
the way the magazine of the Teamsters' Union describes
Jimmy Hoffa and secretary-treasurer John English. English,
it says glowingly, is an "unreconstructed" rank-and-filer.

The rank-and-filer is considered the backbone of labor
and union officials never tire of telling him this. He gets the
credit for its virtues; but as far as its vices are concerned, he
is considered the innocent bystander. This estimate, while
partially true, is much too simple. Admittedly the first responsibility for pulling labor out of its crisis is with the leadership; yet the role of the rank-and-filer is not entirely passive. He may not give his stamp of approval to the sins of

226

omission or commission by labor's brass. He may not *consciously* encourage them. Yet he plows the soil that the leaders reap. He is the transmission belt between the mores of society as a whole and the mores of his union. He is the spur for idealism when he reaches a point of desperation, or for conformity when he becomes apathetic. Neither victim nor hero, he is a reflection of the social world around him as well as the motor power for further labor progress, when and if he rouses or can be roused from his lethargy.

The evils of business unionism and the remoteness of social unionism could never have occurred if it were not for the apathetic attitude of the average unionist, or, in some instances, the outright acceptance of these conditions.

Somewhere in the subconscious of every union member there goes on what can be called a "saturation process." The workingman absorbs in that subconscious, as if on a wax record, the various pressures of his environment. When the stress of economic pressure is mild, or when there are social and economic factors that make him fearful, he doesn't act. From 1929 to 1933 there were relatively few strikes in America because workers were terrified of being replaced by the unemployed. At other times, after long periods of silence and seeming indifference, the rank-and-file worker is engaged in a "spontaneous" strike or some other "sudden" action. In reality this is not sudden at all: it is the culmination of an internal accumulation of abuse and grievances, climaxed by a moment of desperation. Only at the breaking point does this translate itself into action.

One of the remarkable features of the 1930's was the suddenness with which workers went from one extreme to another. Few people, for instance, expected the eruptions of sitdown strikes in the auto plants. The CIO itself looked for the big organizing drive to be in steel. Lewis assigned his top lieutenant, Philip Murray, to that task and contributed millions of dollars to its operation. In the auto city of Detroit there were only four CIO organizers immediately prior to the sitdowns; the strikes came as a complete surprise to Lewis and Hillman. Overnight, thousands of men who had refused categorically to join the union only a few weeks or months before were now in wild, unrestrained motion. In one plant more than 600 of approximately 650 workers turned up at the first organizing meeting, after only one issue of leaflets had been distributed to them by the union. The same "backward" workers who refused to join unions in 1935-1936 "suddenly" jumped into national prominence at the end of 1936 and early in 1937 with their sitdown strikes and their remarkable demonstration of unity.

Some people point to such gyrations on the part of workers as a sign of immaturity, of not knowing what they want. On the other hand, there is a group of liberals and radicals who point to the final outbursts of action as proof of the worker's basic clear-headedness. It is, of course, neither one nor the other. When workers rebel so sharply against their environment it only means they have absorbed enough taunts and indignities to overwhelm their fears and other motivations. The mid-thirties was a historical moment ripe for the sitdowns and the many bitter battles with the police. There was a mood of despair, born of years of frustration, combined with a feeling of hope, born out of the first CIO victories, which bestirred the rank-and-file worker to sustained action. He didn't need much prodding from his leaders; in fact he brushed aside hundreds of old-line business-unionist leaders and established a new leadership. The Walter Reuthers, Emil Mazeys, George Baldanzis, Harold Gibbonses, Harry Bridgeses, and thousands of others were, in fact, the rank-and-filers of the mid-thirties brought to the fore by their fellow workers in the process of revolt, not only against the employer but against the conservatism of their union leadership as well.

Harry Bridges was established as leader of the West Coast

longshoremen when the longshoremen had had enough both of the "shape-up" and other ill-treatment on their job, and of Joseph Ryan, the racketeer head of their union. Auto workers, tired of procrastination by employers, swept aside Francis J. Dillon, the moderate leader appointed by William Green to head their union. Not only did millions of unorganized become unionists overnight, but old business-union "empires" either toppled or were in jeopardy.

More than anything else it was the mood of the rank and file, so volatile, so susceptible to radical leadership, that made possible the CIO and the unionization of this period. The "saturation process" had brought them to the point of action. It wasn't the leadership of labor which electrified the rank and file; the workers of this period superimposed a new leadership on top of the old one. Looking back from the 1950's, it is easy to forget that Walter Reuther was merely a tool-and-die worker or that Emil Mazey was an employee of the Briggs plant in the thirties.

After a few years of heightened interest in union affairs, the mood of the average unionist began slowly to alter. By the late 1950's it had made a full turn around. The subtle social process of the past two decades, which changed the character of the leadership of American labor, also changed the character of the rank and file. The dues-paying member reflects that change more fully even than his leader.

II

There is, of course, no such thing as an "average" union member. Joel Seidman, Bernard Karsh, Jack London, and Daisy L. Tagliacozzo, who studied the motivations of union members for many years, claim that there are seven types of unionists: the *ideological* unionist, who joins because he believes in unionism in principle; the *good* union member, who may not belong for ideological reasons but accepts the union rationale completely; the *loyal but critical* member; the *crisis activist,* who rises to the occasion when there is a strike or other crisis; the *dually oriented* member, who is both pro-management and pro-labor; the *card-carrier or indifferent* member; and the *unwilling* unionist, who belongs because he has to—either because there is a union-shop contract in his plant or because of strong social pressures. These seven types no doubt compose the rainbow of union membership, but at each stage in labor history there are more unionists at one end of the rainbow than the other. It is certainly true, for instance, that the percentage of ideological unionists has fallen since the thirties and that of the unwilling unionists has risen. So has that of the "dually oriented" member and the "card-carrier or indifferent" member. What is so pronounced in the American labor movement of the late fifties is the shift toward the indifferent member.

Two basic factors account for that shift: the further dehumanization of both the work process and the worker himself; and the changing personal goals of the individual member.

Today's worker is, on the one hand, a martyr of the most oppressive feature of our industrial society, bigness; and on the other hand, in lashing out against the dehumanization of his personality he has accepted some of the worst vices of the society that victimizes him. He is, in the words of Dr. Erich Fromm, an "alienated" personality, shorn of his creativity, seeking escape in an endless number of pleasures, and dreaming of earning enough money so that he can achieve an ever-elusive "security." Karl Marx was wrong a hundred years ago when he predicted that more leisure would make the worker more radical; the history of the last quarter of a century has shown just the opposite; more leisure has made him more conformist. Marx believed that if a worker had more time to himself he would study social science and become a rebel. What has happened is that the worker has used his extra time not to study social philosophy but to play. He caters to the child in himself rather than the mature adult, so that in formulating his political views he is guided decisively by the "conventional wisdoms" of the period rather than by his own self-analysis.

Not a few students of the labor movement seriously doubt that a shorter work week—say, thirty hours in five days—will bring the American worker real benefits. It may merely compound his frustration. From an economic point of view, what with automation and the prospects of harnessing atomic energy for peaceful use, a shorter work week is both inevitable and necessary. But from the *human* point of view it will not, by itself, solve the basic problem that confronts the average worker and the average unionist.

After a century and a half of industrialization the worker has lost the joy of creativity in his work. Aldous Huxley could correctly say that: "Every efficient office, every up-to-date factory is a panoptical prison in which the worker suffers . . . from the consciousness of being inside a machine." In the early nineteenth century the craftsman may have worked long hours in a "manufactory," but he made the product from beginning to end and when it was done he could take pride in his work like an artist who finishes a painting. His problem was that he didn't earn a "living wage," that he was at the mercy of his employer. But he did experience creativeness.

In the twentieth century all this has changed. The factory worker now not only does not make the whole product but frequently does not even know what the product will be. The girl who winds the foil in a capacitor factory does not know whether her capacitor will ultimately be part of a telephone or a guided missile. The giant industrial machine—under communism as well as capitalism, incidentally—makes of the worker an abstraction. Like the prisoner, he does not enjoy his work, he merely "puts in time." If work does not make him "stir crazy" it is only because of the camaraderie of his fellow workers, and the many distractions—such as television—after work. The type of fragmented work in the big factory reduces the intellectual capacities of the worker, rather than enhances them. It remolds the man in the image of the machine, makes of him an automatic conformer, rather than an individual with full personality.

Frederick W. Taylor, the theorist of time-study, once made the harsh estimate that "one of the very first requirements for a man who is fit to handle pig iron as a regular occupation is that he shall be so stupid and so phlegmatic that he more nearly resembles an ox than any other type." Many years before Taylor, Adam Smith wrote that "the understanding of the greater part of men is necessarily formed by their ordinary employments. The man whose life is spent in performing a few simple operations . . . has no occasion to exert his understanding. . . . He generally becomes as stupid and ignorant as it is possible for a human creature to become."

The terms "stupid" and "ignorant" are certainly not justified, for workers often show miracles of ingenuity on and off the job. But there is no doubt that, under our industrial system, the employee is "alienated." His own needs and desires are subordinated to the time clock.

"Throughout U. S. industry today," writes Daniel Bell, "the lives of millions of persons are ordered by production standards which most managers feel are as unarguable as the 'time and place of the rising and setting sun.' " The worker must attune himself to the tempo of the machine, his every move charted and engineered by the company's managerial staff. Even the non-factory worker is governed by this same emphasis on time, this same emasculation of personality. As Bell observes: "The majority of Americans may not work in the factories, as the majority never were on the frontier or in the Georgian homes, but the distinctive ethos of the time lies in these archetypes."

An Australian sociologist, Niall Brennan, spent a number of years working at various jobs to determine what they do to the human personality. What started him on this study was the experiments conducted in the United States and elsewhere with mentally retarded people. In 1917, when the New York textile factories were short of labor, the Utica Knitting Mill made an arrangement with the Rome Institution for Mentally Defective Girls, to employ twenty-four girls whose mental age was only six to ten years. Few people thought these workers would do a normal day's work, but to everyone's surprise they did as well or better. The managers insisted they were better-behaved than the normal girls, more punctual, more regular in their habits, and they worked more uninterruptedly because they did not engage much in "gossip and levity." Similar experiments elsewhere proved that morons can do simple, repetitive factory work as well or better than workers with average intelligence.

Ethelbert Steward, once a commissioner of the United States Bureau of Labor Statistics, quoted by Brennan in his book, *Making of a Moron* summarized the findings of industry on this subject as follows:

Personnel managers of textile mills took the view that textile mills formerly were operated by children and they saw no reason why adults of child-like intelligence should not do perfectly acceptable work. And after experiment, they reported that they did. Then along comes the automatic machinery which accomplishes mass production. We are told that "it is of course fortunate that a great many jobs made no particular call on mental alertness because this fact gives even dull minds a chance to find assignments at profitable jobs." Today we find the literature of efficiency and industrial managers full of suggestions as to the preferability of the employment of those men and women with a mental age of ten or less.

Brennan, after working at many tasks both manual and nonmanual, concluded that "if the demands made on a man by society are no greater than those which can be satisfied by a moron, then the unwanted faculties of a normal man will atrophy, and the next and near stage is the conversion, more accurately the subversion, of a normal man into a moron."

Oddly enough, he found white-collar work as unsatisfying, or more unsatisfying, than routine manual work. "If the laborer has been reduced to the status of a horse, the clerk has been reduced to the status of an adding-machine." The most satisfying job he had was that of a wood-carving handicraftsman. The handicraftsman, Brennan said, "is the only type of worker whose work helps him to remain sane. He of all workers sells his work rather than himself."

Perhaps this picture of the modern workingman seems exaggerated but it is attested to not only by trained psychologists such as Fromm, but by men closely associated with the labor movement. The analogy between work and prison is a recurring one in the literature on labor. Harvey Swados, a novelist who worked in an auto factory, wrote this about his fellow workers in *The Nation,* August 17, 1957:

The plain truth is that work is degrading. . . . Almost without exception the men with whom I worked on the assembly line last year felt like trapped animals. Depending on their age and personal circumstances, they were either resigned to their fate, furiously angry at themselves for what they were doing, or desperately hunting other work that would pay as well and in addition offer some variety, some prospect of change, some betterment. They were sick of being pushed around by harried foremen (themselves more pitied than hated), sick of working like blinkered donkeys, sick of being dependent for their livelihood on a maniacal production merchandising set-up, sick of working in a place where there was no spot to relax during the twelve-minute rest period.

To offset the dull monotony, assembly-line workers in auto plants often "double up." One man works furiously for one hour, doing not only his own task but that of his fellow worker next to him, while the second worker "goofs off," so that after the hour his partner can "double up" while he "goofs off." In the interval he plays cards, reads a newspaper, talks with other workers. Union officials have long frowned on this practice because it invites company time-study men to restudy jobs and increase the work standards. But the young workers, in particular, continue the practice because it is only the rest periods and the camaraderie with other workers that make the job tolerable.

The bigness of a commodity-oriented society transforms the worker himself into a commodity: "labor." Management is interested in him only insofar as that commodity produces other commodities, not for his own human qualities. The worker, in turn, feels himself lost in a welter of bigness—Big Business, Big Government, Big Labor—which he does not understand and which he cannot control. His destiny falls out of his own hands into those of the abstract institutions— unions, government, business—which manipulate him. Instead of expressing his own personality, he merely mirrors the institutions around him. "Man does not experience himself," says Erich Fromm, in *The Sane Society,* "as the active bearer of his own powers and richness, but as an impoverished 'thing,' dependent on powers outside himself, unto whom he has projected his living substance."

Alienation pursues the worker not only in the factory, not only in his union and in his relations with government, but even in his leisure time. "What are we to expect?" asks Fromm. "If a man works without genuine relatedness to what he is doing, if he buys and consumes commodities in an abstractified and alientated way, how can he make use of his leisure time in an active and meaningful way? He always remains the passive and alienated consumer. He 'consumes' ball games, moving pictures, newspapers and magazines, books, lectures, natural scenery, social gatherings, in the same alienated and abstractified way in which he consumes the commodities he has bought. He does not participate actively, he wants to 'take in' all there is to be had, and to have as much as possible of pleasure, culture and what not. Actually, he is not free to enjoy 'his' leisure; his leisure-time consumption is determined by industry, as are the commodities he buys; his taste is manipulated, he wants to see and to hear what he is conditioned to want to see and to hear; entertainment is an industry like any other, the customer is made to buy fun as he is made to buy dresses and shoes. The value of the fun is determined by its success on the market, not by anything which could be measured in human terms."

A graphic description of a "representative" auto worker was given in *Dissent* (Summer, 1957) by Frank Marquart, educational director of United Auto Workers' Local 212 in Detroit:

He is around thirty years old, has a wife and two small children to support, earns a take-home pay of around $75 a week (more when he works overtime). The family lives in a modern house, bought a few years back for about $11,500. This worker's payments on his home come to $75 a month. Another $7.20 goes for the monthly installment on a fence around his lot. Itemized in the budget is $9.90 for storm window payments and $14.67 goes towards paying off the inevitable television set. Heat costs $12 a week and another $20 will be spent for food, not including milk. He will pay $5 to the credit union each month to liquidate the debt incurred when laid off last year for over three months. A small sum is set aside each payday for the future education of his children. "If I can help it, my kids are going to get a college education when they grow up . . ."

For recreation the family will of course watch television and go to a movie occasionally (when the husband isn't working overtime). Except for scanning his daily newspaper and his monthly union paper, the worker seldom reads, and when he does it will probably be a paperback—a mystery, a western or a Mickey Spillane story. Skilled tradesmen, who are usually better educated than production workers, may sometimes read more "egghead stuff"—books on labor, history, politics, science. The Michigan CIO Education Department reports a relatively large demand for how-to-do-it books. Some part of the worker's basement is sure to be made into a "workshop," equipped with work bench and a shelf of tools. When working in his basement on some repair job, this auto worker finds a sense of satisfaction such as he never derives from his job in the factory assembly line. . . .

The alienation of the work process and of life generally drives the worker to excessive pleasure-seeking: television, movies, bowling, "do-it-yourself." Since he cannot effectively control his environment, he escapes from it. This mood and attitude carries over into his union. He recognizes the value of the union in improving his standard of living, but he does not feel himself a full participant in this process. "Our people," says the president of a Rubber Workers' Union local, "tend to hang on to the coattails of our stewards and depend upon them to handle all their problems."

In a survey of five locals of the Steelworkers' Union the University of Chicago found that 88.6 per cent of the entire group of workers felt that "the union had made the company a better place in which to work." In a similar survey of Local 389 of the oil workers, over 90 per cent of those who replied said that "the workers in my plant want a union." Yet attendance at union meetings in most locals is generally less than 10 per cent. Often a union of 10,000 members must call off a meeting because less than the 125 members needed for a quorum show up. "With a few members attending," says George Meany, "it's easy for officers to get into the frame of mind that they're running the union and nobody else really cares much."

It isn't that the worker fails to participate only in his own union affairs, but he fails to participate in all other big important activities of the real world as well. He is alienated from social problems; in running away from bigness he focuses more on his personal problems, his family, his home, his pleasures. The important issues of the time he leaves for others to cope with, and he accepts the views of the "father-images" in politics as his own, with little question. Thus there evolves in our times a tendency toward conformity which is *self-imposed,* a tendency which is perhaps even more dangerous than the state-imposed conformity of dictatorships.

III

Against this general background, there has been another important change in the outlook of the rank-and-file worker these past two decades—a basic shift in aspirations for that section of the labor force which has become the "second aristocracy of labor." William F. Schnitzler, secretary-treasurer of the AFL-CIO, made a point a few years ago that the "living wage" is no longer the primary goal of union members because in many instances they have already passed it. The steel, auto, oil worker who earns $100 a week gross or more, like the skilled craftsman of the "first aristocracy of labor" is not in dire want, desperately trying to make ends meet like his brother of the thirties. What he seeks now, according to Schnitzler, is an "improved living standard." He wants to buy his own home, save enough money for a rainy day, purchase adequate life insurance, and even invest some money in corporate securities. For the first time there are now many millions of workers in the United States who have surplus funds above the necessities of existence. Many thousands own real-estate property and stock, which gives them a "dual" economic outlook—as small businessmen and workers simultaneously. This is, of course, still a far cry from the "people's capitalism" that many writers suggest, because only 3 per cent of all workers, and only 5 per cent of all spending units of $5,000 or less, own stock; yet the number of organized workers with secondary economic interests does have an effect on the outlook of the union membership.

The members of the "second aristocracy of labor," just like the first, tend to think in middle-class terms—homes, cars, status, "keeping up with the Joneses." They have gained a sufficient amount of economic security to make them more cautious and far less militant than two decades ago. In the 1930's the mass-production worker was fighting on picket lines out of desperation; today he walks picket lines to earn his strike benefits. Therein lies the difference. The National Industrial Conference Board, in a 1958 survey of seventy-eight unions, found that forty-three of these paid strike benefits. An eleven-week strike at General Motors would cost the auto union $80 million, doled out in sums of $12 to $30 a week per worker. This perhaps isn't much money for the worker to live on, but it is enough to tide him over until work resumes. The rank-and-file worker realizes that he must support his union; but his sense of participation is limited. If he could, he would avoid picketing or taking on other strike duties; he would go fishing. The strike benefits act as a discipline on him.

The change from the 1930's to the 1950's is both psychological and philosophical. Millions of workers, two decades ago, thought that capitalism was hopeless—and doomed. The number who believe that today is infinitesimal. The average worker in big industry in the 1950's is not happy perhaps, but he is relatively satisfied in a material sense. He may be fighting psychological demons because he is alienated and abstractified by big industry, but he does have a measure of economic well-being. There have been three recessions since

World War II but none that approaches the severity of 1929-1939. Furthermore the cushions of unemployment compensation, union-won supplemental unemployment benefits, social-security pensions supplemented by union-won company payments, health and welfare programs, and of course full employment (except for the relatively short recessions up to now)—all these have changed the outlook of the average worker. The very successes of Big Labor have helped to rob it of its missionary élan.

The small, but effective, United Packinghouse Workers' Union listed in March, 1955, the "dreams come true" since the organization was formed as an autonomous international union in 1943. They included thirty-six items ranging from fifty cents per week work-clothing allowance to pensions, improved life insurance, sick leave with pay, and severance pay. If an employee reports to work at the beginning of the week he is assured thirty-six hours of work or pay. If he is asked to work beyond a certain time, the company buys his meal and pays his wages while he eats it. Men who a few decades ago received no vacation, no premium pay for overtime, no holiday pay, now receive eight paid holidays a year, as much as three weeks vacation after fifteen years, time and a half for overtime, night-shift premiums, double time for Sundays and holidays, and "earned vacation pay" even if they are discharged or die. Other benefits are somewhat technical, such as the reduction of "geographical differentials" or the inclusion of "average earnings" in computing vacations, but the list is certainly imposing and it no doubt has made a fundamental change in the lives of the 100,000 members in this union. They are still plagued by the threats of lay-off when their plants are further automated or during a recession, but, while working, their lot has improved to the point where their outlook on life and the American social system must have changed drastically.

In Akron, Ohio, America's rubber center, seven of ten families live in their own homes. According to Swados, who made a study of the situation in early 1958, "The bowling alleys are jammed, the poolrooms do well, the neighborhood waters are stocked with power boats, and last year Summit County sold the fantastic number of 67,400 hunting and fishing licenses to local residents." Rubber-union contracts in Akron provide for a six-hour day, six-day week; but approximately 15 to 20 per cent of the workers hold down two jobs. These "moonlighters" either work on a second shift in another rubber factory or as taxi drivers, bellhops, garage attendants, butchers, clerks, barbers, bakers, even engineers.

While it is working, the "second aristocracy of labor" no longer feels the pinch of poverty. Very frequently the wife in a family takes a job to swell the household income. In a heavy-industry city like Akron there are 52,000 women in the labor force—60 per cent of them married. This would indicate that perhaps 100,000 people are in families with two incomes—and perhaps three if the husband is "moonlighting." Nationally, more than one of every twenty workers, 3.7 million in all, have second and sometimes third jobs.

Making as much money as possible and taking care of "number one" first has become part of the average unionist's credo—not too different from the credo of the businessman. There is a serious question as to whether today's worker truly satisfies more of his personal needs with a $100-a-week wage level than he did a generation ago when he was still struggling for a "living wage." He has become consumption-conscious to the point of disease. Samuel Lubell, making a survey among workers in 1958, for the Chicago *Daily News,* found them weighted with installment debts. When they lost their jobs, or merely had overtime cut, they were in serious difficulties. "They ought to pass a law," one laborer told him, "to prevent suckers like me from buying too much. . . . All I've been doing . . . is borrowing from one finance company to pay another." Consumer credit rose from $8 billion in 1946 to $42 billion in 1956. Nonfarm mortgage debt rose by five times from 1945 to 1956. The average worker was seduced by the glitter of advertising to spend next year's pay this year. When his union called a strike he became obsessed with fear that he might lose his new automobile or television set, bought only a few months before on the installment plan.

The experience of the United Auto Workers with their $25-million strike fund three or four years ago is perhaps symptomatic of the growing materialism. Strike relief for most unions, until recently, has been an *ad hoc* matter. Union officials stalked the highways and byways begging pennies from liberals and fellow unionists for the men and women who manned picket lines. Appearing before a friendly group, they pictured the plight of harassed workers in the warm, meaningful terms of individual hunger, and each sympathizer who dropped a quarter or a dollar into the hat also dropped a tear. During the various coal-miner strikes of the 1920's hundreds of thousands of friends of labor all over the country contributed small sums to relieve men who were actually starving.

The $25-million fund of the auto union, good in itself, nevertheless brought out some of the greedier instincts of men, rather than some of the nobler. In strikes against International Harvester and others in 1955, the new middle-class approach of the mass-production worker manifested itself somewhat ingloriously. Before the strikes were a week old some members were already storming their headquarters for relief. "We paid our money into the $25 million fund," they said, "now where is it? It's our money, let's have it." Though they still had an uncashed pay check in their pockets, they nevertheless were already at the trough, waiting for the $25-million feed bag to be poured in.

UAW rules at this time provided that relief was to be given only to workers in *need*, rather than to everyone. Many rank-and-filers objected to this principle; a few became bitter at the union and walked out on the Harvester strike disconsolate. Some simulated "back-to-work" movements so that they could press Emil Mazey, secretary-treasurer of UAW, for relief funds. Though such threats were not meant too seriously they hurt morale in other places; the strike fund, instead of being a factor of strength, often acted as a pressure for settlement. In one Southern city a few strikers beat up an international-union auditor because of his presumed niggardliness in dispensing funds; Mazey had to threaten to withdraw relief as a retribution. It became next to impossible to limit payments for "need." With this bonanza in the union's bank hundreds became destitute as if by magic. The union paid specified sums for food—$8 weekly for the man in the family, $4 for his wife, $3 for each child. Childless couples thereupon inherited families of four or five, and those with two or three children were suddenly blessed with six. The chiseling was certainly not universal, but it was enough to leave a bad taste in many mouths.

Workers berated one another because one received a chit to buy three gallons of gasoline, while the other received four. Subjected to the pressures of their rank and file, local-union leaders bargained with the international union for more relief, somewhat in the same way as they were bargaining with management for more wages. The strike fund became a damper to militancy rather than a spur. Finally, at the 1958 convention of the union, it was decided that strike relief was a "right" and that each striker henceforth would be paid it whether or not he was in "need."

This attitude to strike relief is becoming widespread: there is a growing and insistent feeling that the union is *obligated* to support a man on strike, rather than being committed to *seek* support, as in the old days, from among sympathetic layers of society. The potential striker asks most frequently "how much will I get if I go out?" rather than the more per-

tinent questions relating to the significance of the strike itself. He is far less in need, far less driven by hunger, than in
the 1930's, yet much more concerned with money. It is as if
the strike is now detached from him, merely a machination
of the leadership, to whom he is willing to grant the right
to call the strike in return for the obligation to support him
while out.

IV

A similar decline in the feeling of solidarity is evident
among the skilled craftsmen in the mass-production unions.
After the 1955 negotiations of the UAW a reported fifty
thousand craftsmen who worked for the big auto companies
formed the Society of Skilled Trades in Michigan, and another group of twenty thousand joined the Maintenance,
Construction and Powerhouse Council as a protest against
"inequitable" wage increases. What these skilled men were
angry about was the fact that they received raises only two
and a half times as much as their unskilled brethren—fifteen
cents and sixteen cents an hour as against six cents. These
"rebels" were not poorly paid or starving; they were earning approximately $2.70 per hour. Their rates had improved
many times over since they had been recruited to the union in
the thirties. But they were annoyed that they were earning
only 34 per cent more than the unskilled, and that the
skilled men in job shops were earning still more than they.
To compensate for these "inequities" the skilled men asked
for increases of thirty-six cents or thirty-eight cents an hour
as against the six cents for the unskilled.

The discontent was so great it spilled over into a number
of strikes. Some groups switched allegiance from the UAW to
craft unions. The patternmakers at Ford joined the AFL Pattern Makers' Union. The die-sinkers in two General Motors

plants joined an independent union. Many more defections would have taken place except that the rules of the National Labor Relations Board bar elections when there is a collective-bargaining agreement in force. By 1958 the particularist sentiments among skilled workers was so strong that Walter Reuther had to yield to it. He gave them the right to negotiate separately on their problems. Yet despite that, the issue flared up again. Twelve thousand craftsmen petitioned through five craft unions (one of them an AFL-CIO affiliate) for ninety-three separate Labor Board elections. The Labor Board threw out the petitions. But when the Ford contract was negotiated, providing an additional eight-cents-per-hour raise for tool-and-die makers, some of them—at Ford's River Rouge plant—showed their dissatisfaction by continuing their strike for a short period. The fact that they were receiving about twice as much in wage increases for the year 1958 as the unskilled did not appease them.

The United Auto Workers, in its formative days, and the skilled men themselves took a different attitude. They felt then that the union ought to do most to lift the levels of the lower paid. The tool-and-die workers made some notable sacrifices in building the union; in 1939 they perhaps saved it when they struck against General Motors to stop management from recognizing Homer Martin's splinter union. But a new era evoked new reactions.

Such individualism may have some merit in the world of business, but it runs directly opposite to the charted course of a labor union. The slogan that "in unity there is strength" presumably implies that each member subordinates his own individual interest for the common good. Certainly no one can argue that the common good is better served by a $2.70 worker receiving a thirty-six-cent raise while a $1.80 employee receives only six cents. This is the same kind of individualism which underlies business unionism.

V

At the 1955 convention of the CIO, the last one before the CIO and AFL merged, Walter Reuther coined a priceless phrase: "unionize the organized." He was referring to the low level of union consciousness on the part of union members. Millions of workers who joined the unions during the war never participated in the vital struggles of the thirties or pre-thirties period. Millions more joined after the war, in a period of moderation when strikes usually involved only staying away from work, with little bitterness on either side. The old generation of militants is passing on, while a new "responsible" and quiescent generation takes its place. The old generation fought out of anger at its intolerable conditions; the new one fights merely for "more."

The story of two strikes illustrates the contrast. A group of shirt makers went on strike in the thirties against "sweatshop" wages. In the words of Stewart Meacham, writing in *The American Friends Service Committee Bulletin:*

Management sat tight, refused to bargain, and waited for the strike to collapse. When days stretched into weeks and the girls gave no sign of weakening, the rumor spread that the company was going to move all its machinery to another town and re-open completely non-union. . . . Finally . . . trucks drove up and began loading the sewing machinery and other equipment from the plant. The little band of last ditch strikers on the picket line stood and watched. It was a wet, cold day. . . . At last the loaded trucks began to move in convoy toward the highway. At the very last moment one of the girls suddenly broke away from the picket line, rushed to the bridge, and threw herself full length into the mud. Immediately everything came to life. The other pickets followed her lead, and by the time the first truck reached the bridge there was no longer a roadway but only the bodies of the pickets pressed together in the mud and wet. The trucks stopped and everything was dead quiet except for the idling motors. There was no use honking or shouting. It was clear that those girls were not bluffing. For years they had tried to speak but their voices had been lost. Now they were speaking with the weight of their own lives. Now it was "come what may." Slowly the trucks backed up and turned around. Soon the machinery was being hauled back into the plant. The strike was won and everyone knew it.

In March, 1958, on the other hand, 105,000 dressmakers in seven northeastern states went out on strike for the first time in twenty-five years. In the quarter of a century before that, the same garment workers had had ten major walkouts, most of them heated and violent. This time, however, *Business Week* could report: "Garment workers strike but nobody is very mad at anybody." The union was well-padded with a $35-million treasury and every striker received benefits. After six days, except in Pennsylvania, it was over. The strikers had held a giant meeting in Madison Square Garden, addressed by George Meany. There had been no violence, arrests, attempts at strikebreaking. An employer in New York's garment area who tried to take a rack of dresses past a picket line of women was dissuaded from doing so by a policeman who told him: "I know you're within your rights, but if you don't want to start a riot, take those dresses back inside."

The workers of the 1950's are not different human beings from those of the 1930's; they are merely motivated differently. Everything has changed for them. A generation ago the police, in strikes, were harsh, often brutal. Now, with labor an accepted segment of society, police seldom give unionists the third degree or beat them with truncheons. A Flint union official, reminiscing with Mary Heaton Vorse, one of the well-known labor publicists of the thirties, told her in 1954: "Now all the city officials are cooperating with us. The Chief of Police, I'll say without reservation, he helps us in everything." This was a far cry from the "battle of bull's run" in the thirties when the police attacked a picket line composed primarily of women. Most of the eighty civic organizations in Flint now have representatives of the labor movement in their leading bodies. The same is true in most other major cities. The rank-and-file unionists—in the big Northern cities at least—are not harassed in the same way they were a generation back. They are the beneficiaries of the innumerable gains of the New Deal era and they feel no impetus to fight in the same way as their fellow workers of a few decades ago. Their sights might be raised if a dynamic leadership in the union movement were to shift away from bread-and-butter issues to more fundamental social ones. But reluctance to change permeates both: leaders *and* rank and file.

A few of the unionists of the earlier period are nostalgic about the past without knowing how its mood can be revived. Frank Marquart records a conversation with one of these old-timers. "It gets me down," said this unionist, "when I see what's happening to our UAW summer school. . . . The old spark is gone, the old spirit has faded. Now everything is becoming grooved, standardized. We get lots of techniques— buzz techniques and mock meeting techniques and many other kinds of techniques—but there is a poverty of thinking. There are ready answers, controlled discussions, with neat, pat outlines mechanically arranged. Brother, someday you'll learn there are some things that are more important for working people than efficiency."

An old-time leader of the 1939 strike at Dodge told Marquart that he seldom or never attends meetings any more. He complained that the old spirit of fire and fight had been replaced by one of: "What's in it for *me?*" . . . "Many chief stewards and committeemen," he went on, "are no longer interested in fighting for the workers who elected them, but are primarily interested in the benefits that go with those shop level union posts: top seniority, higher classification

rates, the chance to get in on the overtime, freedom of physical movement, and the possibility of moving up the career
ladder. Moreover, stewards and committeemen are afraid to
'stick out their necks'—afraid to take a militant stand for fear
it will lead to a slowdown or walkout that, in turn, might get
them fired."

Whether such nostalgia for the "good old days" is justified
or not, it does indicate the complete turn of rank-and-file
thinking. Labor's values have changed and they have changed
at the grass roots as much as anywhere else. The temper of
the times is no longer one of conflict but of accommodation,
and the rank-and-filer too tends to accept the values of the
business community.

David Dubinsky, the president of the Ladies' Garment
Workers' Union since 1932, touched on the nub of the new
era at the last convention of his organization when he took
issue with those who looked back to the "good old days":

"When I became president of this organization," he noted,
"I became head of a small, bankrupt union, as far as number
of members and finances was concerned, but I became an
officer of a union rich in spirit. . . . That is why it was pain-
ful for me to hear some of the old-timers sigh for the
old times. What do they miss? The dirt? The sweatshop?
. . . In the old days—thirty, forty years ago—when an
ILGWU convention was attended by a small group of delegates, everybody knew everybody else. And no Governor
came to our convention. No Senator came to our convention.
No British labor leader came to our convention. What is there
in that past to sigh for? Now, instead of words of pity there
are words of respect. Why? Because the world loves strength.
The world respects power. We are a big—and strong—
union."

Not only the world, but most rank-and-file unionists "respect power." The union has moved away from them and
they don't care too much about participation or identifica-

tion. Glenn W. Miller, an associate professor of economics at Ohio State University, who made a survey of unionists in his area, wrote in *The Nation* in March, 1958 that "probably the most important factor in discouraging union-member activity is the general satisfaction with—or at least absence of strong objection to—the way in which the affairs of the union are progressing. . . . Perhaps their attitude can best be described as one of 'inactive allegiance.' "

The worker has innumerable problems that are unresolved —the psychological one of alienation, the fear of unemployment, the danger of war—but he does not look to his union to do anything about these broad social and psychological problems. In the limited area that American unionism functions—primarily at the bargaining table for higher wages and better conditions—the unions seem to the average worker in the mass-production industries and the more established crafts, as having achieved their full purpose. He does not expect more out of it. Nor does he have any major impulse to drive the union along a more independent political road, as in Europe. He does not regard capitalism as an enemy. He has, in fact, accepted its values on making money, individualism, status, and the like. He recognizes that there is an area of conflict in short-range matters with management, but as Miller points out, his "attitude cannot be construed . . . as 'anti-employer' in any long-range sense."

Sincere union leaders try to explain the sluggishness of their rank and file in a dozen different ways. President Russell White of UAW Local 652 claims that "the union shop and dues check-off are a contributing factor in the lack of interest by the membership, primarily because they don't have to come to the union hall anymore to pay dues, etc." According to labor writer Jay Campbell: "Other local and national leaders in labor blame long-term contracts, the lush earnings and overtime of the postwar era, the motor car and TV, the growing complexity of collective bargaining and the necessity of utilizing specialists in negotiations and grievances." Still other people attribute it to the greater distances workers have to travel to union meetings or the dullness of the meetings themselves. In reality, however, these are all effects— not causes. The cause lies deeper. It lies first in the crisis of leadership of Big Labor, its inability to make a new historical turn that will involve the rank and file. And it lies in the changing character of society itself.

Apathy is the prevailing mood of our society. Despite the bombast of politicians and the noises of a country in cold war, the mass of the population feels lost in the morass of politics, uneasy but relatively satisfied, worried but not moved to do anything drastic. This is the mood of conformism in society as a whole on which many politicians have capitalized. And it is a mood that has taken root among unionized mass-production workers. Everything in their lives, beyond their personal domain, has become distant, unclear. Although the rank-and-file worker is a "little" man, a mere cog in a great wheel, he also manifests that same quality of remote "bigness" that characterizes his union.

10
Little Labor

HOW STRONG IS AMERICAN LABOR?

Just before the AFL and CIO merged in December, 1955, a representative of a large employers' association stood before a Chicago audience and made the dire prediction that labor was about to take over the country. Fifteen million members, each with two or three more voters in their families, would be an irresistible force, eclipsing in power the big corporations and the two political parties themselves. Once united, he argued, labor would form its own party and within a few years control every political subdivision of the nation from the White House down to the smallest hamlet.

The first three years since merger have, of course, revealed how shoddy was this estimate. The united Federation had not grown stronger but a bit weaker. From the fifteen million membership at birth it was down to thirteen and a half million, having expelled its most powerful affiliate—the Teamsters' Union—and two other unions. Progress in organizing the unorganized was so disappointing that, at the end of 1957, AFL-CIO cut its organizing staff by almost one-half. No labor party had been formed, and none was contemplated. Labor's weakness on the political front was patent. In the midst of the 1958 recession it was unable, through its friends in Congress, to extend unemployment compensation beyond the forty-three million now eligible to the millions not yet covered. It failed even to secure passage of President Eisenhower's bill to make compensation mandatory for an additional thirteen weeks for those who had exhausted their benefits; a diluted version passed instead, making it optional with the states. No improvement was made in the Taft-Hartley law; the right-to-work laws were still on the statute books in nineteen states; and labor still had not captured its first hamlet, let alone its first state.

The strength of the labor movement is highly exaggerated by its opponents to make it appear like an ogre towering over society. A myth has been carefully cultivated that whereas labor was an unequal adversary to capital in the early thirties when it had three million members, it has now closed the gap and has capital at its mercy. Labor is frequently called a "monopoly," and some writers insist that it ought to be curbed.

The facts, however, belie this myth. Compared to yesterday, the labor movement is certainly a more significant force. But how cohesive is it? The thirteen and a half million members belong to 135 different national unions and they never vote as a bloc. A survey some years ago indicated that only about three out of five unionists cast their political ballot the way their leaders do. Even in economic matters there is no full-scale cohesion in the AFL-CIO. After the AFL and CIO merged, the Sheet Metal Workers' Union continued its twelve-year boycott against the products of the Burt Manufacturing Company in Akron because it was under contract with another AFL-CIO affiliate, the Steelworkers. Viewed superficially and by itself labor's power may seem impressive, but it far from matches that of Big Business. In its weaker links—the unions in the sparsely organized industries—it is completely outclassed in the conflict with management.

The United Auto Workers and the Steelworkers, part of the million-member fraternity, are certainly powerful organizations. The titans they deal with, however, such as General Motors or United States Steel, are even more potent. If it were otherwise the profits of the great corporations would fall, while the wages and fringe benefits of the laborers would pyramid. In actuality what has happened is that both wages and profits have risen, with profits doing as well as, and usually better· than, wages. As already noted, United States Steel reported a net profit in 1957 of 20 per cent better than the year before and the highest in its history. In the same period its employment costs rose only half as much. General Motors' gross profit in that year was almost equal to its total payroll—$1,648 million as against $1,855 million. Its return on net capital was a solid 17 per cent, hardly indicating callous harassment by any labor union. Nor are either of the two unions these corporations deal with invincible. The United Auto Workers, despite an expenditure of $10 to $12 million, is a long way from winning the strike against Kohler in Wisconsin after four and a half years on the picket line. The steel union has been on strike against a stove company in Huntington, West Virginia, for more than a year without results, hampered by two injunctions, one limiting pickets to four, and another ordering teamsters to cross their picket line. In contrast to the $2.50- and $2.75-per-hour rates of the union in the steel industry proper, these strikers average only $1.35.

Below the level of the auto and steel unions the relationship of forces is much more adverse to labor. James B. Carey's International Union of Electrical Workers is a weakling compared to such firms as General Electric. The big corporation has, in fact, developed an attitude to IUE that is highly frustrating. Known as "Boulwareism," after the former industrial relations head of GE, the technique consists of giving the union a single, final offer. The union has often rejected this ultimatum, but management has gone ahead and put it into effect for nonunion and rival union workers; and IUE usually had to accept it belatedly. In 1954, for instance, the company offered a raise of 2.68 per cent and stood firm until the union either had to agree or face the prospect of a grueling strike. Boulware criticized the "misguided and disappointed IUE officials" for trying to extract "some political face-saver," and penalized the union by putting the raise into effect two months after nonunion GE workers had begun receiving it. This hardly indicates that the company is at the mercy of Carey's organization.

Another union at obvious disadvantage is the Communications Workers of America, headed by Joseph Beirne. CWA deals with the richest corporation in the United States, the American Telephone and Telegraph Company, for most of its 249,500 members. But the corporation refuses to negotiate a national agreement with the union; it insists that CWA bargain with the separate A.T. & T. affiliates. Since its inception the union has never been strong enough to close down completely even one of these affiliates, let alone the whole Bell Telephone System. It is further handicapped by the fact that approximately 300,000 workers belong to independent unions, many of them company dominated. The company has a field day, pitting one union against another and dispersing the bargaining power of its employees.

The oil workers' union, headed by O. A. (Jack) Knight, is a forceful and effective organization, but it has never been able to organize the employees of the industry's giant, Standard Oil. Most of them are in independent unions which sometimes cooperate with Knight, sometimes don't.

The big unions, admittedly, are big. But they have a long distance to travel before they can equal either the economic

or political power of their adversaries at the collective bargaining table. A few, like the Teamsters and Mine Workers,
may be more than a match for the individual employers they
deal with; yet even in these fields the employers have formed
associations that tend to balance their bargaining power
with that of the union. The rest of the union movement, however, is in a less favorable position. Many unions are plagued
by technological and other unemployment, seriously curtail-
ing their effectiveness. Railroad employment for January,
1958, for instance, was 885,971 as against more than two million four decades ago.

II

If labor were as strong and as solidified as its opponents
insist, it would long ago have unionized workers in such unorganized fields as white collar, retail, agriculture, textile, the
chemical industry and, of course, the South. From 1945 to
1957, union membership grew by four million. But that
growth is highly deceptive because in the same period the
labor force grew by some twelve or thirteen million. As a percentage of the labor force, the union share actually declined.
Measured in these terms unions have progressed only at a
snail's pace, if at all. The big gains were in the thirties and
during the war, not since. From 1933 to 1938, the percentage
of nonagricultural workers in unions grew from 11.5 to 27.8.
From 1938 to 1945, it went up to 35.8 per cent. But by 1957
it was only 30 per cent. In considerable measure labor's
growth is due to "filling out," rather than new organization.
As the big corporations themselves enlarged and as they
agreed to union-shop contracts, some unions expanded automatically. The number of workers covered by General Motors contracts increased in one decade from 225,000 to 375,000

as the corporation itself pyramided in size. Little of this was due to new unionization. When a plant with 1,000 employees adds 500 to its payroll, the union, if it has a union-shop clause in its agreement, automatically grows by 50 per cent, but it has organized no new employees.

When the AFL and CIO were merged there was optimistic talk of doubling its membership—to thirty million—by 1965. John W. Livingston, a vice-president of the United Auto Workers, resigned his post to take what was considered to be the most important job in the united labor movement, that of organizational director of AFL-CIO. A staff of 265 men worked under him, and various unions, mostly from the old CIO, pledged a fund of $7 million to "organize the unorganized." Livingston's assistants made broad surveys of the situation in the South, of white-collar workers, department-store employees, unorganized chemical workers, but the surveys were never converted into successful drives. The Textile Workers' Union, aided by AFL-CIO, made a sustained effort to unionize its jurisdiction in the South, but after a string of losses abandoned the project. Even more, it lost many of the old plants that had been under contract; from 1955 to 1957 its membership dropped by 79,970.

The addition of the "second aristocracy of labor" to the labor fold in the thirties and forties has stabilized the movement and given it status. The government deals with it, and employers have learned to live with it. Lemuel Boulware of General Electric said a few years ago: "We believe in the union idea. We think unions are here to stay. We think some among even the best of employers might occasionally perhaps fall into short-sighted or careless employee practices if it were not for the presence or distant threat of unions." But the mere acceptance of unions by the industrial magnates does not make them storehouses of power. Compared to its adversaries at the bargaining table unionism is still a decidedly secondary force. And viewed in the light of both its potential and its needs, it is painfully weak both quantitatively and qualitatively.

III

It must be conceded there is such a thing as Big Labor. But there is also such a thing as Little Labor; and there is Unorganized Labor which comprises almost two out of every three workers in the country. Union strength is concentrated in manufacturing, mining, construction, transport, and public utilities. Of the 2.8 million in transport and the 2.4 million in construction, 80 per cent are organized. Seventy-five per cent of the miners in this country carry union cards. But of the total twenty-six million in wholesale, retail, government, finance and the service industries only 1.7 million—perhaps 7 per cent—are union members. Of the nation's agricultural workers less than one-half of 1 per cent are members.

What makes it even more unfavorable for the movement is the consistent shift of the labor force away from the organized fields to those that are unorganized. In the early part of 1957 the federal government reported that for the first time in American history the number of people employed in the production of goods was fewer than those in the so-called nonproductive industries—government, trade, services, finances, ultilities, transport. White-collar and service jobs in the decade from 1948 to 1957 grew twice as fast as blue-collar-production jobs. The latter increased by 2.6 million while the former shot up by 5.5 million. As industrial production became more complex and as automation made significant inroads on traditional manufacture, the number of office workers and skilled technicians grew more rapidly than did factory jobs. Government payrolls continued to rise as the role of the state itself broadened from year to year. Service industries, relatively unorganized, continue to enlarge as the nation's rising living standards demand new hotels, motels, repair shops, auto-servicing stations, and the like.

The picture emerges, therefore, of a labor movement that is strongly entrenched in those industries that are relatively contracting, and has hardly a foothold in those that are expanding.

Side by side with the reasonably powerful unions are the painfully weak ones, unions that have organized only a minute part of their jurisdiction. An example is the Agricultural Workers' Union, headed by H. L. Mitchell. Though there were some two million organizable employees in this field, his union paid per capita tax for little over 4,000 members in 1957—one-fifth of 1 per cent of its potential. His own salary of $5,433 (in sharp contrast to that of Steelworkers, McDonald, Teamsters' Hoffa, or AFL-CIO's Meany) reflects the general poverty and impotence of the agricultural workers.

Mitchell's problem is not that he faces small, decentralized employers with only a few workers each. On the contrary, agriculture is rapidly becoming a "factory in the field." In California, citrus fruit is a billion-dollar industry, employing a half million wage earners, selling $3 billion worth of products and paying out $500 million in wages. In its packing plants are 130,000 men and women, working on highly mechanized, and in many instances, automated equipment. Even the 400,000 field hands increasingly work with machinery. In lettuce and asparagus harvesting, conveyor belts are used for assembling and packing. The corporations that own land include some of the nation's biggest firms. Standard Oil and Southern Pacific Railroad together own 123,492 acres. The DiGiorgio Fruit Company, which broke a bitter strike some years ago, owns 15,000 acres and is listed on the New

York Stock Exchange. The Kern Land Company owns 231,000 acres. In San Joaquin Valley alone thirty corporations own more than 5,000 acres each.

Many years ago the La Follette Senate Investigating Committee said of the California State Chamber of Commerce that it was "equivalent to a top holding company of employers' associations in industrialized agriculture." This united employer force has been successful in warding off all major efforts to organize its field hands even though they usually earn below $1 an hour. It has used vigilantism, intimidation, blacklisting, and coercion, reminiscent of the harsh pre-CIO days in industry. Twenty years ago, when the AFL Citrus Packing House Workers attempted organization, the owners assessed themselves a fixed amount on each carload of shipped products to fight the union.

In the early thirties the communists made an effort at organization through their Cannery and Agricultural Workers' Industrial Union, but their drive collapsed after eighteen of the union's leaders were arrested and charged with "criminal syndicalism" in July, 1934. Three years later a CIO union emerged, but it had little more success. The teamsters have organized some cannery workers, but the overwhelming majority of the field hands are without union protection. They are not covered by the provisions of the National Labor Relations Act, although the industry is interstate in scope and fairly centralized. The Packinghouse Union tried to unionize the Sunkist growers beginning with 1954 but found itself bogged down because the employers refused to bargain. It has been fighting in the courts for more than three years to win contracts for five of the 132 Sunkist plants, but so far without success. The AFL-CIO convention in December, 1957, voted to join with the Packinghouse Union in a national boycott of Sunkist lemons but it is doubtful if even this will have the desired result.

Novelist John Steinbeck, commenting on this general situation, wrote years ago that "the large growers' groups have found the law inadequate to their uses; and they have become so powerful that such charges as felonious assault, mayhem and inciting to riot, kidnapping and flogging cannot be brought against them in the controlled courts. . . . [They practice] a system of terrorism that would be unusual in the Fascist nations of the world."

The situation has improved but little since then. The conditions of the migrant workers are appalling. The *Miami Daily News* on February 22, 1958, reported that "whole families are forced to live in the open. . . . Many are making homes in cardboard and other kind of makeshift shacks in the woods. . . ." The *Atlanta Journal-Constitution* on January 12, 1958, noted that "literally thousands of farm families in the 'Mississippi bottoms' area are hungry and facing starvation unless help comes quickly. . . ." The *San Jose Mercury*, having made a survey of the California migrant camps, described them on January 23, 1958, as the "longest slum in the world . . . village conditions in Pakistan no worse than some of the California camps . . . migratory families living under conditions similar to refugees in Seoul [Korea]. . . ." This is a chapter in the labor story that is seldom publicized. Yet there are three times as many organizable agricultural workers as there are basic auto workers in the UAW. The impotence of unionism in agriculture and its frustrations are typical of those of Little Labor.

IV

Another example is in the textile industry which employs 962,000 production workers. This is certainly one of the major industries in the country, employing considerably more workers than either the basic steel mills or the auto plants. Yet the Textile Workers' Union, once a major force within the CIO, has shrunk to a mere 190,000. There is another textile union, formerly in the AFL, but it claims only 40,000 members and probably is even smaller. Between the two, therefore, less than 25 per cent of the nation's textile workers are unionized. Their conditions are far from ideal; yet they cannot be enrolled. Their average hourly wage, both North and South, skilled and unskilled combined, was only $1.45 in 1956.

Great strikes against the nonunion textile fortress were led by the I.W.W. in Lawrence, Massachusetts, in 1912 and in Paterson, New Jersey, in 1913. The communists conducted bitter walkouts against extreme exploitation in Passaic, New Jersey, in 1926 and Gastonia, North Carolina, in 1929. None of the efforts struck roots. The United Textile Workers, which numbered as many as 105,000 members in 1920, dwindled to 27,500 by 1932. In the autumn of 1934, a national textile strike was called and 475,000 workers responded both in the North and South; but the strike ended indecisively at the request of President Roosevelt. By 1937 the CIO Textile Workers' Organizing Committee, successor to the old union, had initiated a spirited campaign and won contracts for fully 160,000 of the mill hands. In 1940, the union reported a membership of 314,000 and in 1943 of 400,000. But, despite the favorable winds of general union growth in the following fifteen years, textile unionism suffered a catastrophic decline. It lost half its membership. It was unable to overcome the combined opposition of the mills' moving to the Southern states, the right-to-work laws in most of those states, and persistent harassment and terrorism.

In August, 1957, the South Carolina General Assembly approved six ordinances which required "a permit in writing" before any union organizer could solicit members. In Baxley, Georgia, annual union license fees were enacted costing $2,000, plus $500 for "each member signed up." In nearby Carrollton, organizers were required to pay $100 a day for the privilege of "doing business" and in Osceola, Arkansas, $1,000 a day. At Darlington, South Carolina, after the Textile Union had won an election for the 600 workers employed by one of the biggest textile chains, (Deering, Milliken) the company merely suspended operations rather than bargain with the legally chosen representative of its employees. The closing of this plant did more to hamper further unionization than any event in the South in many a year.

In Fredericksburg, Virginia, the Textile Union won an election for more than 300 employees in September, 1957, but after negotiating until the following January the company involved summarily discharged the forty-two members of the union committee, and forced the employees out on strike to defend their leaders. From the first day of the strike the majority of the town's police force showed up at the plant and distributed leaflets to the strikers reproducing sections of the state's right-to-work law that makes picketing virtually impossible near plant entrances and prevents strikers from talking to strikebreakers. Although the union finally offered to go back to work without a wage increase if the company would reinstate the union leaders, management refused. Unless some concerted effort is made by the whole labor movement on the scale of the 1935-1938 effort of the CIO, unionism in textile seems doomed to many more years of frustration.

V

The newspapers headline the victories and emphasize the power of the successful big unions, but seldom point up the maddening discouragements of Little Labor. The American Federation of Technical Engineers, with 11,586 members, has only five full-time organizers on its national payroll and four more on its local-union staffs. In the last three years it has added about 1,000 engineers, draftsmen, technicians, and researchers a year to its rolls, but there are 600,000 technical engineers. The American Federation of Government Employees has a membership of 55,708 out of a white-collar potential of 950,000. It too can afford only five full-time organizers. The American Federation of Teachers has only four staff organizers and a membership of less than 50,000 of a national teaching staff of one and a half to two million. In one year it lost 2,500 members below the Mason-Dixon line because some local unions there refused to desegregate.

The one "Little Labor" organization that has made some progress in the last year or two is the State, County, and Municipal Workers' Union, headed by Arnold Zander. In August, 1956, his union absorbed the former CIO Government and Civil Employees Organizing Committee, giving the merged group about 130,000 members. Thirteen months later it had grown to 184,000, an increase of more than 4,000 a month. Compared to what other unions—even the Teamsters—were doing, this was sensational. Flushed with success, AFSCME raised its dues and employed some hundred organizers on the international, regional council and local-union payrolls. It was helped considerably by new labor-relations policies in New York, Pennsylvania, Louisiana, and Wisconsin where local and state bodies agreed not only to recognize government unions but in many instances to check-off dues. But despite its progress, AFSCME has a long way to go: there are 4,962,000 state and local government employees in the country—most of them within its jurisdiction.

The construction workers who organized in the nineteenth century had the advantage that they were skilled men who were not easily replaced. The mass-production workers who joined the CIO in 1935-1938 had the advantage that they were clustered in large groups and could stop production completely through their own efforts, by merely refusing to work. But the twenty-six million workers in trade, government, agriculture, service, and white-collar fields do not have these economic advantages. Most are unskilled and easily replaced in case of a strike. Government workers, unlike their counterparts in most West European nations, are often prohibited from striking by law, and at any rate by custom. They must confine their union efforts to lobbying with legislators. The economic power of office workers is weak because they have only a secondary and tertiary effect on production, rather than a primary one. Most companies can do without their stenographers, typists, secretaries, and bookkeepers for a much longer period than they can without their lathe hands. Supervisors can do their work, particularly for short periods. The result is that unionization efforts among these large groups have foundered for many decades.

There are in the United States some eight and a half million clerical workers, but the Office Employees' International Union has a membership of only 44,647; the two insurance unions number less than 20,000. It is only where a strong blue-collar union tries to enroll its white-collar brothers that there is a modicum of success. The United Auto Workers have unionized 90,000 members in this category; the Steelworkers, 40,000; and three other large unions, perhaps another 100,000. But Little Labor has been batting its head against a stone wall. In 1953, the office union acquired an energetic new president, Howard Coughlin. It now boasts thirty organizers on its staff, as well as another thirty employed by subordinate bodies. In 1955, twenty of these organizers distributed leaflets to the employees of New York's banks, but once again, as on a number of occasions in the past, the campaign came to naught. In 1957, the union claimed to have expanded by 16,000 members, a sizable number considering its current forces, but this was still a long, long way from any significant penetration of the field.

In 1958, Jimmy Hoffa announced a joint campaign with

the office union by which the stock clerks and "pickup" de-
liverymen would be enrolled in the Teamsters' Union while
the clerical help would go to the smaller union. Optimistic
estimates of the number of workers to be unionized were
given to the press, but—even assuming the office workers can
violate AFL-CIO policy and collaborate with the Teamsters'
Union—it remains to be seen how far this drive will go. Similar joint drives with the teamsters by the butchers' union
were highly unsatisfactory.

In the 1951-1952 insurance agents' strike at Prudential, the
teamsters respected the picket lines of their white-collar
brothers and refused to deliver heating oil to the company's
headquarters in New Jersey. But management chartered
some barges, transferred the oil to some nonunion trucks with
covered license plates, and brought the fuel in under police
escort. The big firm was more than a match for the tiny union,
even though the agents received substantial financial and
picket aid from the teamsters, marine, and ladies' garment
unions.

In 1929, salaried workers earned 30 per cent more than
manual workers. But by 1943 they were left far behind. As
Business Week put it: "In manufacturing, the salaried workers' wage advantage has disappeared. It may be gone forever.
. . . The white collar is no longer the badge of respectability—and now it's lost its edge in income." Yet, despite this
visible evidence that unionism has paid handsomely to the
blue-collar worker, the office employee still stands aloof. In
part this is the result of the realization that white-collar
strikes are difficult to win. In part it is the result of a feeling
of status, and identification with management to a degree unknown among factory workers. But whatever the cause, the
fact remains that there is a very significant disparity in the
strength of the tiny unions in the white-collar field and the
goliaths of management they must deal with. Multibillion-
dollar banks like Chase Manhattan or multibillion-dollar in-

surance companies like Metropolitan or Prudential are obviously more than a match for a union with 44,647 members.

VI

Still another large area where Little Labor struggles along
at a considerable disadvantage is in retail shops and department stores. There are approximately eight million workers
in this field (more than half as much as in all manufacturing
put together), but only a half million, or 7 per cent, carry
union cards—and of these, 280,000 are in the food stores. A
quarter of a century ago the average retail worker earned 20
per cent more than the factory hand. By 1956 the factory
worker earned 34 per cent more than his retail brother, $82
a week against $61. Hundreds of thousands of retail workers
didn't even do that well. The average wage in general merchandising and department stores was only $45 a week. A
study made in Ohio, a relatively high-wage state, indicated
that fully 45 per cent of the retail employees in 1956 were
earning less than $1 an hour. Nationally there were 750,000
to 850,000 earning less than $1 an hour. Yet, here as in so
many other unorganized fields, Little Labor has been hope-
lessly beaten in trying to unionize its jurisdiction.

The story of retail unionism in the United States is a story
of persistent hardships and painfully slow progress. The largest union in this field, the Retail Clerks' International Association, boasts 291,000 members, but more than half of these
are in food stores. RCIA has made steady gains since 1941,
when its ranks numbered only 85,000, but again its successes
have been primarily in the food-store field where it had some
roots to begin with. In the department stores it has netted
only meager results, claiming to represent some 40,000 workers. Its impotence was clearly illustrated when in early 1958
it came to grips with the large mail-order house, Montgom-

ery Ward. The company refused to grant a wage increase to RCIA, and after months of maneuvering, the union went on strike in a handful of stores while putting pickets around scores of others to enforce a boycott. The union came to terms with the company only when the Teamsters' Union signed a five-year pact with management. Hoffa's union saved it from ignominious defeat by insisting that Ward's agree to the same pact with the clerks' union.

The second largest union in retail is the Amalgamated Meat Cutters and Butcher Workmen, which numbers some 120,000 skilled retail butchers among its 311,000 members. The next union in size is the former CIO Retail, Wholesale and Department Store Union—104,654. Outside of New York, however, this organization is relatively weak and it has suffered one reverse after another. In Chicago it initiated a promising campaign among department-store and mail-order firms back in 1940. Perhaps 1,000 workers joined at Marshall Field, the largest department store in the city, and contracts were eventually signed at The Fair and the Boston Store. Labor Board elections were won at the Montgomery Ward warehouses and retail stores in this city, but the bitter resistance of Sewell Avery, then president of Montgomery Ward, and two indecisive wartime strikes resulted in the loss of these units. Recurring factional strife, in no small measure spurred by frustration, finished the job, so that today the RWDSU has only one department store in its ranks in Chicago. The Fair is still unionized, though it is now in another union, but the Boston Store is out of business and no other advances in the department-store field have been made since the few victories in 1941. Two attempts to organize Marshall Field clerks have failed, though the company does bargain with the Building Service Union for 800 to 900 nonselling employees (of a total work force of 6,000). In 1948, a joint effort by the Retail Clerks and Building Service unions to unionize the Goldblatt Bros. chain also foundered when the company discharged 150 unionists around Christmas time and the two unions were forced into an abortive strike. After a few hours on the picket line the teamsters withdrew their support from the beleaguered retail groups and the strike collapsed. The teamsters themselves eventually enrolled the Montgomery Ward warehouses and a few hundred employees in the Ward stores, but tens of thousands of retail workers in Chicago, earning $1 to $1.25 an hour, are still outside the ranks of organized labor.

Little Labor is in the same dire straits relative to the retail and white-collar fields that auto, steel, rubber, oil, and other unions were relative to mass-production industry a generation ago. It just can't make a break-through. American employers had to yield ground to the great offensive of the factory workers in the thirties. The sitdown strike and the general militancy of the depression era made victory possible in this primary field. But in the secondary and service industries, management has put up far greater resistance. There is a strong suspicion in labor's ranks that department-store employers have a secret national fund to subsidize stores on strike. Confirmation for this was the McClellan Committee exposé of the activities of Nathan Shefferman, formerly in charge of industrial relations for Sears Roebuck. Shefferman's clients in the retail field read like a "Who's Who" of the industry, indicating some kind of general understanding or at least coordination of policy amongst these employers. At the Hecht store in Washington, Shefferman drew up such detailed plans for checking union organization that it included instructions as to where to place trash baskets for the union leaflets, when and how supervisors were to "pump" certain employees for information, and when and how to grant wage increases so as to cut the ground from the organizing campaign.

Indicative of retail problems is the victory won by the Retail and Wholesale Union at the S. H. Kress stores in Bessemer,

Alabama, in 1958. Bessemer is a highly unionized steel- and coal-mining center. In 1951, the clerks at Kress tried to organize but after a seven-month strike were defeated. Seven years later the company, rather than face a similar ordeal, recognized the union and granted a ten-cents-an-hour increase—a sizable raise that year. With the ten cents added, however, minimum wages went only to seventy cents per hour!

VII

The number of small, relatively weak unions in the United States is far larger than most people realize. When speaking of the labor movement it is customary to refer to the AFL-CIO as an aggregate single body of 13.5 million members. But AFL-CIO is merely a federation of some 135 autonomous national unions. It is, so to speak, the propaganda and lobbying voice of the movement but it has no mandatory powers over its affiliates in the decisive matters of strikes, collective bargaining, grievance machinery, or even political action. It receives only six cents per member per month in per capita payments, whereas the national unions are paid seventy cents to $2 a month for each member in the local union.

Since its formation the AFL-CIO has centralized power to a significant extent, particularly in enforcing ethical practices. It has expelled from its ranks unions it considered corrupt and it has appointed "monitors" over such unions as the Distillery Workers when it felt they needed supervision. But the center of power in the movement is still the autonomous national union. Of these there are only nine unions with more than 400,000 members and only twenty with more than 200,000. At the other end of the pole are such midgets as the Asbestos Workers with 10,000 members; Bill Posters with 1,600; Brick and Clay Workers with 25,123; Broadcast Workers, 3,738; Cement, Lime and Gypsum Workers, 35,288; Cigarmakers—Samuel Gompers' old union—8,038; Coopers, 4,012; Doll and Toy Workers, 16,980; Window Glass Cutters, 1,600; Horse Shoers, only 266; Hosiery Workers, 9,917; Glove Workers, 3,063. A famous unionist like AFL-CIO Vice-President A. Philip Randolph of the Sleeping Car Porters heads an organization of only 10,000 members. At the 1957 AFL-CIO convention there were twenty-eight organizations with less than 10,000 members each, and another forty-four that had between 10,000 and 50,000 members. The overwhelming majority of the national unions had memberships of less than 100,000.

Each of the national unions lives in its own separate world, connected to the rest of the movement by tenuous threads. None of them is the invincible goliath that is often referred to in the press. Its day-to-day fare of activity is restricted to relatively simple problems, covering small numbers of people—and monumental difficulties.

Two issues of the *Hosiery Worker,* January and February, 1958, perhaps give some inkling as to the scope of that activity. A report on finances indicates that the Hosiery Union had assets as of December 31, 1957, of $269,167.93, of which a mere $6,000 was in cash. The president, Alex McKeon, head of the organization for eighteen years, earned $6,500 a year. Employment seems to weigh heavily on the minds of the hosiery workers because the newspaper reports a decline of 3,200 workers in the North Carolina full-fashioned-hosiery mills. There were 21,000 in December, 1957, as against 24,200 the year before. Average wages also fell, from $1.56 an hour to $1.54. On the more hopeful side, the paper lists a 1 per cent gain in employment at the seamless mills, and a rise in wages from $1.38 to $1.42 an hour. The paper notes that the "Do Not Buy" Chadbourn Gotham hosiery campaign is picking up. That would indicate that it had lost a strike or organizing drive there and has fallen back on the boycott as a last resort. A strike of full-fashioned knitters at the Morton Hosiery Mills in Runnemede, New Jersey, is also reported. The company reduced the knitters' rate of pay and changed their work week to six days, six hours. The employees spontaneously refused to work, joined the Hosiery Union, and petitioned the Labor Board for an election. So far, we are told, the company has refused to consent. In another column the story is told of the Wytheville Knitting Mills in Virginia, where the union, after an election, was certified as the bargaining agent on December 8, 1955, but the company has refused to negotiate a contract ever since.

Issues of the *Chemical Worker,* organ of a medium-sized union with 71,688 members, list similar problems and items. The union, it is reported, has helped twenty workers at the Summers Fertilizer Company in Maine "bust a company union" and regain their jobs. This campaign has been going on for two and a half years, since the workers were discharged, but the Labor Board has now ruled in their favor and they stand to collect several thousand dollars apiece. The company, however, is still fighting the issue in the courts and it may very well be another year—perhaps two or three —before the matter is resolved. Another item gives details of the Koppers strike in Kearny, New Jersey. Forty-five members of the union there have been picketing against this Mellon subsidiary for eleven weeks because management insisted on transferring high-seniority employees to lower-paying jobs, at its own discretion. "It ended," says *Chemical Worker,* "when management DID budge and granted security provisions which covered thirty-four men in the work force." A report that 500 zinc miners had joined the International Chemical Workers' Union in Tennessee rates the whole first page of the February, 1958, issue. A few other items tell of eight-cents-and ten-cents-an-hour raises at the Clorox Company, 6 per cent wage boosts at two Louisiana plants, and "beating back" an attempted raid of the Teamsters' Union at the Melamine Plastics Corporation in Winona, Minnesota, where the workers voted twenty to seven to keep the Chemical Workers' Union.

None of this is on a big scale or indicates any tremendous power. The union's jurisdiction, if federal statistics are accurate, covers at least 555,000 workers; but it is only a pygmy against its potential. Such giant firms as DuPont have comletely eluded its grasp. One of the interesting sidelights in the newspaper is the plea that each local union "adopt a plant"—organize an unorganized shop. This is Little Labor at its typical pace, fighting hard against insuperable odds, tilting at windmills, trying desperately to hold on, hoping for the great day when perhaps there will be a new swing toward unionism. Meanwhile it organizes a few shops, negotiates a few wage increases, conducts—under the capable guidance of Otto Pragan—one of the best educational programs in the labor movement—and waits.

This is the fate of most of the organizations of the labor movement. They have a small toehold in an unorganized industry, having missed the opportunity in the thirties, and they are waiting for the next big organizing upsurge. When the CIO was first organized Sidney Hillman proposed to the few retail unions in its ranks that they set up an organizing committee under his leadership; in return he promised to supply the funds and manpower to launch a major campaign. The leaders of the Retail and Wholesale Union at the time, however, preferred to be big fish in little ponds, rather than be relegated to obscurity. They turned down Hillman's proposal and remained stagnant. Perhaps even with such help the retail union might still have been unsuccessful, but since then it has made only minor gains. Until its current president, Max Greenberg, took the helm it appeared as if it might fragment completely. But Greenberg has been able to weld it together and to bring back some of the unions in New York that had deserted it. At one point there was a possibility that Greenberg would form some kind of alliance with an old friend of his, Harold Gibbons, who is now Jimmy Hoffa's key assistant, and jointly organize the retail field. At the moment, however, that possibility has receded, particularly since the Teamsters' Union has been expelled from the AFL-CIO. The union picks up a new store here, a new one there, but nothing significant. It has a number of the large department stores in New York City under contract—Macy's, Boomingdale's, Stern's and others—as well as food stores and specialty shops. But outside of the metropolitan New York area it is very weak. As of December 31, 1957, its total assets were approximately $2.50 per member, or $280,978—hardly a sizable sum for enrolling the missing millions who are still outside its ranks after a quarter of a century of heart-breaking effort.

VIII

Our American culture is so enamored of bigness that it seldom puts the spotlight on littleness. But not only is there a large segment of the labor movement that is in the little category, but Big Labor itself is in truth only a veneer over something essentially little, weak, tenuous. The international unions of auto workers, teamsters, and steelworkers are centralized, powerful, big. They have taken over many of the tasks, such as collective bargaining and general servicing, which formerly were handled at the grass roots. But the grass-roots local unions still have a certain area of small, nerve-wracking activity. There are some 75,000 local unions in the labor movement; tens of thousands of them—even in the big national organizations—that cannot afford a full-time organizer, sometimes not even a full-time office girl. Glen W. Miller and Edward J. Stockton made a study a year or two ago of the local-union officer and his background, activities, and attitudes. Polling 291 such officers in the Columbus, Ohio, area they found that in most cases they received less than $25 a month and regarded their work as a "labor of love." On the average they spent eight hours a week doing the odd jobs involved in running their union—after finishing their work in the factory.

The tasks these and other men handled were the small problems that never get publicity. A worker is classified as a machinist but is doing tool-and-die work, rating a higher wage scale. The grievance committeeman takes the problem up with the department supervisor and tries to adjust it. If the company is adamant he arranges for a grievance meeting of his whole committee with the industrial-relations manager and attempts to resolve it at this "second stage." If that is unsuccessful the matter goes to his international representative and is processed further, through arbitration by the national organization. Or, a member has taken a leave of absence for pregnancy and has overstayed her leave by three days. The committeeman tries to make a deal with the supervisor to overlook this transgression and reinstate the woman with her full seniority. Another case involves a three-day lay-off of a member for doing bad work or swearing at a foreman or perhaps fighting on the job. These are the routine problems of labor in its lowest echelons, far removed from the marble palaces in Washington and Detroit where hundreds of thousands of dollars are spent and where great plans are laid.

The leaders of Little Labor at this level are busy day and night trying to mobilize their members to come to meetings; busy attending conferences of their city-wide industrial-union council, participating in minor political action, collecting $1 from members—if they can—for COPE, the political arm of AFL-CIO, and similar chores. On rare occasions they go to conventions or attend conferences out of their cities to coordinate efforts with their counterparts in other plants.

At this level, too, there is little that is big, rich, or corrupt.

The number of corrupt union leaders exposed by various federal legislative committees over a period of five years was only forty. Their influence was, of course, far greater than this small number, and should not be underplayed. But the stigma they cast certainly does not include the half million active secondary leaders of the 75,000 local unions in the country whose work on behalf of their union is primarily a missionary one.

The mores of our times have affected this secondary echelon just as they have the rank-and-file worker generally or the top leadership. Materialism has made its imprint here too. Ralph Helstein, president of the Packinghouse Union, spoke of this in 1957 in a ringing speech on "Moral Values and the Fast Buck."

"How many devoted members," he asked, "will still distribute handbills unless there is a dollar or two in it for them? What of those situations where the drive for piecework earnings force people out of gangs so that those remaining can increase their earnings? . . . What about lost-time practices—is it always for union business or does it provide an opportunity for a quick drink or a ball game? . . . It is my purpose to outline these practices not just to add my voice to those who condemn the few in the labor movement who indulge in the blatant behavior of a Beck, but more importantly to point up with as much precision as I can the fact that the day-to-day actions just referred to are a form of corruption, part and parcel of the values of this commercial age. These are the kinds of practices that make ours the age of the 'fast buck,' the age where you get yours while the getting is good."

Even at the secondary levels there are officials who make a couple of pennies out of their union position. They charge the union for "lost time" for union business when in reality they have taken the day off to go fishing. Or they take a small present from the man who installs the coffee machine in their headquarters. But these are the minority. The majority of

Little Labor's leaders are men of nobility, self-sacrificing and idealistic. Their idealism no longer has the vision that it had in the 1880's or the 1930's; but in their personal attitudes these men are "true believers."

What has been called "Big Labor" is a centralized structure grafted onto the decentralized hulk of "Little Labor." Down at the bottom in the local unions, and among the unions that are struggling to unionize their jurisdiction, there is still a flavor of littleness.

11
The Unfinished Revolution

WHAT—IF ANYTHING—IS WRONG WITH THE AMERICAN LABOR movement?

Leaving aside the racketeers, who constitute a very small percentage of union officialdom, what *is* wrong with business unionism? What *is* wrong with social unionism? Both have greatly improved the wages and hours of ten, twelve, or fifteen million American workers. Both have added to their security and dignity. With all their faults, both have been major pillars of American democracy; and social unionism has helped win important social improvements not only for labor but for the rest of the nation.

It is true that to greater or lesser degrees the two major forms of American unionism have become institutionalized. Both evolved from a measure of radicalism to a greater or lesser moderateness. But what is wrong with a moderate union movement so long as it improves the lot of its members? The leftist can argue that labor should fight for social-

278

ism as a matter of principle, but even socialism, if it has any merit—and the term certainly needs serious redefinition—must have a concrete meaning. If the lot of the worker is good, then why change it? What difference does it make what name his social system bears—whether capitalism, socialism, communism, feudalism, or what have you—so long as it serves his best purposes?

The answer to these questions is, first of all, that a majority of the working class is outside the union fold and does not enjoy the benefits that the established organizations may win for their members. The fact that a construction worker earns $3.50 per hour hardly helps the unorganized retail clerk who earns only $1. Second—of greater significance—is the fact that we live in a changing world. A stable, institutionalized union movement can in its own limited way serve labor, or part of labor, only so long as capitalism is stable. The AFL served the skilled worker well for forty years, but it did progressively less for the unskilled, and it finally was unable to meet the test of a changing America at one of its three great historical turning points, the depression.

The CIO succeeded in giving a new impetus to American labor. It provided something that the AFL couldn't. The reasons for this success have some bearing on the present stagnation of the American labor movement. What accounts for the sensational growth of the CIO in a period of two or three short years? Different reasons are given by different people: The CIO had millions of dollars at its disposal; it was given a lift by the Wagner Act; it had a friendly government in Washington; it charged only a dollar a month dues. All these things undoubtedly contributed, but the outstanding reason for CIO's progress was its crusading spirit, its evangelism, idealism—or whatever name you choose to call it.

At given moments in history the crusader has the ability to bring out the nobility in men, to unite them in a passionate campaign against injustice. He wins their allegiance be-

cause he himself is willing to sacrifice anything and everything, his possessions, his time, even his life itself, on their
behalf. The thin little man with a "diaper," Gandhi, can
bring millions of Hindus exultantly to boycott British goods
because he himself is willing to fast unto death or spend years
in prison on their behalf. Throughout history crusaders have
given electrifying impulses to tens of millions of people, have
welded them together in a way which solid, stable institutions could never do. The texture of life is made up of dreams
of a beautiful tomorrow. The crusader gives reality to that
dream. The Walter Reuther of 1936-1937-1938, arrested by
police, beaten up by Henry Ford's goon squads while dis-
tributing leaflets, walking picket lines and living in poverty
to serve his fellow worker—and the hundreds of other Walter
Reuthers of the 1930's—brought out in hundreds of thousands of followers a similar willingness to sacrifice for a cause.
Workers ran through police gauntlets, submitted themselves
to tear gas and clubbings, some even to death, for the vision
of a world free of exploitation. The flat exhortations of the
old AFL leaders in favor of higher wages could not at that
turning point compete with the ringing call of CIO evangelists for recognition, dignity, a better world.

By contrast to the crusader, the institution cannot evoke
selfless sacrifice. It cannot unite people for bold new action;
it mobilizes them only for routine patterns of behavior. The
crusader is a known individual, the institution an anonymous
thing. The institution can function well in a milieu of stability, when it does not have to confront the unexpected; but
put it into a situation of crisis and it is immobilized. When
there is a strike the crusader denounces injustice and offers to
fight to his very last breath to eradicate it. The institution
mathematically calculates how long a $38-million strike
fund will last and makes its plans accordingly. The crusader
makes his sacrifice in the name of humanity, not for himself;
it does not matter what happens to him personally. The in-

stitution may fight vigorously, but only to defend itself; humanity is secondary.

Perhaps the fundamental problem faced by the labor movement, as well as other social movements, is how to keep the crusading spirit alive in periods which are *not* historical turning points. Can the crusader or the crusading spirit make any contribution in stable times or stable circumstances? This is a philosophical problem of great import, but for the purposes of this study it is a moot question. America and American labor are no longer in a period of stability but in a mounting instability. This is an era of crisis, requiring the rekindling of the fires of idealism. For labor the challenge results from three factors:

1. The second industrial revolution around automation and atomic energy, which threatens to change both the character of the work force and work itself.
2. The tens of millions of unorganized workers.
3. Most important—the permanent world crisis which places the United States at its fourth great historical turning point.

II

Iron Age of June 12, 1958, headlines the fact that "union growth lags as automation begins to take its toll." The beginnings of the electronics age are changing the composition of the American work force. Blue-collar production workers are being laid off, white-collar workers are being added. One aluminum company, which doubled its sales from 1947 to 1957, cut its production staff from 36,000 to 33,000 but raised its office staff by a full 5,000. Though national production in this decade enlarged by 43 per cent, the number of factory employees remained almost stationary—only seven-tenths of 1 per cent higher than in 1947.

The electronics industry lost 200,000 of 900,000 workers in the short period of four years from 1953 to 1957. An ore mine which had 5,000 workers eight years ago now operates with 1,200 mechanized miners. Where 45,000 sheet and tin workers were employed in one strip mill in 1940, 4,400 do the same work today. The steel industry, auto, rubber, can, mining, and many others have steadily reduced their hourly paid force as the new wonders of modern technology made the laborer redundant. By 1956, for the first time in history, non-production workers exceeded direct producers on American payrolls.

Even more dramatic changes impend. On the drawing boards of the automation engineers are new control devices that will make it possible for acres of factory or office space to be depopulated of workers entirely. Automated equipment will process raw materials, assemble them, package them, and load them onto freight cars without their being touched by a human hand. These machines can adjust to various conditions, inspect their products, correct their mistakes, and even change parts when they break down. One writer visualizes the day when a factory becomes so compact it can be operated on a railroad train, making its deliveries while it is manufacturing its product on flatcars. The change is likely to be even more dramatic in the white-collar field than in the factory. The great insurance-company offices of the future may be consolidated into three or four large rooms instead of the current twenty-five-story buildings. Automation has been making great strides in this field. Tomorrow's wonderworld includes innumerable plans for lightening the load of labor: automated grocery stores where the "checkers" are no longer trim young ladies but mechanical monsters who take money, "read" the bills, test it for counterfeit, make change, and wrap the packages in half the time that it takes a person to do it today; automated butcher shops, with the meat already sliced, packed, weighed, and priced by giant machines in the packinghouse plant rather than human labor; and many similar miraculous innovations.

What these technological changes mean for labor's bargaining power must be clear. As the proportion of organized (blue-collar) workers declines in favor of the unorganized technicians and office workers, established unions lose members and finances. In each plant they become weaker relative to the employer with whom they deal; for in case of a strike five hundred men in the automated shops can be replaced more easily than five thousand today. Further, the machine tends to become more important to production than the man. If the workers strike in a mechanized plant they can shut the factory down, but in tomorrow's automated shops it may be possible for a skeleton force of nonunion supervisors and office help to run the operation for the period of a strike. That is almost true today in telephone offices; the mere walkout of telephone girls and linemen does not cripple services for a long time. Thus labor's most potent weapon, the strike, is blunted. Finally, automation reduces some of the cohesiveness of the union as workers are separated from each other by relatively large distances within the automated plants.

Organization of the unorganized is thus no longer a "luxury" to the labor movement, but a vital necessity. It is no longer a question of adding more numbers to the union roster by unionizing virgin fields, but of protecting the established organizations as well. The unorganized white-collar worker, technicians, and service workers become a threat to the bargaining power of the organized employees.

Beyond this problem there are the more urgent psychological and social ones involved in the second industrial revolution. It is anticipated, for instance, that with full automation 200,000 workers will be able to turn out as many automobiles as a million workers in the pre-automation period. The replaced workers constitute a social problem. They must either retrain for automated jobs or find other work. If they shift to retail and service fields, their wage rates are cut by half, sometimes more. Many new industries would have to emerge to absorb the large numbers whose jobs are made obsolete by the automated giants. These new industries, if they develop—and it is not certain they will—may resolve the national economic problem, but not necessarily the human one. Automation requires different skills from those in mechanical factories, and older workers trained in the mechanical techniques do not make the adjustment easily. One sixty-one-year-old man, who was shifted from the Ford River Rouge foundry machine shop to the automated engine plant at Dearborn, failed to adjust. He put his difficulties this way:

"This machine has some eighty drills . . . and twenty-two blocks are going through. You got to watch. Every few minutes you got to watch to see everything is all right. And they [the machines] got so many lights and switches—ninety-some lights. It's hard on your mind." The intricacy of the new job terrifies this worker: "If there's a break in the machine, the whole line breaks down. They all look to you. They want to keep up production, and I don't blame them. But sometimes you make a little mistake, and it's no good for you, no good for the foreman, no good for the company, no good for the union."

A sociologist, David Riesman, noting this human problem, urges that society set up "some social fund [for] easing the blow to the casualties of progress." In the past, he says, society has "not paid the cost of readjustment," but it should do so in the future.

Automation not only will result in technological unemployment, but in a reshaping of our cities, our factory system, our human beings, and our politics. Factories that require only a few dozen or a few hundred employees will find it more expedient to move out of the big urban centers to the small cities and even rural areas. The shift in population will tend to make one unending suburbia between big cities like Chicago and Milwaukee, changing political alignments and political structures. It will decisively affect the big city machines and affect adversely the farm-bloc vote. It will punctuate such problems as civil rights, with Negroes attempting to move into what are now usually all-white suburbs. It will bring with it a host of new social and behavior patterns.

Automation eventually must change the measurement of wages itself. On what basis shall an employee be paid? Today he is paid for his "time," because time is directly related to his productivity. If he produces one piece a minute, he produces sixty in an hour and 480 in a day. This is the measure of his value to the corporation and the basis for payment. But what is the measure when the worker merely watches lights all day? How is the value of his work determined then? By the number of mistakes he catches? By his mere presence? In estimating costs, the employer no longer has to pay primary concern to the productivity of the worker, but to the productivity of the machine. Under automation, just as under mass production generally, the amount of invested capital will grow, while the share of wages in total costs declines. Presumably, therefore, management should be able to pay what is called a "living wage" without feeling too much economic pressure, since wages will be only a small component of costs. In the long run this may mean a more bountiful living standard; in the short run labor's problem is to get management to shorten hours and raise wages as productivity improves.

Tomorrow's human beings, in an automated world, will also be of a different breed. They will need more education to be sure, but there is some danger that they will become more conformist. History indicates that the machine all too often remakes man in its own image; that man, far from being the master of the machine, is usually its servant. Automation robs the average worker of still more of the satisfaction that work should give him. In the present mechanical system he loses the sense of creativity, but he does maintain some sense of judgment. He must measure to see if an item is the right size or "off" a thousandth of an inch. He must test it for many desired qualities. There is still some "art" to his labor. But in an automated factory the judgment is left to the electronic machine. The electronic machine now judges size, quality, weight, and other factors far better than any human can. It expels faulty tools or products and automatically reworks them. The first industrial revolution made man mechanically minded, money minded. Will the second industrial revolution make him more conformist, less capable of independent judgment?

This deficiency in modern man is already acute, and of considerable concern to many thinkers.

Robert M. Hutchins, president of the Fund for the Republic, claims that industrialism is producing men "who are not free in any real sense and who may not even want to be free. . . . We may say that the aim of industrialization is to get rid of men altogether, except as consumers, and to make them interchangeable parts of an industrial machine. But the interchangeable man is not a man. Since he is not, freedom and justice are of little importance to him."

"The individual worker [under automation]," says Dr. Bernard Karsh, "loses his importance and is replaced by the team, and greater value is placed on the operating unit as a whole. Whyte's *The Organization Man* may indeed replace the traditional individualism which has characterized American society for so long." The trend toward dehumanization of the work process will doubtless continue with automation, unless some means is found to combine creativity and education with work.

Assuming that the work week must be steadily reduced under the impact of automation, there is some doubt as to what the worker will do with his leisure time. Will he "moonlight" with one or two additional jobs in his spare hours? Or will he find some positive means of using his leisure? Will a shorter work week itself really solve the human problem, or must some effort be made to combine work and education?

An experiment along these lines has been conducted by a group of men in a watch-case factory at Boimandu, France. This plant has been cooperatively owned since France was defeated by Hitler in World War II. After only three months of operation the men at Boimandu became the most efficient watch-case makers in the country. They didn't shorten their work week. Instead they added nine hours of education to their job. Instead of working forty-eight hours they actually worked only thirty-nine hours, but the rest of the time was spent studying engineering, physics, literature, Marxism, Christianity, dancing, singing, and basketball. In addition, the group bought a 235-acre farm and each worker and his family worked on it for three ten-day periods a year. Considering that the men had a month's vacation, this meant a total work year of only ten months, all of it designed to utilize more fully the worker's talents, involve him in management, and widen his horizons. The experiment at Boimandu cannot be applied universally or even on a large scale, but it seems obvious that work, education, and creativity must some day be combined.

III

Of far greater consequence for labor than even the second industrial revolution is the historical impasse which America finds itself in today. The United States and its allies won the Second World War, but they have not won the peace. Most of their colonies have gained independence in the greatest wave of national revolutions in all history, and many of their former spheres of influence have defected either to neutralism or to Soviet influence. In a material sense the United States has never been stronger. But strength can be deceptive. The historian Arnold Toynbee has noted that civilizations often decline at the height of their power, when they destroy their "creative minority." Certainly the Soviet challenge is the most formidable one the United States has encountered in our lifetime. The nation knew it could ride out the depression, particularly after Roosevelt came to office. It seldom had doubts about winning the war against Hitler. But there is a pervasive feeling today that victory against the new challenge is far from certain.

Chester Bowles has been arguing for some time that America needs a new "consensus."

"On three previous occasions," he writes, "the American people have come up against new situations which no longer responded to the slogans and political approaches which had been created for an earlier day. . . . Unless I am profoundly mistaken, a similar situation is developing today, out of which a new political and economic liberalism will ultimately take shape. As in 1800, 1861 and 1932, the American people are again starting to blink away their self-complacency and to grope for a more positive role to play in a world that cries for a reassertion of their country's greatness. . . . There are few who will argue seriously that either party as such has yet offered such leadership."

We are living in a revolutionary age, one in which America's role as a great power is seriously threatened. Each national revolution creates a crisis for America, becomes a factor in the intense, full-scale conflict between two social systems, capitalism and communism.

Until World War I capitalism ruled the world unchallenged. The only other social system was a decadent feudal order in the underdeveloped countries, and these nations were firmly held under the boot of imperialism. The great powers dominated the whole planet. After World War I, Soviet communism threatened the capitalist edifice and a wave of revolutions followed for six or seven years—in Germany, Bulgaria, Finland, Austria, Turkey, China, and many other lands. But in the end Soviet Russia remained alone, isolated, relatively weak. Capitalism seemed secure.

Now after World War II all this has changed. Despite the totalitarian character of Soviet rule it has attracted millions of people away from the West; capitalism is no longer unchallenged, it has formidable opposition. The communist world is a great land empire encompassing more than 900 million people. It has broken out of a *cordon sanitaire*. Beyond that, at least twenty noncommunist nations with perhaps a population of 750 million have achieved independence and are currently in the midst of a combined national and social revolution. This is the greatest social tornado in all history and it poses tasks for America of titanic proportions. Not only is there the heightened tension of international relations and the constant danger of war, but all internal problems in the United States now become *part* of the world conflict. The nation didn't relish its periodic depressions a few decades ago, but it could survive. Today a full-scale depression might be fatal, opening the door to communism in the weaker capitalist nations like France or Italy, and estranging America completely from the uncommitted nations of Asia and Africa. A depression might also revive the Communist party here. Though the party has shrunk to five thousand or fewer members, and has alienated most of its sympathizers, any economic cataclysm could bring it back to life.

In the face of this, American capitalism has been modifying its own character to an extent undreamed of either by the stern advocates of laissez-faire or the liberals of just a generation ago. Our nation is changing drastically in front of our eyes.

The first important change is in the military sphere. For the first time in American history we have become a peacetime military power, spending almost 10 per cent of the gross national product—$40 or $42 billion a year—on armaments. We are attempting to gain what C. Wright Mills calls "peace through mutual fright." In the process we are transforming the fiber of our own society as well. General Omar Bradley pointed out that in modern warfare it is "nations, not armies, [that] go to war." It is inevitable, therefore, that the nation emphasize the military theme of obedience rather than that of individualism to which we have aspired throughout history. Conformity, loyalty checks, antisubversive laws and prosecutions are symptoms of this altered emphasis. As President Woodrow Wilson long ago pointed out: "To fight you must be brutal and ruthless, and the spirit of ruthless brutality will enter into every fiber of our national life, infecting Congress, the courts, the policemen on the beat, the man on the street. Conformity would be the only virtue and every man who refused to conform would pay the penalty." The first effect of the cold war has been precisely this trend to conformity.

A second change is in foreign policy. The United States is doing things today which would seem unbelievable to citizens of 1920 or 1910. We are allotting billions of dollars to aid our traditional economic competitors—Britain, Germany, Japan, France, Italy. We have spent $78.5 billion for military, economic, and "dual purpose" aid to the countries of the so-called free world to save them from a fate presumably worse than war—communism. We are not only giving economic and military aid, but political support for a customs union and a political unification of Europe. In the face of a greater challenge we are buttressing the economies of nations we ordinarily would be fighting.

A third significant change is in the attitude toward the colonial nations. Western policy has been confused and begrudging, but the imperialist powers have given up one colony after another since World War II. The old imperialism is finished and cannot be revived. When France and

Britain attempted an imperialist venture in 1956 into the Suez area of Egypt, the United States put its foot down so firmly that its two allies had to get out. In 1958, the United States and Britain sent troops into Lebanon and Jordan, but world opinion and opinion at home forced another withdrawal.

A fourth change, of course, is in our own internal life. We strive to make those changes that will take the sting from communist propaganda both overseas and at home. The nation has become far more conscious, for instance, of the minority problem and there has been a sustained—though far from complete—effort to achieve civil rights for the Negro. To a considerable extent this was a reflex to communist propaganda among the colored peoples of the world. We have fattened the "cushions" of our economy by measures such as increased unemployment compensation, higher social-security benefits, farm supports. And it is quite clear that one of the major considerations in priming the pump during the 1958 recession was to stave off a serious depression that would bolster communism all over the world. When the Russians sent their first satellite to the skies in 1957 the United States reacted by examining its educational system to see why American scientists had failed to achieve this goal first. The federal government appropriated large sums to stimulate youth to study the physical sciences. Every Soviet action has its reaction here.

The competition of Soviet Russia has served to centralize power in the federal government and to push the nation further along the path that conservatives describe as "creeping socialism." The state holds the key today not only to questions of war and peace, but to the whole economy. It is by far the nation's biggest business, and business' biggest customer. Its decisions on armaments, disarmament, fiscal expenditures, almost immediately affect the living standards of all its citizens. If the government were to come to terms with Russia to disarm, thereby cutting its budget by $5, $10, or $30 billion, that would plunge America into severe economic difficulties—unless effective measures were taken to spend these sums for other things. It would also create an immediate political crisis: many business interests would argue that the nation needs tax cuts to "spur business initiative"; labor would probably lobby for public housing for low-income groups, new schools, medical subsidy, higher social security. What the government did finally would determine whether millions would find work or be unemployed.

In the final analysis, competitive coexistence with Russia will either block America's progress or spur it to new great heights. Either way it is evident that the nation will not stand still.

IV

The drastic changes in American capitalism, dictated by the cold war, pose basic problems for American labor as well. The movement, it is clear, has lost its forward momentum. For the third time since the Civil War it is at an impasse. As in 1886 and 1935, it can make no further progress unless it finds a new direction.

Most union leaders console themselves that their problems are essentially moral ones. They feel that once they clean house and remove the stigma of racketeering placed over their heads by congressional committees, they can regain the initiative. A moral purge of the unsavory elements in the house of labor, these men insist, will make it possible once again to organize the unorganized and intensify labor's efforts as a political pressure group. In line with this approach the second AFL-CIO convention in December, 1957, reaffirmed its ethical-practice codes. It directed affiliates to run their affairs democratically, hold conventions at least every four years, and expel anyone "commonly known to be a crook or racketeer preying on the labor movement and its good name." Union leaders were admonished to keep a wary eye on welfare funds and to liquidate any business investments where there is a "conflict of interests." To show that it meant business the Federation expelled three organizations, including its most powerful affiliate, the Teamsters' Union.

There were many deficiencies in the codes. The most glaring was the one on business investments. While the Federation declaims against business investment where there is a "conflict of interests," it does not condemn business activity as such. Can a union official who owns tens of thousands of dollars of property or factories of his own really sympathize with the plight of exploited workers? It seems doubtful. Another deficiency was in the terms of office; almost any bureaucrat can consolidate a machine in four years' time. The codes failed to mention "sweetheart" contracts, nor did they contain rules against crossing the picket line of another union. They set up no independent machinery for policing or investigation. Up to the present the Federation's Ethical Practices Committee has depended almost exclusively on information furnished by the various Senate committees.

Nonetheless, with all these defects, the codes reflect a change in climate within the house of labor, and the new vigilance is no doubt irreversible.

"Labor has no ills," wrote the *Oregon Labor Press*, "that the good medicine of democracy cannot cure." This answer, however, is far too simple. Democracy cannot be injected into the labor movement by fiat, by passing resolutions. It is part of a process of involving the rank-and-file members in struggles for idealistic objectives. As things stand, most national unions and tens of thousands of local unions *are* democratic. Formally they have all the safeguards needed for countervailing power. But labor's democracy today, like that in society generally, is not a meaningful one. It is a manipulative type of democracy. In all spheres of American life democracy no longer seems to mean the full participation of the individual in every facet of government, but the right of the Big State, Big Business, Big Madison Avenue to *manipulate* the individual in any direction they see fit, so long as in the process of manipulation there is no resort to force or police terror. This is the essence of our new conformity. The individual submits to subtle and ceaseless manipulation; he is not an active part of the democratic process.

The same type of manipulative "democracy" prevails in the labor movement. "If one asks," writes Sumner Slichter, in *Challenge of Industrial Relations,* "whether unions give their members what they want, the proper answer is that for most unions the question is irrelevant. The great majority of the members do not have much opportunity or desire to consider and discuss alternative policies. Hence they are not to be regarded as making a choice. The proper question to ask is: 'Do the members like what they get?' The answer to that question is usually 'Yes.' " The rank and file influences the leaders, Slichter claims, but it does not participate in decision-making, except at the lower, and least important, levels.

Neither ethical practice codes nor resolutions on democracy can, in themselves, wake the labor movement from its state of suspended animation. Superficially, it seems to lack nothing for a great new advance. It has the necessary funds (far more than in the 1930's), and the necessary organizers to organize the unorganized. It has scores of competent public-relations men and lobbyists to present its point of view in the right places. It is certainly better placed to move forward than a quarter of a century ago.

What is missing, unfortunately, is what C. Wright Mills calls the "insurgent impulse." Labor has once again exhausted its *élan vital.* It is incapable of galvanizing millions of workers to zealous sacrifices. It is fighting today's wars with yesterday's weapons—very much as France tried to fight the second World War with the Maginot Line concepts of World War I. Today's wars are political, but labors chief efforts are on the economic plane. At least 90 per cent—probably more—of labor's efforts remains in collective bargaining. Labor refuses to face up to the demands of a new era.

In the 1930's labor was still fighting against industrial tyranny and starvation wages. That battle is still far from won —for the unorganized and for Little Labor. But it has been achieved for the mass-production and construction workers. The movement itself is far from the inconsequential force of three million it was a quarter of a century ago; it is now the largest single-interest bloc in the nation. American labor, just like Western European labor a half century ago, needs new objectives. It has, so to speak, exhausted the "old enemy." The new one is essentially—though not completely—a political one; labor must be ready to accept a far broader social responsibility than it has been willing to assume up to now. That is particularly true in an era of hydrogen bombs, cold wars, the second industrial revolution, and competive co-existence. If American workers can be fired with an "insurgent impulse" at all, it is only over such vital issues as peace, full employment, civil rights, welfare legislation. A ten-cents-an-hour wage increase is meaningless if hydrogen bombs begin to fall on Detroit or Chicago. It can't be won at all if there are eight or ten million unemployed ready to take over the jobs of the employed. It can't be won for the unorganized Negro down South until he first wins civil rights. It is decidedly secondary for the jobless, the aged, and the sick. No matter how the issue is viewed, labor's crisis returns invariably to its relative political impotence.

In essence the dilemma of American labor is: Should it continue as a mere political pressure group, lobbying through "friends" in Congress for its objectives, or must it launch a new crusade through a new political party?

V

The objective of politics is state power; every political party must aspire to govern.

A pressure group is justified only when the political objective of the group is a limited one, when its interests are confined to a relatively small area. A lobbying group for veterans seeks only such partial objectives as larger bonus payments, better hospital facilities, or lower-interest rates on FHA loans. A pressure group for the oil industy seeks higher depletion allowances, restrictions on oil imports, stricter enforcement of "allowables." But a labor movement of eighteen million has political objectives as wide and as broad as society itself. It cannot seek special-interest laws merely for labor, because its destiny is tied up with the fate of the whole nation. As a defensive measure it can act as "pressure group" to repeal the Taft-Hartley Act or right-to-work legislation. But, for the rest, anything that affects America affects the labor movement immediately and directly: inflation, peace, disarmament, foreign aid, taxes, the military budget, farm policy, tariffs, welfare legislation, schools, medical laws. Such issues require more extensive activity than lobbying; they are the meat and marrow of a political party's program. Labor, because of its expansive social needs, can hardly entrust them to the hands of "friends of labor" who are not directly accountable to labor. It cannot rest its political cause in the liberal minority wing inside the Democratic party. It needs firmer control over its "friends" than the current *ad hoc* relationship, or the loose alliance through the Americans for Democratic Action. It cannot come to the political table begging for crumbs, because it is too vital and too big a force. Eventually it must make an independent place for itself.

Throughout its history American labor has either formed

its own parties, as with the labor parties of the 1820's, or has been toying with the idea. The notion of a labor party comes up repeatedly. After World War II there were a number of conferences to set up a third party, but all of them came to naught. The United Auto Workers had the issue on its agenda for five or six years, until it was sidetracked by Reuther in favor of a "realignment" within the Democratic party. Emil Mazey publicly advocated a labor party until two or three years ago. When the AFL and CIO merged in 1955, Michael Quill of the Transport Workers' Union demanded that the new organization pledge itself to a third party before his organization would affiliate. "I believe," he said, "the CIO is doing too much bowing and scraping before the Democratic party. They say the CIO has no other place to go. But I maintain we have some other place to go. CIO should declare its position now on an independent party— before the merger becomes final." The Mechanics' Educational Society of America, another AFL-CIO affiliate, has advocated formation of a labor party since its inception. The social unionists as a whole, however, have not yet accepted this position. They insist on remaining a mere pressure group.

One of the obvious weaknesses of this approach is the lack of interest by the rank and file. In the 1956 elections, when the AFL-CIO was asking every member to contribute a single dollar for its political arm, COPE, it collected $623,158. Only one of every twenty-three or twenty-four union members was willing to contribute even $1. Various publicists make much ado about "labor in politics" but the fact is that outside of a few areas, such as Michigan, where the United Auto Workers have done a creditable job of infiltrating Democratic party ranks, labor's participation is minute. Politicians are willing to pay a price for labor support because it lends an aura of "liberalism" to their candidacy. The words, "Endorsed by organized labor," are more important in wooing the middle-class and liberal vote than that of the workingman. The majority of the workers remain pro-Democratic, not because of their union leaders, but because of the New Deal tradition which gives the older party the stamp of "poor man's party." But workers will not ring doorbells in any large number either for the Democrats themselves or for a labor movement which supports the Democrats. Polls consistently show that labor voting in elections is smaller than that of the middle classes. The rank-and-file worker, wary of the politicians of both parties—"They're all a bunch of crooks anyway," he says—does not feel they are fighting his battles.

James McDevitt, national director of the AFL-CIO's political committee, COPE, discloses that less than 40 per cent of American union members are registered to vote. A survey by the Amalgamated Clothing Workers of its ranks in one Delaware and seven Maryland counties showed that only 20 to 30 per cent were registered. Unionists just do not feel they have a vital stake in the traditional politics. They vote with their feet, by staying home. They are not aroused by their leaders' urgings. In an article in *Harper's,* in August, 1958, Dick Bruner, who worked on the political staff of an ex-CIO union, charged that labor is short of political vitality because:

1. It lacks ideas of its own. On many of the most fundamental political and social issues, it is hard to distinguish labor's position from that of the National Association of Manufacturers.

2. It is pathetically weak on political organizing ability.

3. It has adopted the "mass market" concept of many big corporations, and its leaders treat the rank and file with cynicism.

The pressure-group policy has been a lamentable failure. AFL-CIO writers, with a little Madison Avenue sleight of hand, can compile an impressive statistic of how many senators "voted right" this year as compared to last, or how many congressmen "voted right" over the past decade. The union leaders can point to innumerable conferences they have held with successive Presidents, and to thirty or more labor attachés that sit in key American embassies overseas. But the unassailable fact is that labor has been steadily losing ground in the last decade; its voice in the halls of government is less than a whisper. Though it has published tons of pamphlets and held scores of meetings and lobbying sessions, it has been unable to modify the Taft-Hartley law. It has been unable, except in one or two cases, to repeal right-to-work laws. It has been unable to reverse the course of the National Labor Relations Board. It has been unable to secure bold legislation in new social fields, such as, for example, health insurance. Where social legislation already exists, labor has been able with its liberal friends to make a few changes for the better in some areas; in others—such as low-cost housing—it has fallen behind.

Admittedly there is no ground swell for a labor party at this juncture. But labor could pose the problem and take rudimentary steps in that direction. It could cut its ties with the Democratic party and disavow completely its Dixiecrat and center wing. It could run candidates of its own on a limited scale, against both the Democrats and Republicans. It could establish an embryonic independent political structure that would form the basis for the next step in the future.

In St. Louis, Local 688 of the Teamsters' Union has developed a pioneer "Community Action Program." The union members are organized not only at the shop level but at the community level as well. In addition to shop stewards and shop meetings, they elect community stewards and hold regular community meetings. In some wards, where membership is large, a regular full-time office has been opened. Among the day-to-day political activities of community stewards are such political "grievances" as police protection, street lighting, housing, sanitation, sewage, safety, and all other neighborhood problems. These stewards meet with aldermen, councilmen and other local officials, and they are organized city-wide into a Community Stewards' Assembly

which meets regularly to take up problems such as rat control, city-country coordination, transportation, a free city
college, and the like. The program is so extensive that it takes
thirty-five cents a month out of each member's dues and has
a full-time coordinator.

Such political action, of course, is on an elementary level.
It does not come to grips with the problems of war and peace
or economic reorganization. But it is a beginning toward
what Harold Gibbons calls a "new·look" in the house of labor. It is a method of involving the rank-and-file worker,
rather than the leader alone, in political life. In many respects it performs some of the activities of the labor-represen-
tation committees in England, prior to the formation of the
Labour party there. Community political activity has given
the St. Louis teamsters real political power in that city. They
were successful, at one point, in defeating a proposed new
city charter. "For the first time in metropolitan area history,"
wrote the *East St. Louis Journal,* "Labor's rank and file followed Labor leadership in defeating the proposed new St.
Louis City Charter. . . . If there are those who fear this
Labor experiment in grass roots participation in government,
let them go into the hinterland themselves and woo the citizen where he lives."

Unfortunately all too few labor leaders have enough confidence in the rank-and-file worker to organize him for such
political action. The old-line unionists are afraid that it
would sweep them from power in the union itself; it would
shake up the bureaucratic machines of the business unionists.
The newer leaders, around Reuther, are not so much afraid
of the rank and file, as inflexible. They continue to fight only
a defensive battle as a tail to the liberal Democrats. With
such an approach the best they have been able to do is moderate some of the blows against labor. They are not re-invig-
orating either the labor movement or society as such with any

evangelical impulse. They are only entrenching traditional forms of politics that are historically outmoded.

The Democratic party is really two parties, and the Southern Dixiecrat wing not only controls the key congressional committees, but has a veto power over all forward-looking legislation. Furthermore, the American concept that "you vote for the man not the party" is woefully immature and inadequate. Who can look into the lives and views of the hundreds of candidates from which one must choose on election day? The only sensible type of politics is one where a party program is sacrosanct, and all members of the party pledge to work for that program if elected. In that way the voter knows *what* he is voting for, rather than just *who*. He votes for ideas rather than names. The "vote for the man" type of politics offers the voter only little choice and great confusion. It does not really involve him in political decision; it is part of the "manipulative" democracy of our conformist era. An independent party of labor would not only have a consistently liberal or radical program, but would of necessity be a different kind of party as well: it would be a "responsible" party whose voters would know in advance what they were voting for.

V

The purpose of a labor union is to fight against injustice. At each period in history it must find new objectives and new organizational forms to fire its membership with an idealistic *élan*. To accomplish this the leadership of labor must be able to rise above its milieu, to chart a new course. Once this happens the old, conservative union forms are immediately on the defensive. The new course charted by Peter McGuire and Samuel Gompers in 1886 swept aside the old Knights of Labor. The new course charted by Lewis, Hillman, and the radicals in 1935 forced the AFL seriously on the defensive, and for a time threatened to engulf it. It survived only because it bent sufficiently with the winds to ride out the storm. Now, as we enter the 1960's and a historical turning point for capitalism itself, a new course of political unionism can destroy business unionism and rehabilitate the institutionalized social unionism. The point is that no simple structural changes, adoption of ethical codes, or mechanical attempts at infusing democracy into the undemocratic sectors of the movement are enough. Business unionism can be checked only to the extent that the rank and file is involved in union affairs to act as a real countervailing power. And the rank and file can be involved only if it receives an insurgent impulse.

In the process of forging a political unionism, the movement will inevitably change its structure and impose a new moral self-discipline. As the old behavior patterns are jettisoned, radically new ones will take their place. It is impossible to blueprint the forms of tomorrow's unions but we can—tentatively—outline some of the changes.

Until the AFL, the city central bodies were the power center of the movement. Then the national unions became the power center. The centralized structure of these unions today is a halter around labor's neck. The national unions are necessary to labor to match economic power with management. But their power must be checked by the countervailing power of other labor bodies and the rank and file. To make a new turn, labor will inevitably add new bodies and alter its structure. Side by side with the national union there will evolve, on the one hand, the political labor club, and on the other, the council of unions. Thus the members of ten or fifteen local unions in various internationals that deal with Montgomery Ward would form an autonomous council to deal with the same employer. The six or eight unions at

Borg-Warner—in the United Auto Workers, Steelworkers, Machinists, Allied Industrial Workers—would form a Borg-Warner council. The Industrial Union Department of the AFL-CIO is already taking steps in this direction. In July, 1958, an Allis-Chalmers Inter-Union Joint Conference was formed of delegates from the Auto Workers, Steelworkers, IUE, International Brotherhood of Electrical Workers, Machinists, and Firemen and Oilers. Each of these unions has pledged to ask for the same basic package from the employer. We can expect that in the future hundreds more of these councils will be established, and that in time they will gain increasing freedom of action from their national unions.

How the third party itself will be organized is hard to say. If it follows the British pattern, the AFL-CIO will be part of an alliance with labor, farm, church, liberal, socialist, and other organizations who are willing to form the new "consensus" that Chester Bowles speaks of. In that case the individual union would be automatically affiliated with the labor party, paying per capita taxes to it, but the individual union member would be active in his own ward or district political club only if he wished to undertake the additional activity.

The AFL-CIO itself, as part of the new course, would make a number of significant structural and ethical changes. Perhaps the most important would be:

1. Acceptance of direct membership from the councils. This would weaken the centralized hold of the national unions.

2. Provisons for direct elections to the annual or bi-annual AFL-CIO conventions by the local unions, rather than by the national unions. Today the conventions are far from democratic bodies, even though they are conducted democratically. Everyone can speak; every delegate can oppose the leadership's policy. The trouble is that the delegates are not elected but usually *appointed* by the national-union executive boards. The rank and file at the grass roots are not given

the opportunity to discuss issues before they come to the AFL-CIO convention and it has no say in choosing the delegates except the rather ambiguous one of electing the national officers of their union periodically.

3. The city central bodies would be revived as a potent force helping in strikes, coordinating joint activity of local unions, initiating new organizational drives, resolving jurisdictional disputes at the home level.

4. The AFL-CIO itself would be given the right to inspect the books of all affiliates, down to the local-union level, and take disciplinary action against union leaders and organizations guilty of malpractices.

5. The movement would not only adopt a more extensive code of ethics but a code of democracy. To revitalize labor's leadership it is necessary to give it a sense of identification with the rank-and-file workers it represents. Provisions are needed limiting a union official's salary to that of the highest-paid worker in his jurisdiction. That would cut the pay of men like David McDonald, George Harrison, and others by eight- or nine-tenths, but it would bring them closer to the outlook of the members they represent. Another possible provision is that the labor leader go back to the shop for short periods of three months or six months, periodically—again to identify further with the men he represents.

6. The movement would adopt an unequivocal position on industrial unionism, and take steps to merge the building trades into one industrial organization, rather than the many craft groups that exist now.

7. Labor would adopt a policy of collective bargaining by industry or groups of industries, and fight for extension of benefits won for the unionized worker to the unorganized one. This would seriously cripple racketeering, because the racketeer could no longer sign "sweetheart" contracts or perform special services for individual employers or employer's associations.

Tomorrow's labor movement will differ from the present one as the AFL-CIO differs from the union federations of a century ago. Among other things, its activities will include a comprehensive program of adult education. As automation increases productivity and the work week can be reduced to thirty-five, thirty, and twenty hours a week, unions will be conducting "on the job" educational programs to broaden the horizons of their members and give life a fuller meaning. Education will not end in grammar school or high school, but will be a life-long avocation. There is no guarantee that education in itself ensures democracy, but it makes democracy more possible—both in the union and in society generally.

Other programmatic planks for labor, if it reorients toward political unionism, will be in the administration of a national health-insurance program, participation in a federal planning commission to guarantee full employment, a voice in the management of industry, formation of cooperative retail stores and cooperative housing ventures, and the establishment of functioning auxiliaries of women, pensioners, and other groups.

If it charts a new course, labor will also take on a new look. It will complete the unfinished revolution begun in the 1930's.

VI

How will such a change come about? Where are the forces to bring it about? Will it take a depression or war to implement such a program? There is little of the insurgent impulse in America today; the "creative minority" is being whittled down. This, says James B. Carey, "is the new age of conformity. It is an age in which one does not shout against injustice because shouting is impolite and out of style. Poverty and slums at home and hunger abroad cause little or no indignation although they may on occasion be the subject of a wise-crack from some well-dressed juvenile delinquent of almost any age. This is a matter of concern to the entire labor movement and to all thoughtful Americans. Certainly, labor must never become too polite to scream out loud."

C. Wright Mills in his *New Men of Power,* published in 1948, visualizes the "coming slump" as the compelling force of a new idealism. Possibly that is true, though none of the three postwar slumps have been of such proportions. At the height of the 1958 recession 8 per cent of the work force was unemployed, most of whom received unemployment compensation up to thirty-nine weeks. This compares with 25 per cent in 1933, when there was no compensation. No mood of desperation prevailed among the jobless and no new evangelism came to the surface in the house of labor. It is possible, however, that in the years to come this may change. A number of basic industries show the same signs of long-term illness as they did a generation ago. In 1958, the automobile industry, with a capacity to produce twelve million cars a year, was manufacturing only at the rate of four or four and a half million. Economists estimated that not until 1995 at the earliest would the nation be able to consume twelve million automobiles a year. In the meantime the auto workers were suffering greater unemployment than any other sector of labor. More than 400,000 were unemployed in the auto center, Michigan, alone, and according to Dr. William Haber of the University of Michigan, there will be a permanent army of 175,000 jobless in that state even after the nation recovers from the recession. Steel production fell at one point below half its total capacity. Heavy industry in general seems to have hit its peak of employment. Under the circumstances, the American economy may stabilize at an ever-growing rate of unemployment: Four million this year, six the next, and perhaps more in subsequent years. The trend of the thirties, when unemployment was slowly reduced after the New Deal came to power, may very well be reversed. Short of war itself, America can hardly spend much more for military supplies; and short of a new approach in government, it can hardly stimulate greater production in the basic industries. A permanent army of unemployed can emerge later than Mills visualized, but if it does—as seems likely—that may be one of the wellsprings for a new idealism.

Another is the Negro movement. For the first time in history the Negro people in America are developing an effective leadership of their own. Young, well-educated Negroes like Rev. Martin Luther King of Montgomery, Alabama, are not only emerging as leaders but fashioning new techniques of struggle. One of these, the nonviolent resistance used in the Montgomery bus boycott, captured the imagination of the American people and probably did more for civil rights than any single event of this period, except for the Supreme Court decision on school integration. If the effort is sustained it must eventually affect the trade-union movement as well, because on winning civil rights the Negro will certainly insist on economic rights. As things stand now, the Negro usually works in the low-paying and unorganized service industries. A disproportionate share of his brethren are outside the union fold but most anxious to join if the climate inside labor can be improved. In organizing the service industries and the South, the Negro must be a key factor. And in the process of enrolling him, some of the idealism from his civil rights crusade may brush off on the rest of labor.

Another wellspring of idealism may be the South itself. It is still virgin territory, just as were the mass production industries in the 1930's. And just as with the mass industries a generation ago, organization in the South is so difficult, repression by police and legislatures so great, that a large strike wave there must unleash considerable self-sacrifice and stoke the fires of "insurgency."

Still another source, of course, is within the leadership of labor itself, especially in its secondary echelons. During the 1958 recession Emil Mazey, secretary-treasurer of the United Auto Workers, made a series of ringing speeches in his union reminiscent of his talks when he was an unemployed leader in the thirties. Lesser leaders of other organizations were similarly stirred to speech and action of a more fiery type. Their inherent dedication fed on the fuel of unemployment and gave some visionary leadership to many disheartened people.

No one can predict the course by which idealism will be reborn in the labor movement. Most likely it will result from a combination of factors, both objective and subjective. But neither the materialism of business unionism nor the remoteness of social unionism will be altered appreciably until there is a resurgence of evangelism in the house of labor. That resurgence cannot be hurried; history waits its own good time. But it must be anticipated.

Admittedly this is all visionary. But it has roots in reality. This is the inexorable direction of America itself, if it is to survive: more logic in social relations; less anarchy; preoccupation with human problems. It is also the direction of labor as well, if we are to have a *participative* rather than manipulative democracy.

Whatever the specific tactics and the final dimensions of labor's goal, one thing is certain. The only means by which labor can make a new step forward is through new crusades that infuse idealism, more idealism, and still more idealism.

And that, incidentally, applies to American society as well.

Index